The Making of a Country Veterinarian

A Collection of Short Stories

Memoirs of a Country Vet

- 5 -

David E. Larsen, DVM

David E Larsen (signature)

Wiley Creek
Publications

The Making of a Country Veterinarian
A Collection of Short Stories
© 2022 David E. Larsen, DVM
All Rights Reserved

David E. Larsen, DVM
PO Box 117
Sweet Home, OR 97386
email: d.e.larsen.dvm@peak.org
blog: docsmemoirs.com

ISBN: 979-8-9865226-0-9

Cover design :
Eva Long/Long on Books
longonbooks.com

Printed in the USA

Dedicated to the extended family
of Frank and Dolores Larsen
whose continued support and encouragement
ensured the completion of these memoirs.

Contents

Author's Note

These memoirs are gleaned mostly from my memory, as few early records survive. They are presented in a rough chronological order. But in a small town mixed veterinary practice in the 1970s and 1980s, there was little control in what came through the door. And to some degree, these memoirs try to reflect that chaos.

This is the fifth book in a series of five books. The first four books follow the same format, with short stories of specific snapshots in my life. Stories of my early life, my Army experience, and my college days have been pushed back to the fifth book. Those stories will provide a little insight into the making of a veterinarian.

My First Sick Cow

I stood at the window and watched the chicken coop up the hill from the house. Dad and the uncles were in the coop, treating our cow. She was sick this morning. Of course, at four years of age, I knew nothing of the particulars.

Dad picked up the earpiece on the wooden wall phone and cranked the hand crank several times. Then he told the woman on the phone who he was calling. I was never allowed to use this phone. You had to know our ring before you could answer the phone. Otherwise, I would be just like Mary down the road, listening to other people's conversations.

"The cow was staggering this morning," Dad had said into the wooden phone that hung on the wall. "I was able to run her into the chicken coop. She went down, and I can't get her up. It looks like milk fever to me."

We lived on a small acreage on Catching Creek at the time. It was not really a farm, but this cow was our family milk cow.

There was a big concern about the cow in the house that morning. This was our sole source of milk.

It was not long after the phone call that Grandpa and Uncle Dutch arrived at the house. Mom poured them coffee as they waited for Uncle Duke and Uncle Rodney. Rodney was next to come.

"Duke is never on time," Albert said.

They were waiting on Duke because he was the "cow doctor" for the group. Duke had been to college and was respected for his expertise. There was a lot of chatter at the table, about the cow, and about Duke.

When he arrived, everyone was up and out of the house. They all headed for the chicken coop.

I have no real recollection as to how long they were in the chicken coop. Mom was busy in the kitchen, dishing up some pie to go with the coffee. The men would be back when their work was done.

Finally, the first to exit the chicken coop was the cow. She must be well. Everyone in the house was happy. Then in a few minutes, the men filed out the door.

Mom served the pie with thick cream and coffee. All the men relaxed and talked about the treatment and the coming chores of the day. Rodney kidded my brothers and me. It was a happy event.

The mood around the table was almost jovial. It was more than the fact that the cow was well. It was the fact that it had been so easy and so fast.

There was no way for me to know at the time, and I can only speculate today, but this could have been the first time that this group of men had treated a cow with milk fever with an injection of IV calcium.

Before the mid to late 1940s, milk fever was treated by inflating the udder with air to bring the milk production to an immediate and temporary halt. Udder inflation was the first successful treatment for milk fever. It was used initially without a clear understanding as to why it worked.

In the mid-1930s, low blood calcium was found to be the cause. Routine treatment, on the farm, with IV calcium, was slow to replace udder inflation. But by the late 1940s, IV calcium had become the standard treatment.

In the late 1940s, veterinarians were in short supply in western Oregon, especially in Coos County. Duke's skills were heavily relied upon in those years before Myrtle Point had a veterinarian.

This event provided me with an early awareness that we treated sick cows. And, perhaps, most importantly, the elation when everything was successful.

The Broadbent House

To call it the Broadbent house was a little misleading. It was just an old farmhouse, located a couple of miles above Broadbent on a small farm that dated from the early 1900s. Broadbent was more of a place than a town, even in 1950. Broadbent was about five miles from the small city of Myrtle Point.

This house was unpainted, the siding weathered to a steel gray like most barns in the area. The siding was made of one-by-twelves that ran vertically, the entire length of the two stories. These one-by-twelves were lapped with one-by-fours. A porch ran the whole length of the house on both the front and back.

Interestingly, the front door, and the front porch, was rarely used. Life revolved around the kitchen, and the kitchen door opened onto the back porch. We came and went through the back door. Of all things from my childhood, using the back door, the kitchen door, as the main door in the house, is something that we still do to this day.

During the warm summer days, when the upstairs bedrooms were too warm, my brothers and I would use the front porch as a sleeping area. We had an old metal bed with an old, thin mattress on it, and two or three of us would sleep there, most of July and August. We would fall asleep watching shooting stars and the Milky Way.

We moved to this farm in January 1950. I was four years old at the time. That January, we had nearly two feet of snow. Nobody was happy about the snow. But we explored the hill country, snow or no snow.

There were several outbuildings associated with this house. On one end of the backyard were a combination garage and woodshed. These were connected to the house by a plank walkway.

The other end of the backyard was framed with a building that served as a root cellar and pantry. Both of these buildings were of the same construction as the house. Both were unpainted, and all the buildings had a shake roof.

The outhouse was located off the far end of the garage. There was a long plank walkway to it. I have limited memory of using the outhouse, but one night is etched in my mind. My older brother was afraid to make the trip during a late night in February. I was assigned the task of accompanying him to the outhouse.

Standing in the cold, holding a flashlight while he accomplished his business, is not one of my fondest memories.

Straight out from the kitchen, completing the enclosure of the backyard, was a massive cherry tree. Mom's garden was located behind the cherry tree. This garden provided produce and staples for the family for the coming year. My mother could never understand how people could survive without a garden.

Beyond the fields was the hill country. For a group of young boys, this country became a vast playground. It also became my first classroom. I learned more about nature, animals, life, and death in this classroom than from any school. Some lessons I learned on my own, many were taught by my oldest brother.

The creek was also beyond the fields. We fished this creek almost daily in the spring. Fishing was only interrupted by the school, and many Fridays were sick days for me. I had to stay in the house until noon, then I could go fishing. Those Fridays were more productive than any classroom hours.

In the kitchen were the range and counters with the kitchen sink situated so Mom viewed the backyard, the garden, the fields, and hills beyond. This view was framed by Robin's Butte and Neal Mountain in the far distance.

Also in the kitchen was the wood stove. This was the only heat source in the house. In the winter months, there was always a fire roaring in the stove.

Behind the stove was a bathroom that would shortly become the home of our new indoor toilet, sink, and bathtub. Mom and Dad's bedroom door opened off the back wall of the kitchen. The dining room was to the right of the kitchen as you entered from the outside. The living room was through a doorway off the back wall of the dining room. The living room was the coldest of the downstairs rooms. We would later make the door larger and build a fireplace in the living room.

Upstairs were two bedrooms, one on each side of the stairs. My sister had the room over the folks' bedroom, and we three boys had the one over the living room and dining room. There were no doors upstairs. The stairway was accessed either through Mom and Dad's bedroom or from the living room.

The upstairs bedrooms were very cold in the wintertime. I would wake up and blow a large breath of air out from under the covers. How much fog was formed from that breath told you how cold it was in the room. I would jump out of bed and run as fast as I could, down the stairs and through Mom and Dad's bedroom to the kitchen. The heat from the fire was very welcome.

The first summer we were there, they put plumbing into the house. Uncle Dez from California came up to do most of the plumbing. Dad and the local uncles, Dutch, Duke, Toad, and Robert, did the digging for the septic tank and drain field. It was a pretty simple installation by today's standards.

Also, it was during the first year that Ernie Bryant built a plank road along the line fence to a little sawmill up the creek.

A couple of years later, I think my third-grade year, the neighboring farm built a house just across the line fence. This was the first time we had neighbors we could see from the house.

In later years I had friends who lived up the river. It was about six miles to their house by going on the highway, but by going up the plank road and then over Neal Mountain, it was half that distance. And it was a lot more fun by the Neal Mountain route.

We fished, daily at times, hunted and trapped any time after the chores were done.

Today, I still enjoy having neighbors you can just barely see from the house. I have lived inside the city limits only during my Army and school years. We seldom, if ever, use our front door. And of all things, I like to fish best of all.

Gary's Accident

The afternoon was filled with bright sunshine and anticipation. It was the end of March, Friday the thirty-first in 1950, and we were planning to go to the high school tonight to watch the school play. Our cousin, Bill Davenport, was one of the actors. The last two weeks of March had been a welcome relief from January and February's horrible weather.

In January, we had just moved to our place in Broadbent and were welcomed with nearly two feet of snow. The weather remained miserable through February. A couple of weeks of good weather in March had the grass growing and we were enjoying the out of doors.

There was a massive cherry tree in the backyard, and I was sitting in the grass under that tree. Gary, age 8, was on a sturdy wooden table that was under the cherry tree.

"I'm going to jump on you," Gary said. "You better move."

Gary, four years older than me, was always picking on me. I considered myself tougher than him, so I didn't pay much attention to his threats.

Suddenly, he made a leap at me. His arms were spread as if he was going to swoop me up. He landed far short of me, putting his hands down to break his fall.

The next I knew, Gary was screaming and bouncing across the yard, holding his hand, with blood spurting everywhere.

By some stroke of divine guidance, Dad had brought home a first-aid booklet and a tourniquet for Larry, my oldest brother, to study for a first-aid card so he could get a summer job.

"Larry, get ahold of Gary, and I will grab the tourniquet," Mom said as she ran into the house.

Larry's memory was that he tackled Gary, but that may have not been an accurate description of the event. Mom was right there with a towel and the tourniquet.

"Do you know how to use this?" Mom asked.

"I just read that chapter last night," Larry replied as he applied the tourniquet to Gary's forearm. He twisted it tight until most of the bleeding stopped. "This is a bad cut, Mom. We need to get him to the hospital."

"Linda, you need to call Mrs. Hermann and see if she has a car and can take us to the hospital," Mom said as she picked up Gary and sat on the edge of the porch, holding him in her lap.

Gary buried his head in her chest and sobbed.

I looked at Gary's hand as I passed by and followed Linda into the house. The phone was sort of a mystery to me. It was a large wooden box that hung on the wall and had a crank handle that Linda turned three or four times. I was never allowed to use the phone. Everyone on the line had a number coded in long and short sounds. Linda knew Mrs. Hermann's number, and since she was on our line, she could call her without talking to the operator.

"Gary cut his hand real bad," Linda said into the phone. "Dad has the car at work, and we need to get him to the hospital."

"I will be right there," I could hear Mrs. Hermann say.

Mrs. Hermann's car was like our car, but it was black. Larry helped Mom and Gary into the back seat, and then he got in the front with Mrs. Hermann.

"When Dad gets home, you have him call the hospital before he comes," Mom said to Linda through her open window as Mrs. Hermann started down the lane to the highway.

"Okay, David, let's go find what cut Gary's hand," Linda said as we watched the car pull onto the highway and head to town.

I ran over to where I was sitting, and Linda followed.

"Gary landed right there," I said as I pointed to the spot where he had landed. I could see blood on the grass.

Linda looked in the grass where there was blood on the grass. She picked up a broken bottom of a milk bottle, and there was blood on the glass.

"This is what happens when you guys play out where the grass is long and hasn't been mowed," Linda said. "I don't want to see you out here until this grass is cut."

Linda was ten years older than me, and I think she thought she could boss me like Mom.

"We need to go in and call Grandma and Aunt Lila," Linda said.

I don't know why she said we needed to go call. I was not allowed to use the phone. But I followed along and listened to her make the calls.

There was nothing else to do until Dad got home. Linda seemed to be on the phone all the time. I think she was calling everyone she knew.

It seemed like hours before Dad got home, and Linda was crying as she tried to tell him what had happened. About that time, Mrs. Hermann drove up with Larry in the car.

"Boy, what a day this has turned out to be," Mrs. Hermann said while talking with Dad. "They had traffic stopped at Hoffman Wayside, but I rolled down my window and waved. They let us through as soon as I told them we had an emergency. When we got to the hospital, they gave Gary a couple of shots, and Gary got ready for surgery. Anyway, we dropped Deacon and Gary at the hospital. And the doctor said that Larry did an excellent job with the tourniquet. Otherwise, Gary could have lost his hand."

"We can't thank you enough," Dad said. "Can I give you some money for gas?"

"No, I think you will need all the money you have by the time that hand is fixed," Mrs. Hermann said.

Mrs. Hermann had not been gone too long when Grandma and Grandpa showed up.

"We just wanted to make sure you guys were going to be okay the next day or two," Grandma said. "Have you heard from Dolores yet?"

"She hasn't called yet," Dad said. "I think they are probably working on Gary's hand still. Larry and I will do the evening milking now, and Linda will fix dinner. I think Larry and David can get the morning milking done."

"Well, David isn't going to be able to stay home by himself when Larry and Linda go to school tomorrow," Grandma said.

"I'm big enough," I said.

"I know you think you're big enough, but I think we will come over in the morning and pick you up before Larry and Linda go to school," Grandma said. "We can take you two to school, so you don't have to worry about catching the bus."

We were just done with that conversation when Mom called.

"Gary is in surgery now," Mom said. "Dr. Gurney is operating on his hand. We will need to stay the night here. They say that I can sleep in his room, and I think I will be able to come home tomorrow afternoon. The doctor says he is pretty sure that this surgery is just a temporary fix and that we will have to go to Portland to the Shriners Hospital for more surgery. I think Dr. Gurney said he would be sending us to see a Dr. Thatcher."

"Grandma said they can come over and pick you up when you are ready to come home," Dad said on the phone. "You take care and tell Gary to keep his chin up. Grandma also says that she will call Uncle Ferrill. You can probably stay with them if you go to Portland."

Mom came home in the afternoon, the day following Gary's surgery. Gary stayed another day.

During surgery, Dr. Gurney had to make an incision at Gary's wrist in order to pull the tendons back into the wound. They had retracted with the muscle pull after they were severed.

13

"The worst thing about the surgery was when they put a mask on my face and then dropped ether on the mask," Gary said as we sat at the dinner table the day after he was home. "They asked me to count while they did the drops, and I think I got to six."

And so, Gary's ordeal began. At home, we made do. Larry could do the morning milking with no problem. It was early enough in the spring that many cows had not calved yet. Linda could come close to fixing dinner and breakfast, although I am sure she complained a bit. There were days that I stayed with Grandma and Grandpa, and I liked that because I could spend time in the lower barn with Uncle Ern.

"This is the bottom of a milk bottle that cut your hand when you landed on it," Dad said as he showed Gary the jagged piece of glass.

"I don't want to look at it," Gary said.

Dad took the piece of glass and threw it down the hole in the outhouse.

The first trip to Portland was for surgery. Mom and Gary stayed with Uncle Ferrill's family on their dairy farm out of Aurora.

To avoid the discomfort of the ether anesthesia, when they started the drops, Gary breathed as deep as he could so he would be under quicker. Dr. Thatcher opened the wound at the original laceration site and cleaned up the tendon repairs done by Dr. Gurney.

A few weeks following that surgery, Dr. Thatcher signed Gary up for a couple of weeks of physical therapy. Mom and Gary would make daily trips into Portland from Ferrill's farm in Aurora. This involved a trip across the Willamette River on Boone's Ferry to and from Wilsonville.

Gary was testing how well he could throw with his left arm during this stay. His target was the many swallow nests under the eaves of the barn. Uncle Ferrill caught him in the act and was none too happy.

There were follow-up trips for months with a second surgery stuck in there somewhere. I went along and stayed at Ferrill's on the second surgery trip.

The second surgery was through an incision separate from the original injury on Gary's palm of his right hand. And again, Gary sucked in the ether as fast as he could.

The frequent trips were arduous. Dad would take Mom and Gary to catch the Greyhound bus in Coquille at three or four in the morning. The bus trip up the coast to Portland was a long one, probably eight hours. People would flag the bus down at most any location along the route, disrupting anyone trying to sleep.

They did have a stop at Otis Junction that allowed for a walk to stretch their legs and get a bite of food. Then the bus went on to Portland.

They would get off the bus at the central Greyhound station in the middle of downtown Portland and walk a couple blocks to the doctor's office. It was in a high-rise building on the seventh floor.

After the doctor's visit, they would eat lunch, usually a hamburger and fries, at the lunch counter in the Woolworth's store. Then they would have time for a movie before catching the bus back to Coquille. If they were lucky, they would be able to get some sleep on the bus, wrapping up a nearly twenty-four-hour day. They would arrive in Coquille around two in the morning.

"You should see all the movie theaters in Portland," Gary said one evening as we were getting into bed. "There are five or six of them, all in a group, and you can just pick which movie you want to watch."

Gary never returned to school after the accident. His teacher, Miss Wilson, gave the folks the option for him to pass the grade or to repeat the third grade. Mom had a strong feeling that he should repeat the year, so that was how it was done.

Gary's hand was never the same. The laceration was across the entire width of the palm of his hand, severing tendons, muscles, blood vessels, and some nerves. As he went through life, he displayed his Larsen character and never allowed the deficit to dictate what he could or could not do.

Jerd

Peggy was lying on the kitchen floor and reaching as far as possible under the wood cookstove.

"I can almost reach him," Peggy said.

"Leave him alone. He will just scratch you," I said. "Jerd doesn't like us."

Jerd was our grandmother's cat. He was a short-haired, white cat with one blue eye and one yellow eye. He was a loner and spent much of his time hunting and sometimes fighting the other barn cats. And he was death on grandkids. He was fine when we were watching him from across the room. But try to touch him, and he was all claws.

The only time he would tolerate our presence was when we were helping him find mice in the haymow of the lower barn. We could scatter hay, and the mice would run in all directions. He seemed to be able to catch one with each paw and one in his mouth.

Peggy reached a little further, and there was a low growl and then a hiss. Peggy withdrew her arm with a long set of scratch marks on the top of her hand. She was crying by the time Grandma got to the kitchen.

"I have told you kids, time and again, to leave that old cat alone," Grandma said. That was probably the first time I had heard her speak in a stern voice. "Now, let's get in the bathroom, wash this up, and put some Merthiolate on it."

"That stings," Peggy said through tears from the scratch and now the fear of the treatment.

"It helps if you blow on it after putting it on," Grandma said.

***

A year or two later, during silo filling time, we little kids were stuck in the house with Grandma and the other women preparing lunch for the crew. It was more like a Thanksgiving dinner.

Uncle Rodney pulled up to the back gate in his tractor with a sickle mower attached. He came through the gate and up the steps to the back porch. Grandma and a couple of the other ladies were waiting for him on the back porch.

"Mom, I just wanted to tell you that Jerd was out in the grass hunting mice, and the mower got him," Uncle Rodney said. "It cut off all his legs, so we knocked him in the head to put him out of his misery. I think he must have been deaf. Otherwise, he would have heard the tractor coming."

"That was the only thing you could do," Grandma said. "What have you done with him?"

"Duke is burying him over under that big myrtle tree on the creek bank," Uncle Rodney said.

"That's a good place for him," Grandma said. "I'll miss the old guy, but the grandkids will probably be safer with him gone."

***

Many years later, my mind drifted back to that day on Grandma's back porch. I was waiting at the clinic for a client to bring in a cat that had been injured by a sickle mower in the fading light of the summer evening.

As I thought about Jerd and his behavior, he probably was deaf. That was why he was so antisocial with people and why he never hung around the barn with the other cats. White cats do have a genetic degeneration of the organ of Corti in the middle ear. So it is very possible that he was deaf.

And the sickle mower took all of his legs. I am wondering just what this lady will be expecting for the treatment of her cat tonight. And how many legs will it be missing?

"Good evening, Dr. Larsen," Sally said as she came through the door with her cat peeking out of a bundle of towels. "Thank you so much for coming in this evening to look at my Oliver."

I took Sally and Oliver into an exam room and placed the bundle of towels on the table.

"Tell me again, what happened to Oliver," I said.

"Jim was trying to get the last of the field mowed this evening," Sally said. "Oliver must have been out there, hunting in the tall grass. Anyway, Oliver got caught in the sickle blades, and he is a real mess. When Jim called out to me to bring a towel, I was afraid he had been hurt. I saw Oliver trying to walk as soon as I got to the tractor. I just scooped him up and headed back to the house. That's when I called you."

I carefully peeled the towels away so I could get a good look at Oliver. Oliver seemed resigned to his fate but didn't display any obvious discomfort. What a mess, both of Oliver's hind feet were severed just below the hock joints. His right front leg was severed at the middle of his forearm. There was only a minor laceration on his left front leg.

"Sally, there is not much I can do for Oliver," I said. "Maybe we should be thinking of what would be in his best interest."

"Can't you just sew up his wounds?" Sally asked.

"Yes, I can sew up these wounds, but I am not sure how well Oliver will be able to move around," I said. "Are you sure you want to deal with him in that situation?"

"I just can't give up on him over an accident that was not his fault," Sally said.

"I am pretty certain that his stumps won't hold up to any outside activity, and I am not sure how well he will handle the litter box in the house," I said. "I don't have a problem with repairing his wounds, as long as he will be in a situation that is livable for him. We could always rethink our decision later if you have difficulty dealing with Oliver at home."

"Can you do this tonight?" Sally asked.

"Yes, after I get him under anesthesia, I will clean up these wounds and close things up," I said. "I might have to shorten his stumps a bit just to be able to make more functional stumps.

"Will I be able to pick him up in the morning?" Sally asked.

"Probably, but call first," I said. "I will need to check him over and make sure his pain is under control before sending him home."

I gave Oliver a hefty dose of ketamine to start anesthesia and provide some pain control.

In the surgery room, I prepped the wounds and trimmed the stumps on both hind legs, removing all the remnants of the metatarsal bones. This allowed me the ability to form a smooth, well-padded stump on each hind leg that could maybe serve Oliver pretty well.

I smoothed the bones on the right front leg and closed that stump. It would not be as functional as his hind leg stumps, but it would heal well.

I infused a little lidocaine into each repair to help with pain on recovery, but with the ketamine onboard, he should be okay until morning. I settled him into a well-padded kennel.

"We will see you in the morning, Oliver," I said as I closed the kennel door. "We will see what morning gives us."

***

In the morning, Oliver was up and looking for breakfast. He seemed to be doing well in the kennel. Hopefully, he will do okay at home.

Sally came in the early afternoon, and Oliver was happy to see her. We sent him home with instructions to stay indoors and keep incisions clean and dry, and use a pelleted litter.

I saw Oliver once more for suture removal, and Sally reported he was doing well at home. The incisions had healed well, and the stumps looked like they would be serviceable. He didn't use his right front leg stump but moved around on his hind leg stumps and his good left front leg.

After that last visit, I never saw Sally or Oliver again. One can only hope that Oliver's life was tolerable for him.

The Plank Road, My First Job

We had moved to a small (one hundred sixty acres) farm up the river from Broadbent in December of 1949. There was a lot of snow that winter. We had over a foot of snow on the ground that January. That was unusual for Southwestern Oregon. With two older brothers, I learned every corner of the farm.

By the spring of 1950, I was a hardy five-year-old farm boy. Left at home by myself and Mom while the other kids were in school, I was allowed to roam the farm's lower reaches by myself. I was not supposed to go to the creek, and I could not cross the road to the fields by the river.

That spring, I acquired a new job. I became the construction supervisor of the plank road going to the mill being built up the creek. In those days, they often would build a small mill at the timber source, harvest the timber, and saw the lumber right there. When the job was done, they would pull the mill's hardware and move to the next location.

The creek road was gravel, but the lower road that crossed the field was a plank road. This road was being built along the fence on the neighbor's place. I could scurry across that fence in a flash.

Ernie Bryant was building the road. He was a friend of my folks. They had been in school together, years ago.

Ernie knew who I was before I introduced myself. I had him explain everything he was doing on that first day. I wanted to know everything if I was going to be supervising the rest of the job.

Ernie laid out two parallel rows of railroad ties, staggered, so the joints between the ties were never lined up with the opposite joint. Then he would lay the large planks across the ties. These planks were large, rough-cut planks, probably three by twelve inches. Ernie nailed the planks down with large nails that looked about six inches long. The planks were eight feet long. They extended out from the railroad ties about a foot on each side. I am sure the work was hard. Ernie built the entire plank road by himself.

Most of the time, Ernie showed up at eight in the morning. That gave me plenty of time to see the brothers and sister off to the school bus and finish breakfast. The first day I didn't pack a lunch and had to run back to the house when Ernie stopped to eat his lunch.

After that first day, I always showed up with my lunch in a paper sack and a thermos of milk. I stowed these in the old stump on the fence line. This was an old cedar stump with a rather large cedar tree growing out of its center. All the time after that first day, I would sit and eat my lunch with Ernie. We would discuss the progress we expected to make on the road in the coming afternoon during lunch. Sometimes we would talk about Mom in her school days so many years before. After lunch, I would stand partway around the stump as Ernie, and I would pee on the stump.

When the plank road was getting close to the gravel road, I showed up at eight sharp, and Ernie was not there. I had learned from my Grandfather and Uncle Ern that to be late for anything was terrible and to be late for work was the worst thing you could do on a job.

I sat down on the ground by the stump. I would sit on the plank road, but the planks were very rough, and I thought it would probably give me splinters in my butt. I had had splinters in my hands before. I didn't want Mom to be digging a splinter out of my butt with one of her sewing needles.

Finally, Ernie came driving up the plank road. I stood up and greeted him as he came to a stop and got out of his pickup.

"You're late for work," I said. "My Grandfather says you should never show up late for work."

"I bet you have a time clock in that pocket of yours," he replied with a smile on his face. "I figure that if I work hard today that I could finish this road. Then you are not going to have anything to do."

Ernie was right. This had been a fun couple of weeks. I had not thought about the fact the job would be over one day.

"I have lots of stuff to do," I replied. "One of these days, I am going to convince Mom that I am big enough to fish in the creek by myself."

Ernie finished the plank road that afternoon. He was picking up his tools when I came running down the road with a small bag of the large spikes that had been left on the old cedar stump. Ernie finished, reached in his pocket, and pulled out his wallet. He handed me two dollars.

"Here you go, young man. I appreciate all your help. We will have trucks using this road next week. You make sure you stay out of their way," he said as he handed me the two bills.

Two dollars was a small fortune to a five-year-old in 1950. I had nickels and dimes before, but I don't think I ever had a dollar bill, let alone two of them. Ernie was driving down the plank road on his way home when I scrambled across the fence. I stopped and returned to retrieve my lunch sack and thermos from the stump. Then I was off again to show Mom that I was a rich young man.

Chicken Wars

My brothers and I had spent the entire morning cleaning out the old chicken coop. It was one of the most unpleasant jobs on the farm. The dust from the manure and debris made breathing difficult. We would work a bit and then step outside to breathe for a few minutes.

We had just finished when Dad arrived from town with a crate on the back of the truck. He had about thirty chicks in the crate. These were a little older than the just hatched size but still small, maybe a week old. When the crate was opened in the coop they scattered, happy to have some open space.

We spent the next hour setting up the water tank and the feed rack. Dad put some medicine in the water. We had a mash in the feed rack, and we planned to feed some scratch on the floor every morning. This was going to be our summer job. I enjoyed filling the feeder with mash and throwing the scratch out for the chicks to scramble after. They would gather all the scratch before they would return to mash. They seemed to grow as you watched them.

It wasn't long, and they had some feathers. They were all doing well, but there were a couple that the others picked on, pecking their tail stump raw. We had to doctor those wounds every morning and finally had to separate the chicks who were being picked on, sort of like kids at school, I guessed. There was always an odd one that didn't get along.

The summer went by rapidly, and the day came to slaughter the chickens. If I thought the daily chores were a pain, this day was going to be fun but a lot of work. The first job for my older brother Gary and I was to chop off the heads of the chickens. We had to work relatively fast because there was an assembly line of sorts set up and the speed of the chopping dictated the pace of the assembly line.

We went into the coop and started capturing chickens and placing them in a crate. Then we took the crate to the woodshed. My job was to pull a chicken out of the box and hold its head and neck down on the chopping block. Gary swung the ax. Then I would release the headless chicken with a bit of a toss into the air. It would fly around a moment, then run around the woodshed, blood spurting. It didn't take long for Gary and me to be covered with blood, and the woodshed looked like the scene of a horrible crime. The only thing that bothered me was that the head would blink for a short time. I wondered what it was thinking.

We would gather the birds after they were quiet and well-bled out, then take them out to the scalding tub, a large kettle of boiling water set over a fire in the middle of the yard. After a short dip in the tub, we could pluck the feathers.

Then Mom and Aunt Lila would take them into the house, singe the fine feathers and pull the large quills if any remained. After the singeing, they would gut the bird, saving the heart, liver, and gizzard, then rinse them thoroughly, and wrap them for the freezer. While that was going on, Gary and I were starting on the next crate of chickens in the woodshed.

The battles started when the chickens were thawed and cut up for dinner. Mostly fried, one chicken fed the family, Dad, Mom, Linda, Larry, Gary, and myself.

Mom cut up the bird into the breast, two thighs, two drumsticks, two wings, neck, and the back was divided into two pieces. The breast was divided to provide three parts. The wishbone was cut out first, then split the breast into two pieces.

At the table, the meat was distributed. Dad and Larry got a large piece of breast, and Gary got the wishbone. Mom and

Linda got a thigh and maybe another piece like a drumstick or wing. I was left with a drumstick and maybe a wing. Once in a while, I would get the neck and a piece of the back. This was fine until I was old enough to think that I also deserved a part of the breast.

Mom attempted to defuse the problem.

"David, you can have my thigh. I like the wings and backs, and the backs really have a lot of meat, and the wings are white meat also," she said.

"The thigh is dark meat, and I like white meat. I don't see why I can't have some breast meat," I replied.

"The chicken can only be cut into so many pieces," she pointed out.

It was decided that the wishbone would be up for grabs for whoever got to the table first. You can imagine how that went. Mom solved the problem finally by cutting the wings off with a chunk of breast meat attached.

Tripping Up the Bully

Broadbent school in the fall of 1952 had grown to its largest enrollment ever with nearly eighty students in eight grades.

The school board had discovered that the upper part of Catching Creek was actually in the Broadbent district rather than Myrtle Point. In 1952, they started busing those kids to Broadbent. It meant a long bus ride for the kids, but more students for the school.

Tommy, a small blond first grade boy, was one of those students from upper Catching Creek. I was in the third grade that year, and Tommy, being so small, was a kid I watched over somewhat.

"David, that other David in your class has been picking on me," Tommy said to me one afternoon as we were waiting for the bigger kids to get out of class so the buses could take everyone home.

"What is he doing to you?" I asked.

"He pushes me every time he walks past me," Tommy said. "And he says he will beat me up if I tell the teacher."

"My dad says that you have to stand up to a bully, or he will just keep pestering you," I said.

"Yeah, but David is scary," Tommy said. "He almost acts like a wild man."

The other David was a special case. The first two years of school, he and his two sisters were home schooled. They lived at the top of Dement Creek, almost over the hill where Dement Creek, Flores Creek and Catching Creek all started. They had no neighbors.

During those first two years, the family would come to school for testing to make sure they were learning what was expected.

David was a holy terror during those visits. My mother tried to say he just didn't know how to play with other kids. I thought he was crazy.

Starting in the third grade, David and his two sisters came to school full time. And it was a constant battle between David and all the other three or four boys in the class.

"Let's figure out how you can get him," I said.

"He always waits in the hall when we are out of class," Roy said. "He waits there for his sisters to get out of school."

"I bet we could have Tommy hide behind the door while we stand out in the playground and make fun of David," I said. "He will get mad and come running at us full speed with a fist in the air."

"Yeah," Tommy said. "And when he comes out the door, I could trip him, and he will fall down the stairs."

"He is probably waiting in the hall right now," I said. "Let's just do it now. It will teach him a good lesson."

We positioned Tommy behind the closed door of the double doors leading into the main hall of the school. In good weather, the other half of the double doors were always open.

Roy and I stood out in the school playground where we could see David in the hallway. We started hollering names at him. Sure enough he came running at us, full steam ahead.

The plan worked better than any of us expected, one would have thought it had been conceived by Army generals. David came running out the door, going as fast as he could run. Little

Tommy stuck his foot out and tripped him. David fell, head over heels, down the five concrete steps in front of the school.

We were probably lucky that he was not seriously injured. But Tommy sort of pranced by David as he was getting himself up, looking at scrapes on both of his elbows.

We laughed and patted Tommy on the back and went over to the swings. David got up and went back into the hall to wait for his sisters. He never said a word.

For the rest the time David was at school, he was never a problem again, not for us and not for Tommy. At the end of our fourth grade year, David and his two sisters moved to Texas.

Tommy and I, and many of the other kids who watched the event, learned a valuable lesson day. If you ignore the actions of a bully, you just enable him to continue his abuse. In the end, you live with constant fear of what he will do next. There comes a time, you have to stand up to the bully and trip him up the best that you can.

Lessons learned in elementary school often have applications to later, more serious events in one's life.

The Dreaded Pox

"Gary, let me look at that sore again," Mom said to my brother as he was getting ready for school one spring morning.

Gary had a blister-like sore that had developed on the back of his hand. After a couple of days, it had scabbed over and was not bothering him much.

"I don't know how you can stand it," I said to Gary as Mom was looking at the sore. "I would pick that scab."

"This looks just like this sore that has popped up between my fingers," Mom said.

Gary was four years older than me. He and Mom did most of the morning milking when Dad was working, as I had not started school yet. We milked a small herd of cows, but it was enough to pay most of the bills in the early 1950s.

"I think this is a cowpox sore," Mom said. "Grandpa said he had seen these before."

Cowpox is a disease of cattle caused by a virus that closely resembles the smallpox virus. In 1796, Edward Jenner noticed that milkmaids who had contracted cowpox never had smallpox lesions. After some experimentation, he published his findings in 1801. Cowpox virus was used to vaccinate people against smallpox for many years in the 1800s. The vaccine was changed to another virus sometime in the 1800s, but that date is not known.

"I will call Dr. Whitaker and have him look at the cows," Mom said.

The next morning the cows were left in their stanchions after milking. Mom and I waited at the barn for Dr. Whitaker to arrive. I was excited because our farm's rare visits by veterinarians were always filled with mystery and intrigue.

Dr. Whitaker was a tall, thin, young veterinarian who had just moved to Myrtle Point. He moved from cow to cow until he found a sore on the teat of the fourth cow.

"Yes, this looks like cowpox to me," Dr. Whitaker said to Mom. "I will go ahead and vaccinate the entire herd."

"David can stay and watch, and he can show you where everything is located if you need anything. I have chores to do at the house. You can stop there when you are done," Mom said as she left the barn.

"Well David, let me show you how we vaccinate cows for cowpox," Dr. Whitaker said as if he was conducting a lecture.

Dr. Whitaker returned to the cow with a large scab on one teat. He carefully picked the scab off the teat and placed it into a small tin container that looked like a lid off a jar. Then he added a little sand to the container and some water.

With a knife, he cut the scab into tiny pieces. Then he placed it all in a mortar and pestle and ground it into a fine suspension.

"There, that should be good enough," he said as he showed me the finished product. "Now we just have to scratch some of this into each cow. We will do this on the edge of their tail. That way, the sore that develops won't be a problem for them."

We moved from cow to cow, working down the milking string. Dr. Whitaker treated each cow the same. Lifting the tail, he would grab the web of skin on the side of the tail. Then he would scratch the skin with a knife blade until it bled. He had a small stiff brush in the solution he had made from the scab. He dipped the little brush and then rubbed it into the bleeding scratch he had made on the tail.

Each cow took a few minutes to complete the process. It must have taken close to an hour to finish the entire herd.

"Do you guys have any heifers that are going to calve soon that are not in this bunch?" Dr. Whitaker asked.

"No," I said with confidence. Although, I doubt if I had any real awareness of that status.

"Okay then, let's clean up, and I can get out of here," Dr. Whitaker said.

"I better turn the cows out first."

"No, you come with me to the milk house, and we will wash up first," Dr. Whitaker said. "Then you can turn the cows out."

"But I didn't touch anything."

"It is better to be safe than sorry," Dr. Whitaker said.

Dr. Whitaker washed my hands like they had not been washed before. I would have complained had it been Mom doing the washing, but I sensed that it was time to show how tough I was.

"Okay, you can go turn those cows out. They will be ready to get out to the pastures."

I opened the large door on the side of the barn. All the stanchions were connected with a set of boards along the top of the stanchion. I pulled the wooden pin that was holding them closed and pulled hard on the first stanchion. That pull, plus all the cows pulling back with their heads, and the stanchions came open. The cows backed out, and with some degree of order, turned and headed out the open door.

Just as Dr. Whitaker had said, as soon as they were clear of the barn door, they would buck and kick their legs as they ran toward the pasture.

"This barn is a big mess. Those extra couple of hours with the cows in here makes it a big job to clean," Dr. Whitaker. "I suppose your mother does that job."

"I do some of it," I said. "I can scrape and sweep the floor into the gutter, but I can't do the gutter. When my brothers get home from school, we will clean it then. My sister never has to work at the barn."

"I hear that a lot," Dr. Whitaker said as he put everything back into his truck. "Sisters seem to get out of a lot of barn work. But most of the time, they do plenty of work around the house."

Dr. Whitaker stopped and talked with Mom.

"You should notice a scab on the right side of their tails," he said. "And you shouldn't have any more problems. You might want to have a doctor look at your sores if they get worse. Most of the time, they are no problem, but once in a while, they make people sick."

"Thanks for coming so soon," Mom said.

"Thanks for the call, and thanks for the help, David," Dr. Whitaker said as he departed.

The Young Boy and the Creek

When spring finally came in my third grade year I was deemed old enough to fish in the creek by myself. I was nine years old that March. I am not sure why it took Mom so long to come to the conclusion that I was old enough. I knew every inch of the creek from our upper line fence, through our hill country and across to Hermann's field all the way to the bridge at the highway, maybe a distance of a mile or so.

My only problem now was school. The weekend only provided limited time at the creek. Dad had to drive the car to work. I figured that if I was sick until the bus was gone, Mom would have to let me go to the creek. Friday morning came, and Mom came upstairs to wake us boys up. The three of us shared an upstairs bedroom. My sister had the other room to herself.

"I'm sick to my stomach," I told Mom.

"Okay, you can stay in bed," Mom said.

I laid there and listened for the bus. When I was sure it had pulled out and headed down the road I sprang from the bed. I was confident that the monster was not under the bed this morning because I had watched my brothers get up and get dressed. I made my usual trip down the stairs, bounding down several steps at a time, with a final jump from four steps up, trying desperately to touch the ceiling that crossed the lower staircase.

34

Mom was in the kitchen. I stood close to the wood stove, the only source of heat in the house. "I am feeling better," I said.

"Oh, no you don't, you go back to bed. You have to stay in bed at least until noon," Mom said.

I had not counted on that, but that would be okay. Without a breakfast, I could get hungry early then go fishing in the afternoon, I thought as I headed back up the stairs.

Mom finally called me to come down for lunch. She had been working in the garden all morning. We had a large garden, about a half acre. I was already dressed in my work clothes. We sat at the dining room table by the window. Mom always liked to sit where she could watch her lilac bush, flowers in the yard and the distant traffic on the highway. There were seldom more than one or two cars during lunch. Today we had an egg salad sandwich and a small dish of canned pears. Not my favorite; Mrs. Lilly would be serving her chili at the school today.

This year was the first year that we had a school cafeteria. It was added on the back of the gym. All the mothers had worked with Mrs. Lilly during the summer and fall, canning stuff from the garden and all sorts of fruit. But my favorite by far was Mrs. Lilly's chili. Only the chance of catching fish by myself would lure me away from that lunch.

I helped clean up the table after lunch, summoned all my courage and then I spoke, "I'm feeling a lot better now, and I am sure bored."

"You should have gone to school," Mom said.

"Maybe I should go fishing," I replied.

"Okay, you can go fishing. But you don't go too far down the creek. If you can see the highway you have gone too far. And don't you get yourself wet. You stay on the bank, and stay off the logjam."

I was out the door in a shot. I grabbed the willow pole that I had cut and rigged last weekend. I also picked up my little canister of tackle. I opened it to see what was left, one split shot, one hook and small, mostly empty, spool of leader. I would have to be careful in the log jam hole. Maybe I would avoid that hole today, I thought.

The pole was a cut willow branch about five feet long. I had cut a notch in the end and tied a length of line maybe eight feet long. I tied a loop in the end of that line and attached the hook with its short leader there. One split shot above the knot and the rigging was complete. This was precious tackle. This was all there was.

My brother and I would take the wagon on Saturday mornings and walk to Broadbent, about two miles down the road. We picked up bottles along the way. When we turned in the bottles at the store we got one cent for beer bottles, two cents for pop bottles and five cents for large quart size bottles. Mostly there were beer bottles.

With the money we bought our fishing tackle. Once in a while on a good day there would be money left over for a candy bar or something. We could usually make the tackle last until the next trip but the log jam hole could eat a lot of tackle. That hole had the biggest fish. To fish it best you had to climb out on the logjam and fish down the cracks. Mom didn't like to see us do that, but the biggest fish were there. Today I would fish at the falls and be satisfied. I picked up an empty tuna can from the trash and headed for the manure pile beside the barn.

We always just left the shovel stuck in the ground by the edge of the manure pile. If you could turn over a scoop of dirt by the edge there were generally enough worms for the afternoon. It was hard for me to turn that scoop. Sometimes when I was by myself I had to dig in the manure pile. The worms were small there. I jumped on the shovel to drive it into the ground and leaned back on the handle hard. It flipped up one large scoop of dirt, and it was loaded with worms. I filled the can quickly.

I headed across the field to the falls. They were on Hermann's land but that was okay. I could hear the roar of the water as it spilled over the low falls, maybe five or six feet high. The hole here was deep and I could usually catch as many fish as I wanted. Once in a while I would catch one that was ten or even twelve inches but not as often as at the logjam. With my pocketknife I cut a willow fork to hold the fish as I climbed down the bank. I had carried a pocketknife since I was five years old. All the boys at school had a pocketknife. We often played mumblety-peg at school during recess and lunch.

When I got to the hole I sat on the rock ledge beside the falls and threaded a worm on the hook, pinching off the excess worm.

If the fishing was good I would need all the worms I had. I stood up and dropped the line into the water just outside of the bubbles made by the falls. As usual, there was no wait. I had my first fish almost as soon as the worm hit the water. I quickly unhooked it and broke its neck with my finger in its mouth and bending its head back. Then I placed it on the willow fork. I touched up the worm on the hook and added a little more worm.

Returning the line to water, there was another fish, again, almost instantly. In a half hour I had a dozen fish on the willow fork, all of them about eight inches long. I was sure I could easily catch a dozen more, but I wanted to catch some bigger fish. The logjam was about three holes down the creek. It was the last hole before the road was in view. I thought I would skip the three holes and go right to the logjam. Mom would never know.

It was good weather and the sun was out; the logs were dry. I liked to fish from the two large logs near the downstream edge of the logjam. They were the easiest to stand on and had a good gap between them. It always seemed that the bigger fish were under those logs. I lowered my worm into the gap between the logs. Again, almost instantly, there was a hookup. This was a bigger fish than the others, I would guess eleven inches. It took a little longer to tend to fish at this hole because I had to go to the bank each time. In the next half hour I had a total of four more fish, all between ten and twelve inches.

I lowered the wormed hook into the water between the logs. This time there was a funny tug on the line. I raised it again, slowly. A large trout followed it toward the surface before sinking back into the depth of the water. This was a large trout, maybe the largest I had seen in this creek. My heart raced and I lowered the line back into the depths of the water. Bam! There was a big strike on the line. I pulled and the fish pulled. The willow pole bent almost double. He slowly came to the surface and the water between my feet exploded. He made a strong dive. Again I pulled and he struggled. Then my pull was against dead weight. He must have wrapped the line around a snag. I was sick, not only was I about to lose this fish but I was going to lose the tackle also.

When I looked over the downstream edge of the log I could

see the large trout still on the hook, struggling against the snag. If I could get down there, maybe I could catch him by hand and maybe even retrieve my tackle. I laid down the willow pole and went back to the bank, moving down the creek to a point I could get into the water. The water below the hole was not deep, but was very cold. As I approached the hole I could see the trout. He was hung up on a small branch on a short piece of line. When I got close enough to reach him I was in waist deep water. I reached in and grabbed the fish. When I got a finger through his gills I was able to unhook him.

What a prize; it was probably fifteen, maybe even sixteen, inches long. I got him to the bank. He was too big for me to break his neck. I took my pocketknife and severed his spine at the base of his skull. After adding him to the willow fork, I returned to the creek to try to retrieve my tackle. I found the stick the line had been wrapped around but the line was not there now. There was another hook embedded in the same stick, however. When I retrieved this hook it still had some line attached and a split shot. I was able to reach the willow pole from the log. I pulled my line up with no problem, hook, line and sinker still attached.

This had been a great afternoon. Not only had I caught the biggest fish in the creek but I was coming home with more tackle than when I left the house. I gathered everything up and headed home. Even with the sun out, I was already chilled. Mom was going to be upset, but she would feel better when she saw this fish. I remember how excited she was when my oldest brother caught a twenty-inch fish in the river last fall.

Mom was waiting on the porch as I crawled through the fence into the yard. She had her hands on her hips and a frown on her face. Mom never got really mad. She just said she was disappointed.

"I thought I told you not to get wet!" she said.

"Mom, I couldn't help it, this big fish almost got away," I replied, holding up the willow fork filled with fish.

She took the mess of fish and started for the kitchen. "You get out of those wet clothes and get in by the fire before you catch pneumonia," she said.

I stripped down on the porch and put my clothes in the

hamper by the wringer washer. Now I was really cold. I scampered into the kitchen and huddled up to the wood stove.

"You bring your shoes in behind the stove. I will get you a blanket," she said.

I ran out, grabbed my shoes and returned to the stove. As I wrapped the blanket around my shoulders, I could start to feel the warmth return to my body. It had been a great afternoon.

Monday morning, as I was hurrying out the door to catch the school bus, Mom handed me a neatly folded note.

"Here is your excuse for Friday, you give it to your teacher when you first get to school," she said.

On the bus I took the note out of my pocket and carefully unfolded it. It read: "Please excuse David from school last Friday. He was ill."

Brownie, 1953

I woke to an empty bedroom. The sky was clear and the morning sun was out, but there was still a chill to the summer air. I laid still and tried to listen to hear my brothers downstairs. I hated to wake to an empty room. Did the monster get them when they got up, was he still waiting for me? I felt confident that I was safe if I watched them get up and dress, but now, I didn't know.

I stood up and backed up to the far corner of the old double bed. I had to bend over a little because of the slant of the roof on the side of the bedroom. After a deep breath, I ran and jumped, hit the floor on the dead run and made a rapid turn to the open staircase. I bounded down the stairs, taking two or three steps at a time. I didn't look back until I was at the bottom. No monster, I opened the door and entered the kitchen as if nothing had happened. Both Larry and Gary were at the table eating breakfast. I huddled up to the wood stove, the only heat in the house. It felt good after my run down the stairs.

"You need to go get dressed and get back down here for breakfast," Mom said. "Your brothers are planning to go swimming this morning but you guys have to clean the barn first."

"We can ride Brownie to the river and back," Gary said. "That way we won't have to worry about the thistles in the field."

I hurried back upstairs and dressed. Mom had a bowl of Wheat Hearts mush waiting for me when I got back to the kitchen. I didn't like mush but Wheat Hearts were better that oatmeal. The warm mush felt good on a cold morning, and the large glass of milk made it easier to swallow

With the three of us the barn cleaning went fast. Larry was the oldest, and he assigned the chores. Gary scraped any manure on the floor into the gutter. I went along behind him and used the large barn broom and swept the loose dirt on the floor into the gutter. Larry cleaned the gutter, using the shovel to scrape long sections out the door onto the manure pile. With the job done we could head to the river. There was no need for a bath today.

Back at the house we changed into our swim trunks and slipped on a pair of thongs (flip-flops). I hated to cross the lower field in these things because of the thistles. There was no good way to avoid the stickers except when we could ride Brownie. Gary headed to the pasture to get him. With a couple of whistles he came running. He probably knew he would get the whole lower pasture to himself while we swam.

Brownie was a Jersey cross steer, solid light brown with a pinkish nose. This was his second summer and he was starting to get extra grain every evening. We had raised him from a calf and he was very friendly. He came when Gary whistled. I couldn't whistle yet but I was trying.

Gary had no trouble getting onto Brownie in the middle of the field. It was a little hard for me so I would wait at the gate. We didn't need a bridle or rope. We just tapped him on the side of the neck with a switch to tell him where to go. I jumped on and he trotted down the lane. Larry was already across the highway and in the lower field but we would catch up with him now.

The grass in the lower field was knee high. The cows were not allowed in this field until we cut hay. Dad would be a little upset with Brownie being down here but we could tell him that we were just helping to fatten him up.

When we got to the riverbank we slid off and Brownie ran to the middle of the field, bucking with joy. The sand on the riverbank was warm from the morning sun. The river was probably still cold. Larry was already in the swimming hole. He had crossed the river and was ready to dive off the old log on the far bank. I was not supposed to go over to that log but with just us boys here today, I thought I would swim over to it.

The water was really cold. It took a slow walk to get into it. I swam a little up and back. I think I will wait until it is warmer before I swim across. A couple of times up and back was enough for me. I got out and laid down in the warm sand. It wasn't long and everyone was ready to go back to the house.

"You go get Brownie while I dry off," Gary said.

I ran up the riverbank. Brownie was clear across the field with his head buried in the grass. I made my best attempt and out came a weak little whistle. Brownie raised his head and looked. He had heard my whistle. Here he came on the run. This was going to be a good ride home. He came to a stop in front of me. I nuzzled up to his belly for a little warmth. I would need some help getting on him here in the field. Pretty soon Gary came up and jumped up on him with no problem. I jumped and Larry gave me a little boost and I was on also.

Brownie trotted toward the gate. His trot was a little rough, not like a horse, but we were used to it and had no problem staying on his back. He stopped at the highway and waited for our heels to tell him to go. He gave a long look back to the lower field as he started up the lane toward the house.

We rode Brownie every day that summer. He enjoyed the rides. We covered the hill on Brownie and went to the river on all the good days. When we had company everyone wanted to see how well he was trained. As the summer wore on, I was able to get myself onto his back in the middle of the field. He was a better companion than a dog.

But fall came, and the second fall of all good steers would be their last. The day for Brownie's slaughter finally came. We slaughtered on the farm. It was a common event that we were used to watching. We generally helped where we could. The steer was shot in the head and hung in the machine shed. He was gutted and skinned there. I had helped in this part in the past but today I waited in the house. Brownie was different from the other steers. After he was skinned and gutted, they would split his carcass with a handsaw, then cut him into quarters. The quarters hung from the large cherry tree in the back yard. It would hang there in the cold fall air until the weekend when Uncle Ern would come and cut him up. Uncle Ern was an old man now but he had been a meat cutter in his younger days. He knew just how to do it.

It was hard to see Brownie hanging there in the back yard every day. In farm families, life revolves around the kitchen and the back yard. We never used the front door, and the front yard was seldom used. Finally Saturday came and with a lot of help from Uncle Ern, Brownie was in the freezer in a short time.

Dinnertime that winter became a challenge. With every meal, I would fiddle with the meat on my plate. I knew it was Brownie and I knew I had to eat it. It proved to be a long, hard winter.

"Is this Brownie?" I would ask, almost every meal.

"Yes, this is Brownie," was always the answer. "Now eat your dinner."

"This meat is tough," I would say.

Dad would answer, "It would be a damn sight tougher if you didn't have it."

Fast Ball Pitch in the Bullpen

I enjoyed lying in the haymow, resting before evening chores and pondering the mysteries of the world and reliving the day's events. The fresh hay was warm and chewing on a stem of grass yielded a pleasant taste. I could lie here, and nobody would bother me as I let my mind wander over the events of the morning before getting to the mysteries of life.

As soon as the barn was cleaned following the morning's milking I had hurried to the house to change out of my barn clothes. I gathered my willow fishing pole and a can for worms and raced out of the house and off the back porch. That was one of those mysteries. Every home I knew of used the back door to come and go, usually through the kitchen. If the front door was never used and the back door was the main door in life, why didn't the back door become the front door and front door the back door?

I ran to the manure pile at the corner of the barn. I was anxious to get to the creek before the sun was on the water. The fish would be biting better early in the morning. I drove the shovel into the ground at the edge of the manure pile and jumped on it a couple of times to drive it deeper into the earth. Then with both hands near the top of the handle, I pulled back with all my weight. After a brief resistance, the shovel flipped over a large scoop of dirt. It was loaded with worms. Breaking the dirt apart, I filled the worm can quickly. These worms were large and wiggled a lot. They had that bright reddish color that the fish seemed to like. This was going to be a good morning for fishing.

The run to the creek was several hundred yards, but I covered it in no time. I practiced my moves that I learned watching Crazy Legs at the movie last year. I scrambled over the fence at the wooden section and ran down to the creek. This first hole was the largest and the best. There was a four-foot waterfall at the head of the hole. The water was deep under the waterfall. I fished from a rock shelf that ran the length of the hole on this side of the creek. These early summer days were great fishing. The flow was just starting to slow a little, and the water was crystal clear.

I put my stuff down and untangled the line on my willow pole. My hands were shaking in anticipation as I threaded a worm onto the hook. The free end of the worm wiggled a lot. I would break this portion off if the worm supply was low, but I liked to leave it on for the first couple of fish. The larger fish would tend to seek out this squirming worm. I dipped the worm in my vial of cod liver oil. I was less than convinced that it made a difference but my Uncle Duke was sure that it did and Dad said that it couldn't hurt.

With everything ready, I lowered the worm into the water at the deepest end, just a foot from the foam from the waterfall. Bam, there was a sharp tug on the line before the worm was halfway to the bottom. I struggled a little, and the willow pole bent with the tip touching the water. But then with the spring in the willow branch and my pull, the fish came flying out of the water. Such a nice fish, probably fourteen inches long. I quickly dispatched him with my pocket knife, driving the blade into the back of his neck at the base of his skull. He didn't even damage the worm much.

The morning went quickly, I had twenty fish and had wished only two of the main holes. I gathered up my stuff and the willow fork of fish and headed back to the house. Mom would have lunch made, and after I cleaned the fish and finished lunch, I could head out to the barn until it was time to do evening chores.

I cut the heads off the fish with Mom's large butcher knife. She was always quick to remind me not to cut a finger off.

"David, you be careful with that knife," she would say, "You could cut a finger off before you know what happened."

It was good for her to remind me I guess, but you would think she should know that I would remember her warning by now.

Uncle Duke left the heads of his fish on and cooked them that way, but Mom said she didn't want them looking at her from the frying pan.

It didn't take long, and the fish were cleaned and in the refrigerator. They would make a good dinner tonight, enough for everyone. Mom fried them after dipping them in egg and then flour. They came out golden brown and tasted great. There was nothing better than fresh trout unless it was really fresh trout, cooked over a campfire.

I washed and sat down with Mom and my brother Gary for lunch. Bologna sandwich and a glass of milk. We ate quickly without a lot of conversation. Gary had not wanted to fish this morning. I bet he regretted that decision after seeing the mess of fish I brought home. Anyway, I finished lunch and headed to the barn.

The fresh hay was warm and smelled sweet. I pulled a long straw from a bale and casually chewed on it as I laid back and tried to decide if I should take a nap or solve some the mysteries that seemed to bother me a lot these days.

I wonder why girls are so different from boys. I mean the farm girls are not bad, they can do stuff like ride horses and do barn chores. They even fish sometimes. But the town girls, they play jacks and do hopscotch, that's about it. Last summer when two LA cousins visited and I took them on a hike around the hill, they complained most of the time. They were not impressed with the duck pond on top of the hill, and then when they had to scale down the face of the cliff on the back side of the hill, you would have thought the world had come to an end. I thought we were going to have to turn around and go back the way we came. I ended up taking them down the cliff, one at a time. Almost had to place their every step but we all got down okay. To hear them tell the story when we got back to the house, you would have thought we had climbed down into the Grand Canyon.

And then, maybe the biggest mystery of all, how does this barn roof shed water without leaking a drop. Lying here I can see cracks between every shake. At night you can see stars through the roof. I asked Mom once; she had no idea how it worked.

"All barns are made that way," she said.

When I talked to Grandpa about it, he just chuckled.

"David, they have been building barns that way my entire life," he said. "I guess there must be a draft that keeps the water out of the cracks."

Grandpas are pretty smart guys; if he couldn't answer, I was at a loss of who to ask. Then Uncle Ern, Grandpa's brother who had been listening to the conversation, came up with a reasonable answer.

"David, the hay is warm, that makes the air inside the barn warmer than outside, the warm air rises and goes out the cracks in the roof, that keeps the water out," he explained.

Made sense, but how come the hay was warm? I guess some things in life just are too complex to explain. Answer one question, and it leads to another question.

I must have drifted off to sleep for a time. When I woke with a start, I could hear the cows coming into the barn for the evening milking. I would have to hurry to change clothes or I would be late for my chores.

I hurried to the house, passing Gary on the way. He had just brought in the cows and was now trying to practice hitting a baseball, throwing the ball up in the air and swinging the bat at it when it came down. He actually hit it once in a while.

After changing into my barn clothes, I hurried out of the house toward the barn. Just then Gary connected with the ball for a good hit. The only thing wrong was the ball landed in the middle of the bullpen.

Of all places for it to land. The only place on the entire farm that was strictly off limits was the bullpen. All bulls were dangerous just like all guns were loaded. We were never allowed to touch the bull and even bull calves were off limits. Get caught playing with a bull calf, and your name was Mudd for some time. I never did know why Mudd was such a bad name, but that was the way it was around our place. This particular bull in the bullpen now was a young Hereford bull. The main concern on the local farms was with Jersey bulls. The Jersey bulls had the reputation of being the meanest of all the bulls.

"What are we going to do now?" Gary said. "We will never get that ball out of there."

"Just go in and get it," I said. "This bull is not mean, and Dad will never know."

"Not me," Gary said. "I am too scared to go into that bullpen. What would you do if he came after you?"

The bullpen was made with a high fence, two rows of woven wire with barbed wire on top. It was a large square pen, about a hundred feet on a side. Right now the bull was standing at the corner near the barn talking to a few of the cows. He wasn't paying any attention to us or to the ball.

"I'll go get the ball for you," I said to Gary.

I climbed over the gate and looked at the bull when my feet hit the ground. The bull glanced at me briefly and then turned back to the cows. I walked to the center of the pen and picked up the baseball. Again, the bull glanced at me but did not move and returned his attention to the cows. I started back to the gate. As I walked I made one fatal mistake, I started throwing the ball in the air and catching it as it came down. This caught the bull's attention. The second toss and bull turned and kicked up his heels. Here he came at a fast trot.

I first turned to run but immediately realized that being in the middle of the pen, I had nowhere that I could run to and make a getaway before the bull would catch me. I stopped, turned and took my stance. I had watched Don Larsen pitch his perfect game on TV last fall when visiting Mom's cousin, Margery, and Mid Johnson, in Smith River. I had been practicing my pitching ever since. I concentrated on the bull's forehead.

Things were in slow motion now. The bull was closing the ground between us at a rapid pace. I could see Gary coming across the gate with the baseball bat, and I could see Dad jumping off the end of the milk house platform; he would be really pissed. I concentrated on the bull's forehead. I took my windup and threw the ball as hard as I could. I completed my follow through and immediately assumed an athletic stance, ready to move in any direction if the pitch missed its mark.

The ball struck the bull squarely in the middle of his forehead. It bounced off hard. The bull stopped in his tracks, shook his head a little, turned and walked back to the cows at the edge of the pen. I quickly retrieved the ball and ran to the gate. Now my next obstacle was Dad. I think I would rather face down the bull.

"You damn little buck fart," he said as he reached out to bat the back of my head. "What do you think you are doing in the bullpen?"

I ducked my head just at the right moment to avoid most of the blow to the back of my head. That was from years of practice. "Gary was afraid to get his ball, so I went in after it," I replied. "That bull is too young to be mean."

"You are just damn lucky. That bull could just as well knocked you down and mauled you to death by the time I got there to help," Dad said.

"I hit him with my best pitch," I said.

"Your best pitch. I haven't seen you throw very many good pitches. You are just lucky it hit him. Now you get your butt in the barn and get your chores done and give some thanks to the fact that you're lucky to be alive," Dad said. "You can daydream about you pitching while you work."

I tossed the baseball to Gary and went to the barn and grabbed the bucket of milk for the calves. I was thinking while I portioned the milk out into the calf buckets.

Dad was just like all my teachers. He just thought I was lucky,.But just maybe, I am good.

The Camping Trip that Wasn't

I stood up to peddle harder as the last half mile was steeper. I wished I had one of those new bicycles with gears to shift. When the advertisement said you sell to your neighbors, they didn't remind you that your neighbors were two miles away, uphill.

At twelve years of age, I had embarked on my first venture as a salesperson. Lured by a flashy magazine ad, I was going to sell garden seeds and earn enough to purchase a pup tent. It sounded simple, I had a few neighbors, and they all had large gardens. And I had a large family. Grandmas can always be depended on to buy stuff.

"And who are you selling them for?" Margaret asked.

What a dumb question, I thought. You think I would ride my old bike for two miles up that hill to sell them for somebody else?

"I am selling them for myself," I said. "I am going to get a pup tent."

"I thought you might be selling them for the Boy Scouts or church or something," Margaret explained.

This is going to be more challenging than I thought. She would donate to some group, but she was hesitant to help some kid achieve his goal.

"That is why I need a pup tent," I explained. "I have to work at home so much, I don't have time to join the Boy Scouts. So I have to go camping by myself."

I thought that was a good comeback. Margaret knew I worked in the barn and in the fields. But then, she also knew my parents. And they would not deprive me of joining the Boy Scouts if that was what I wanted to do.

"I will buy a couple of packs of the peas," Margaret said. "I don't have my seeds yet, and it is probably close to the time to be planting peas."

I figured I would have to come up with a better storyline if I was going to sell all these seeds. And tomorrow, I was going to go the other direction. There were only a couple of small hills on the way to Broadbent.

As the spring progressed, I did manage to sell the necessary allotment of seeds. Although, I would guess my mother bought more than she planned to buy. I placed my order for the pup tent and waited anxiously for its arrival.

I tore open the box when it did arrive. The tent was much larger than I expected. And it was heavier also. Made from heavy canvas, at least it would be durable. It would be difficult for me to carry along with a pack, that was for sure.

I quickly had it set up in the back yard. There was plenty of room for two people that were my size. You couldn't stand up in it, but that was no problem in my view.

It rained the second day after I had pitched it in the backyard. It didn't leak one drop, but it took three days to dry out.

Summer came, I planned a camping trip to the back of our hundred and sixty acres with my friend from up the river. Dana and I could easily carry the tent, sleeping bags, and my brother's pack with all the necessary supplies.

We were all packed up and ready to head up the hill when Dad came out to wish us well.

"We are planning to go to the movie tonight," Dad said. "You two can stay up the hill if you like, or after you set up camp, you can come back and go to town with us. I have a good flashlight, you could go back up the hill when we get home."

What a dilemma, a movie was hard to pass up in the mid-1950s. Movies were really our only source of outside entertainment. My Dad liked to go to the movies, and we would go a couple of times a month. I knew that Dana did not go that often.

"What do you think?" I asked Dana.

"I think it would be a good idea," Dana said. "We could go set up camp, come back and go to the movie, and then walk back up in the dark to sleep."

"Okay, we will go to the movie," I said to Dad. "We probably will be back in time so we can eat dinner before going."

With that, we were off. The trek was not long, we crossed the upper fields and crawled over the fence at the pasture's end. Then we followed the cat road along the creek until it turned up the hill to the burn.

The burn was where they had logged the timber and burned it over to make good pasture for the cows. It was a good-sized area and open so we could watch the deer and other animals.

We picked a spot on the old landing and set up the tent. We threw everything else into the tent and headed back to the house for dinner.

"We don't want to be late," I said. "Dad won't wait for us."

We hurried along and got to the house just as mom was setting the table for dinner.

"This is a whole lot better than eating that can of pork and beans you would be heating over a fire," Dad said. "You never know what you are missing until you don't have it."

My older sister pulled the car into the garage and came rushing into the house.

"I just had a cougar run across the road in front me," She said, trying to catch her breath. "I was right down there at the end of Hermann's field."

Dana's eyes were large, as we turned around and tried to see if anything was in the field, some half-mile distant. There was nothing there.

"Are you sure it was a cougar?" Dad asked.

"We should call Uncle Robert," Mom said. "He might want to get his dogs on its track tonight."

"Yes, I am sure it was a cougar," Linda said. "It had a long tail, and it moved like it didn't have a care in the world. Are you boys camping up on that hill tonight?"

"We are going to the movie first," I said. "We already set up camp. We will walk up there when we get home after the movie."

"Well, I sure would not be walking up on that hill tonight," Linda said. "That cougar probably is headed right up the creek."

"They are brave boys," Dad said. "We will find out tonight."

When we got home from the movie, the night sky was clear, and the stars were bright. The moon was not up yet, and there were no lights around to distract from the Milky Way.

"So, do you boys want my big flashlight?" Dad asked with a little chuckle. "It is going to be pretty dark up along that creek. Or are you a little concerned about that cougar your sister says she saw?"

That was just a little hint that he was not sure he believed my sister. But it was still possible and something to think about.

"I guess we could probably sleep here tonight," I said. "And then we could go up and cook breakfast at the campsite in the morning."

"I think I would feel a lot better about things if you slept here," Mom said. "That cat could carry you off before you even knew it was there."

That was all we needed to hear. If Mom thought we should sleep in the house, we would sleep in the house.

We were up at the crack of dawn and headed up the hill. We were both well versed in the out of doors. We had a cooking fire going in no time, and I mixed the pancake batter.

"I am not sure those are going to look much like pancakes," Dana said as he watched me trying to turn over the pancake in the little cook set fry pan.

By the time we sat back to eat, the pancakes were in a jumbled heap on the plates. But it was cooked, and a little syrup made it all better. We ate quietly, both of us thinking that Mom would have made a better breakfast.

After watching a few deer and the digger squirrels, we packed up the camp. Dana just folded the pup tent into a square and threw it over his back. It was all downhill to the house. We started off, chuckling about looking for cougar tracks down at the creek. That made us walk a little faster.

A Leap of Faith

Preface: The summer following my sixth-grade year, Dana Watson and I thoroughly explored all the lands between Broadbent and Gaylord and over the hill to Yellow Creek. That covered a circular area of about fifteen square miles. We climbed cliffs, traversed Neal Mountain, followed streams, and marveled at the engineering of beaver dams. We were vaguely aware of property lines but had no concept of trespass in those years.

***

I could hear Mom moving about in the kitchen as I laid in bed in the upstairs boys' room. I nudged Dana awake.
"Dana, I have been thinking that we should go home to

your place over Neal Mountain today," I said as soon as he stirred.

"That would be a good idea," Dana said. "I could show you that large beaver dam I was telling you about."

We both bounded out of bed and dressed quickly. It was a cool summer morning with a dense covering of coastal fog. That meant that we had a few cool hours before the fog would burn off and expose the bright sun. But with the morning fog, even the hottest days would only be in the low eighties.

Mom had a plate of pancakes and bacon on the table when we tumbled down the stairs to the kitchen.

"When we go to Dana's this morning, we are going to go over Neal Mountain," I said to Mom, more to inform her than to ask permission.

"You two have been that way before, haven't you?" Mom asked.

"It is a steep climb, but other than that, it is an easy route," I said. "Once we cross over onto Mr. Neal's place, it is all downhill."

"What does Mr. Neal think about you traveling across his place?" Mom asked.

"We just go down his far fence line," Dana said. "He wouldn't say anything, and if he wanted to make a thing of it, we could just cross the fence. It's just that there is a lot of brush on the other side of the fence."

"Maybe I should call your mother," Mom said. "Just to let her know where you guys are going to be."

"They were going to Coos Bay this morning," Dana said. "She probably won't be home until after we get there."

"Okay, but you be careful," Mom said as we finished eating and started out the door.

We headed across our upper field on a trot. Our plan was to reach the top of the shoulder on Neal Mountain before the fog burned off. The heat from the sun would make the climb up the steep slope difficult.

We crossed the line fence onto Hermann's and continued up the road to the old mill site. We gave the sawdust pile, left from the mill, a wide berth. Smoke rose from several holes around the parameter of the sawdust pile.

56

We knew these sawdust piles burned for years from spontaneous combustion. There were many horror stories of kids getting too close and falling into a burning hole. I doubted the truth of the stories, but not so much as to want to get too close.

We crossed the creek here and rested in the cool breeze coming up the stream. Now it was all uphill to the crest of the shoulder of the mountain.

We took a deep breath and started up the slope. Dana led the way, almost crawling at times. We used branches to pull ourselves along on the really steep spots. Finally, we hit a well-worn trail, probably made by deer, but we liked to think it was an elk trail.

"Wow, this is so much better," Dana said. "This is wide enough. It has to be an elk trail."

The only place I had seen an elk was in the higher elevations of Eden Ridge and Bone Mountain.

"I don't know, Dana," I said. "I don't think we have elk down here."

"They could live on this mountain, and nobody would ever see one," Dana said.

"I bet this is a cow trail," I said. "We have cows that come to our place, and to Hermann's, from over the mountain. But it doesn't matter. It makes the trip easier."

Sure enough, we followed the trail to the crest of the shoulder, and there was a hole in the fence. We threaded our way through the fence and almost ran down the other side.

When we came to the fence at the bottom of the hill, we were careful in crossing it. These old ranchers would complain if we stretched the wires.

"That beaver dam is up the creek at the bottom of this hill," Dana said as we continued on down the hill.

There was still a good flow in the creek for mid-June. We followed the stream through some pasture land for about a half mile before coming to the beaver dam.

This dam was about three feet tall and made with barked tree sections three inches in diameter and four feet long. There was a large pond behind this dam, and the water flowed over the top. This dam was solid as could be. We crossed the creek on the dam, jumping up and down in a few places to test its construction.

"My folks aren't going to be home until later this afternoon," Dana said. "Why don't we go over and climb those cliffs by Gaylord?"

"Maybe we should stop by your house and let them know where we are going," I said.

"My brothers don't care," Dana said. "And it would take us twice as long to get to the cliffs. Let's just cut across these fields."

And off we went, again at a trot. We were at the base of the cliffs in no time. These were exciting cliffs. This solid rock wall was pockmarked with shallow caves halfway up the cliffs. Some said it had probably been on the edge of an ancient ocean.

We went from one shallow cave to the next, almost in a stair-step fashion. There was a deeper cave in an indentation of the cliff wall. We climbed up to it and found that it went about ten feet into the rock wall before narrowing to an impassable passage. We found some bugs on the walls of this cave. They were nearly an inch long and were strange looking. Sort of like a cross between a long sowbug and a grasshopper. When we would try to catch them, they would jump at us like a grasshopper. That was enough of that, and we went on to explore more of the cliff.

That is when we found it. We could see what looked like a nest of a hawk or eagle on the ledge above us. We needed to get onto that ledge.

The problem was, the ledge was sort of an overhang. We tried several approaches but could not get up to the ledge. Finally, Dana climbed onto my shoulders, and he could then pull himself up to the ledge. Then he laid on his stomach and extended his arms where I could just reach them. With Dana pulling and me digging for every toe hold, I finally made it up to the ledge also.

This ledge was five feet wide and had a shallow cave on the cliffside. What we had thought was a nest may have been one at one time. But it was long abandoned at this time. We looked at every crevice, thinking we could maybe find an arrowhead or something.

After spending nearly a half hour on the ledge, we thought it was time to get down. Suddenly, the overhang loomed large.

"I don't think we can get down without falling," I said as I looked at the smaller ledge below us. The ledge we were on hung out a foot or two beyond the ledge below us.

Dana laid down and looked. "There is no way we can land on that ledge."

"Now, what are we going to do?" I said.

"Nobody is going to miss us until dark," Dana said. "And then they are going to be looking on Neal Mountain, not here."

We sat and pondered our situation for a time. Then it was time to do something. Anything was better than nothing.

"Let's start looking for another way down," Dana said.

I went to the right side, I could see a route up to another ledge. Maybe there would be another way down from that ledge.

Dana went to the left side and disappeared as he crept along on a narrow ledge that ran along the cliff wall. I waited for his report before climbing up to the next ledge.

Suddenly, Dana called out from below. He was on the ground.

"Just follow that little ledge around the corner, and you can jump to the top of a fir tree," Dana said. "Just grab the branches and slide down the outside of the tree. The last branch will put you almost to the ground."

I started around the ledge with my back to the cliff wall. It seemed to get narrower the further I went. When I was across from the tree, I stood on my heels.

The top of the fir tree was just a little higher than my head, and it was a full thirty feet to the ground. Dana came back to coach my jump.

"Jump hard, and you will catch the tree about five feet below where you are standing," Dana said.

"Jump hard," I thought. "How the hell do you jump hard?"

I squatted down by sliding my butt down the wall to give my knees some flex. Then I exploded into the air with outstretched arms. When I slammed into the tree, I grabbed an armful of branches.

I stayed put for a moment, clutching the branches to my chest.

"Now, just relax and slide down the branches," Dana said, reminding me that I was still twenty-some feet from the ground.

I relaxed my grip, and to my surprise, I slid down to the next set of branches. After that bit of a confidence builder, I slid all the way down, with the last large branch lowering me to the ground.

"See how easy that was?" Dana said.

I smiled and wiped my hands on my shirt. Pitch, I was covered with pitch. There was almost nothing on earth that I hated worse than pitch. That is, except for squash. I really hated squash.

"I have pitch all over me," I said. "I hate pitch."

"That's alright," Dana said. "Dad has some soap that will take it all off with no problem."

We started off toward Dana's house.

"I wonder how long it would have taken them to find us?" I asked.

"I don't know," Dana said. "But I don't think we should be telling anybody about this."

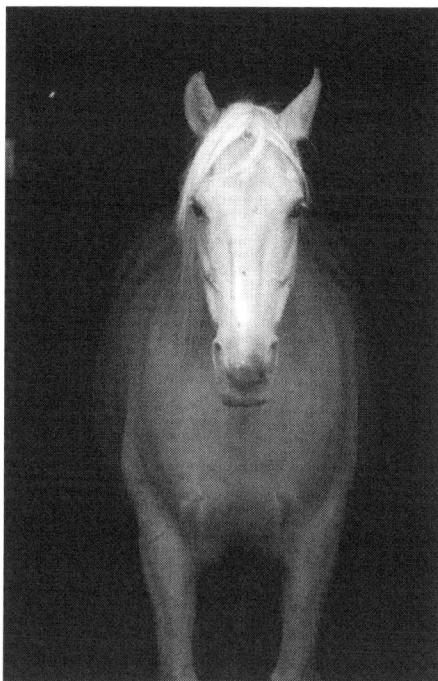

The Big Horse Race

I purchased Judy the summer following my sixth grade. It took a lot of chittum peeling to come up with the purchase price.

She was a light palomino and had a big scar on the back of her neck like she had been bitten by another horse when younger.

Our neighbor trimmed her hooves and shod her for me. He would not take any money for the chore.

I rode Judy everywhere. She required a strong hand on the reins to make her do what the rider wanted. Judy was barn sour. She was uncomfortable away from the barn. When we would turn toward the barn, and I let her have her head, I knew I had better hang on tight.

One afternoon, Dana Watson and I rode Judy down the creek to Hermann's new barn. We met Jack and Larry Hermann there and rode the horses up their hill a bit. The Hermann horses made Judy look like a pony. Both were outfitted with full saddles, while Dana and I were riding bareback and double on Judy.

When we got back to the barn, we tied the horses and looked over the barn and the haymow.

"Why did you buy such a small horse?" Jack asked.

"I really wasn't looking for a horse," I said. "My cousin Peggy had a friend selling her, and the price was something that I could afford."

"She doesn't look like much of a horse," Jack said.

"She might not look like much, but she is the fastest horse I have seen," I said. "I have been around horses a lot, and I don't think I know a horse that could outrun her."

"Our horses are quarter horses, and they are pretty fast, too," Jack said. "And they are so much bigger than that little thing, I don't think she could begin to keep up with them."

"Well, the only way to know is with a horse race," I said. "What do you think, Dana. Do you want to ride with me?"

"Sure, those big horses are all weighed down with saddles and everything," Dana said.

"Okay," Jack said. "We will start on the road here, race down across the creek and up the field to where it starts uphill. Do you want to do this, Larry?"

"Sure, I have wanted to see which one of these horses is the fastest for a long time," Larry said. "The only problem will be if Dad sees us. He will be furious. You know he doesn't like us to gallop the horses."

"He is in town," Jack said. "We will be able to get these horses cooled down and turned out before he gets home."

I jumped up on Judy, and Dana got up behind me. We rode out to the road where the race was going to start. I had to hold a tight rein on Judy because we were pointed at her barn.

"You have to hold on tight, Dana," I said. "Judy is barn sour, and when she is headed home, she runs like the wind. These Hermann horses are going to be left in her dust."

Jack and Larry pulled their horses up beside us. I was holding a tight rein on Judy, and I could hear her heavy breathing. She was excited to be headed home and had no concept of a race.

I looked up at Jack. For the first time, I realized just how much taller their horses were.

"You say the word," I said. "Something like ready, set, go."

"Go," Jack said as he and Larry spurred their mounts.

I released my grip on Judy's reins and let her have her head. I leaned forward with my head against her neck and took a firm grip on her mane. Dana leaned forward and tightened his grip around my midsection.

I looked back, and the Hermann horses were thundering along on our left, but they were at least two lengths behind. Judy was headed home, and nothing was going to slow her down.

The creek was approaching. This time of the summer, there was only a trickle of water that ran between the deeper holes. The road crossed the creek, but there was a substantial bank on this side and a rocky creek bottom before going up on the other bank and then out into the field.

Judy flew down the bank and did not slow across the rocks. The downward force when she hit the creek bed caused Dana and me to slip. We were off Judy's back and hanging on her left side. I still had my grip on her mane, and we were both desperately holding on with our right legs still over her back. I looked back, Larry's horse had slowed at the creek, but Jack was spurring his horse, trying to catch up with us. If we fell, there would be no way his horse could avoid running over us.

Judy did not slow with our slippage. She was up the far bank and turned up the field. Her barn was in view, and I felt a surge in her speed. Dana was able to pull himself back up on Judy's back first, and with a bit of tug, he helped me right myself. Judy was oblivious to our struggle to remain mounted.

Once back in a normal position, I looked back. Jack's horse had faded a bit, and Larry's horse was abreast with him. The distance at this point was probably a half-mile, and the quarter horses had spent their best energy. Judy continued at her wicked pace. My only problem was going to be in stopping her when we reached the hill.

When we came to the hill, I sat up and pulled back on Judy's reins.

"Whoa, whoa," I said as I pulled her to a stop.

Jack and Larry pulled their horses up beside us.

"You guys should join the circus," Jack said. "How did you get up on her back?"

63

"I had enough of a grip with my right leg that I was able to pull myself up and then help Dave," Dana said. "I thought we were goners."

"Ha," I said. "I was just looking at your horses' hooves that would be running over us."

"Well, you were right about how fast that horse of yours is, and she didn't slow down a bit," Larry said. "Our horses just about were done for when we got halfway up this field."

"I have to admit, it would have been a different race if we were going the other direction," I said. "Judy is barn sour, and when she is going home, she goes like the wind."

"Maybe so," Jack said. "It sure would have been a different race if you guys hit the ground."

Notes on My Mother

My mother was born on August 14, 1913, as Dolores Lorrene Davenport. She was born on the family farm on Catching Creek, out of Myrtle Point, Oregon.

The fifth child in a family of ten, she learned how to work at an early age. But by today's standards, her childhood was idyllic. There was hard work, shared by many hands, and many lessons learned that served her for a lifetime.

There was no electricity on Catching Creek until the late 1930s, and the family had a three-hole outhouse. My mother never lived in a house with indoor plumbing until 1950.

She went to elementary school at Twin Oaks School. At this one-room school, her family accounted for a large portion of the attendance. Then she went on to high school in Myrtle Point.

She met my father in high school, and they were married a couple of years later. Graduating in 1932 in the depth of the depression, Mom worked at several jobs until she married Frank Larsen in September 20, 1934. Dad attended OSU that fall and winter before running out of money. They hitchhiked home from Corvallis to Myrtle Point. Mom was pregnant with my sister by then. Some thirteen months after my sister was born, my oldest brother came along.

Dad went to work in the woods, and they lived in logging camps in Coos County for a time. One shack they lived in, they purchased for forty dollars. It had a dirt floor, no water, no plumbing, no electricity. They couldn't sell it when they were leaving, so they just left it.

In those years, one car was luxury, two cars were unheard of for most people. Once, when they lived out of Allegany on the Coos River, my sister was whittling on a door frame, dropped the knife, and it stuck in her eye. Dad was at work with the car. Mom had no phone, no car, no close neighbors, and my oldest brother was too young to run for help. Mom held my sister on her lap with a washcloth over the knife until Dad got home from work. They took my sister to the doctor then. The injury looked far worse than it was, but imagine the stress of that situation.

My second brother was born in 1941, and I followed in 1945. Shortly after I was born, we moved from the Coos River back to Catching Creek. And then they purchased a small ranch above Broadbent in December of 1949.

Things like a telephone and electricity were commonplace by the late 1940s. And most houses had running water by then, gravity fed from a spring on the hill in our case, both on Catching Creek and at Broadbent. The telephone hung on the wall, and you cranked the handle to contact the operator who would connect you to who you were calling. Party lines only, and that meant ten or twelve parties on the line. Don't plan on making a call on Saturday morning, and don't think anything you say is private.

To make a go of it on the ranch, Dad continued to work in the woods as a donkey puncher. Mom milked the cows in the morning with the boys' help, and then she did her housework. Dad would be off work in the afternoon, and he did the evening milking. Mom and the kids did all the other chores, including changing irrigation all summer long.

A full dinner just seemed to happen, every night. Everybody was at the dinner table, and that was what you had to eat for the night. If you didn't like something for dinner, that was fine, but there was nothing else to eat until breakfast.

With the labor of a bunch of uncles, the folks installed a bathroom in the house at Broadbent in the summer of 1950. No more late-night trips to the outhouse and no more weekly baths in the washtub. Mom was thirty-seven years old at the time.

In 1950, my brother cut his hand badly. We had no car, and an ambulance did not exist. Mom was able to call a neighbor, and she had a car. She drove Mom and my two brothers to the doctor. Larry was in the back seat tending to Gary's lacerated hand.

That laceration required several surgeries, most of them in Portland. Mom and Gary would catch the Greyhound bus at two in the morning in Coquille, change buses in Coos Bay and arrive in Portland about ten in the morning. They would do the doctor visit, eat lunch, and maybe go to a movie before catching the afternoon bus back to Coquille. Dad would pick them up when they arrived at some time after midnight. I have never heard how they got around in Portland, from the bus to the doctor and back. I could not imagine them using a taxi.

I have no memory of eating at a restaurant as a family. A couple of times, I remember eating at a restaurant when we were traveling and visiting, but those events were rare. When my sister got married, we went to LA. We went to a Chinese restaurant with an aunt and uncle. Even when we traveled long distances, we would eat a packed lunch in a park somewhere.

In 1958, we moved from Broadbent back to Catching Creek, where the folks leased the Lundy place, and Dad quit the woods and milked cows only. Mom did not have to milk cows there, but she kept plenty busy with a massive garden, canning, and housekeeping.

There was silo filling twice a year and hay hauling once or twice a year. Lunches for the crew of uncles and friends and maybe a hired hand or two were something akin to a holiday dinner. The women worked as a crew in the kitchen, similar to the crew in the fields.

I was the last to leave home, for college in 1963 to 1965, where I was home and gone from time to time. Then I joined the Army in 1965. In 1967, the folks sold the dairy cows and moved back to Broadbent and ran beef cows. Dad worked at the feed store for a time, and then he tended greens at the golf course. Mom went to work at Myers and Myers Department Store in town.

They fully retired in 1978. Dad had contracted brown lung disease from the silo and got to the point that he could not go to the barn. Mom had to do all the feeding, so they decided to sell the cows.

When they were loading the cows to go down the road, Mom started to cry. Dad asked her what was wrong.

"I wanted to keep that little heifer," Mom said.

So, of course, they kept the heifer. And in so doing, they learned that feeding one cow is just as hard as feeding twenty cows in the winter. The following spring they sold the heifer. And Mom was without cows for the first time in her life.

My mother was loved by everyone. She was a favorite aunt, commonly called Auntie Deacon. I think there were other names. Deacon, also used by my father and her brothers, was a name given to her by a childhood friend, Connie Felsher.

My mother seldom said a cross word. We were always instructed, "If you can't say something good, don't say anything at all."

As I grew older, I could read her body language better. When she was bothered by somebody's comments or the event of the moment, she might wring her hands. It would be rare indeed to hear her speak in unfavorable terms.

Maybe the most consistent way to get her to comment would be to say something was the mother's fault. "The kid was bad because it was the mother's fault."

Then Mom would say, "That makes me so mad, for them to always blame the mother."

Mom struggled with my father's death. Dad had wanted to die at home. When the doctor in Eugene told him that there was nothing more they could do for him, he immediately said, "I want to go home."

Mom could not allow nature to take its course with Dad. Every episode where Dad would approach death, she would call the ambulance, and it was back to the hospital. Each trip left him weaker and frailer, and it did nothing but buy a few more days or another week. Finally, Dad died in a care center.

Mom's family was long-lived, although her mother had died at eighty-four after suffering a stroke. Her father lived to be ninety-four. Six of the ten kids lived into their nineties. Mom was the longest-lived, at ninety-eight.

We had to move her into the care center in Myrtle Point for the last few years of her life because we could not find competent in-home care in the area. The last year she was home, she was in and out of the hospital with digestive issues every few weeks. The caretakers could not boil water.

Initially, in the care center, the converted Mast Hospital, she had a room upstairs where the full nursing care was located.

"David, I think this is the room we were in when you were born," Mom said to me on my initial visit. In those years, birthing mothers were often kept in the hospital for an entire week or more.

Later, when a room came available, we moved Mom downstairs to the assisted living portion of the center. She was happier there, but she would have preferred to be home.

At one point, two of her sisters were in the care center with her. Lila and Audrey were both there. Of the three, Mom was the oldest, and she took personal responsibility for the care of her sisters.

Once, she said, "I would like to escape this place, but I can't leave Lila here by herself."

Mom became somewhat bitter as she recognized her approaching death. She had enjoyed many years where she was the matriarch of the large extended Davenport and Larsen families. She said to me during one visit, "People are just going to have to learn to get along without me."

"Mom," I said. "Your example will guide many people for the rest of their lives." I am not sure that helped her cope with her pending death much.

The care centers tend to eat through a person's assets quickly. We were very close to the point of going to state and placing her on Medicaid. She was down to her last few dollars when she had a stroke. She was in the hospital for almost a week following that stroke and then returned to the care center in Myrtle Point, where she died a few days later. On my last visit with her in the care center, she was able to sit up and stand with assistance, but she did not acknowledge anyone. And she never spoke.

She lived ninety-eight years, six months, and eleven days. She left four kids, thirteen grandchildren, and twenty-seven great-grandchildren.

Columbus Day Storm, October 12, 1962

The day started like any other fall morning in western Oregon. The sky was mostly clear with just a few clouds. There was no wind, and there was no major concern about the weather as I headed out the door to school. My 1955 Chevy started with no problem, and I put my work clothes in the back seat and my stack of books in the front seat. I always brought books home from school. But I never did any homework or reading. I guess I just wanted to look like the other kids leaving school.

I had Physics class right after lunch each day. This day, Mr. Oglesby came to class late. This was unlike him, and he was a little excited.

"We will be leaving early this afternoon," Mr. Oglesby said. "There is a big storm coming, and I have to get home and secure my roof."

This was the first time we had heard any information on a storm. He had no sooner told us the news than the principal came on the intercom and said they were dismissing school and everyone should go directly home. School buses would be out front shortly. This was great news. I would get out of school early, but I could go to work rather than home.

Mr. Oglesby had his stuff together and was heading out the door.

"You guys go home like the man says. This looks like it will be a big storm," he says as he heads out the door.

I took things to my locker and put on my light jacket. No books this weekend as it is hunting season, and I don't have to look like I am going to study. It seemed like everyone was leaving the building at once. I was glad that I had parked on this side of the street this morning, and I didn't have to turn around. I jumped in the car, started it up, and was one of the first to pull out. It was a short trip to the cheese factory.

Working at the cheese factory was a great job, and it provided good money and about as many hours as I could work. This was my second year working there.

I had quit football this year when the coach was upset that I went pigeon hunting on Labor Day and missed practice. It was better for my knees anyway. A good off-shoot of that action was I could work for another couple of months at the cheese factory after school and on weekends. We were generally laid off in the winter when the dairies dried up most of their cows. Then when spring calving started, we were back to work. My brother could work a summer and pay for his year at college, and we didn't have to work in the woods. I hated pitch on my hands.

When I got to the cheese factory, most of the work had been done. All the cheese was made, which meant that milk production was falling. Often there would be a vat of cheese to be made when I got there after school. Jim Taylor, the late shift foreman, said they held a lot of the milk in the holding tanks because of the storm coming. I guess they got the news also. I changed clothes quickly and helped finish cleaning up. We had just finished when the lights began to flicker.

We opened the large garage door in the front receiving area to have some light in the building if the lights went out. Standing in the open doorway, we could see that the wind was much stronger than earlier.

There were four of us standing there. Jim Taylor, a young guy not long out of the Navy, had long dark hair that he wore in an Elvis style, and he was thin and muscular.

Ray Sturdivant is a big guy with short-cropped hair. I believe Ray was from Pound, Virginia.

Roger Gary was the last guy in the group. Roger was a couple of years older than I. He was about five feet ten inches, very muscular, and he had a large square head that made him look even stronger.

The wind started to pick up pretty strong. We watched as it slowly peeled the aluminum sign off the building across the street. Then another sheet of metal came blowing down the street like a tumbleweed. The tall fir trees in the city park on the north side of the cheese factory were bending over in the wind.

About this time, Mom came driving down the street, heading home. Her car, a 1961 red Chevy, was bouncing from the wind. When she saw us standing in the doorway, she stopped behind my car and rushed inside.

Mom was a short but nice looking woman. I considered her old. She must have been almost fifty.

"Do you think I will be able to make it home?" she asked, no one in particular.

Jim was the first to reply, "I think you better wait for the worst of the wind to be over."

She stood by me and said she was in town to help my brother, Larry, and his wife, Maggie, get to the hospital. "It looks like the baby will come tonight, with or without electricity."

Now the trees in the park started to fall. It was a slow fall, uprooting their large root wads and hitting the ground. One tree followed the other. Not all of the trees fell, but probably twenty out of thirty fell in five minutes. There was not even a flicker of lights anywhere.

Finally, the wind slowed to a gusty wind after nearly an hour. We changed clothes and waited outside as Jim closed the large door and found his way to the front door with a flashlight.

"Follow me home, and don't get out of the car on the road," I said to Mom. "There might be downed power lines."

We had about a mile and a half along the river to the ranch. Only a couple of trees could be a problem along that road, so if we were lucky, it should be no problem.

After getting Mom home, I opened a can of tuna fish and made a couple of sandwiches for dinner. Dad was finished at the barn. There were little branches everywhere but no significant damage. There was no power, and Dad had to finish milking using the vacuum from the tractor. Most of the cows were dry or in the process of drying up, so that was not a big issue. The milking chore was much reduced. I told Mom I should return to town. Some of the guys would probably be thinking about cutting trees out of the roads.

I put the power saw in the trunk and went back to town. A group of us went around the roads out of town. Some roads had almost no trees, and other roads had many trees down.

The first road we cleared was Stringtown Road. It ran in a loop, out across the river from the cheese factory, then along the hillside for a mile before turning back to the river road. The part that ran along the hillside had a bunch of trees across the road. We had three or four power saws running all the time, and we cleared a path in a short time. We had to worry about the power line in only one spot, but being careful and working on the far side of the road, we got it open.

The next road was the road to Arago. This was about six miles, but most of that was across open country, only a couple of areas through the trees. We cleared that road pretty quickly. We had a string of cars following us on this road, and they were pretty thankful for our efforts.

After Arago, we went out Gravelford Road and back down the North Fork Road. Like Arago, these roads only had a couple of small sections through trees, and we only had to cut a couple of trees out of the way.

That was enough for us as the evening was getting long. We bumped into a couple of older guys, and they were happy to furnish us with a half case of beer, Blitz, I believe. It put a good ending to a night's work. The rest of the trees could wait for the highway crews or the power company.

The aftermath of this storm left some tremendous damage to Western Oregon. Friends working in the woods told stories of salvage logging stands of timber that were blown down in all directions, a big tangled mess.

"I was bucking trees, standing on logs that were forty feet in the air," Jim Luhrs told me.

The City of Myrtle Point had salvaged the trees that blew down in the park across from the cheese factory. By Halloween, there were many limbs were scattered in the park. They came in handy as we were looking for trouble to cause on Halloween.

"Let's stack those limbs on the highway," someone said.

What a neat project that was. The group of us, maybe twenty guys, pulled those limbs out of the park and made a pile in the middle of Highway 42 beside the cheese factory. This was no small pile, probably fifteen feet high or more, and it covered the better part of both lanes of traffic. Cars could still get through by using the parking lanes. We were proud of ourselves.

It didn't take the city cop, Mr. Dietz, long to figure out who had done the job. Dietz was a massive man with a large nose and a large belly. He talked fearsomely but controlled us with a gentle disposition. Mr. Dietz found the whole group of us down at the corner ice cream shop, gloating over our recent project. He pulled up and slowly worked himself out of the car. It almost looked like he would never quit coming out of that car until he finally stood and took a deep breath.

"He looks pissed," Dick said.

"Damn you, little Yahoos, I give you every break in the book, and you go and do something like that," Mr. Dietz said in a gruff voice, pointing down main street. "You can't shut down a state highway! Now you guys get your butts down there and clear out that pile of limbs, or I will run the whole damn bunch of you down to city hall."

We didn't have to be told twice. We all knew when a man was mad. We loaded into our cars and headed down to the pile of limbs. We pulled the limbs off the stack, dragged them through the park, and piled them up on the street on the other side of the park. It didn't take long for the job to be done, and we thought we got the last laugh. As it turned out, the city was pleased with our work. They could load the limbs much easier than if they had been scattered in the park.

I Are One

Dad was drying his hands as he entered the kitchen. He had just finished the morning milking and had washed up for breakfast.

Looking over Mom's shoulder as she stood at the stove, he asked, "What's for breakfast? I am hungry as a horse."

"David wanted hotcakes, but I also cooked some bacon and eggs for you," Mom said.

Dad sat down at the table to wait for breakfast.

"Vern stopped by the barn this morning to pick up a jug of milk," Dad said. "He said that Shorty Shull sold his place yesterday."

"Oh, that's great," Mom said. "He has been trying to get it sold ever since he hurt his back last fall."

"Yes, but the price he got is almost obscene," Dad said. "These damn Californians keep coming up here and paying these high prices for a place, and it just drives the prices so high that a young man can't get a start anymore."

"It will help Shorty get his back taken care of and allow them to move to town with no problem," Mom said.

"At these prices, a place can't pay for itself," Dad said. "It doesn't matter how many cows you milk. You would have to work out also. And not just to feed the family, but to pay the mortgage."

***

This was the same conversation that I had heard my entire life. The influx of money into the local real estate was ruining the market for local folks. Of course, it was true, but it was unavoidable in a free market society.

It was also the beginning of the end for the family farm, at least in our little corner of southwestern Oregon. To some extent, farmers became little more than land speculators. All they had to do was struggle to pay the mortgage and provide a living for their families for a decade or two before cashing in on the inflationary spiral for the price of their land.

***

Years later, Sandy and I started exploring the family histories and soon became engrossed in genealogy.

"Sandy, look at this article," I said as I placed the old newspaper article in front of her. "This is an article showing the taxpayers in Coos County in 1910 who paid more than a hundred dollars in property tax."

"So, who is of interest to us?" Sandy asked.

I pointed to a name on the list, Joseph Davenport.

"There is my great-grandfather," I said. "I looked through this list. He paid three hundred thirty-seven dollars, which ranks him about 68 on the list. But forty of those above him are companies. This guy was well to do. We need to investigate this some more."

***

Over the next ten years, we gleaned all the family information we could get from family members. Still, it was not until the internet became available that we really started on the road to mapping out our various family groups. Joseph Davenport proved to be interesting.

Joseph was born in England in 1835, and he came to this country with his family in 1847. He lost a brother and a newborn sister at sea on the trip.

After settling in Wisconsin, his father traveled to California during the gold rush. He returned to Wisconsin after a year of limited success in the goldfields.

Joseph married his wife, Libbie, in Wisconsin in 1866, and he came west to Grizzly Bluff, California, in 1871. There he had a dairy farm and raised a family of five children.

He built a creamery in Ferndale, California, when the dairy farm needed to expand its market, and shipped butter to San Francisco on lumber schooners sailing up and down the coast. I often wondered if he ever met my Larsen grandfather. The latter sailed one of those lumber schooners in the 1890s.

Sometime between 1900 and 1903, he sold out in California and moved to Coos County. His son, my grandfather, was married in Grizzly Bluff in March of 1904. He then followed the rest of the family to Oregon.

***

"Look at this, Sandy," I said as we scoured documents on the computer screen. "They bought four ranches, two on Catching Creek, one on Fat Elk out of Coquille and one below Cedar Point just out of Coquille. He also built a creamery and ice plant in Coquille."

"They must have had a bundle of cash when they came to town," Sandy said.

"Their house in Coquille is one of those classic old houses," I said. "Very large and elaborate for being built in the early 1900s."

"We will never know what people thought of them when they came to town," Sandy said. "I wonder if people complained about the Californians in those days?"

"It is just like Mike Enright said, the most ardent environmentalist is the guy who has just built a new house on Big Sur," I said. "I have heard nothing but complaints about the prices the Californians pay for property in Oregon."

"Maybe those people didn't know the family history," Sandy said.

"It is just a little upsetting," I said. "After I heard all those complaints about transplanted Californians, for all those years, and repeating them myself at times, and now I find out that I are one."

One Day at the Cheese Factory

P epper Baker folded his book and turned off the projector. Chemistry class was over. I quickly gathered my books and hit the door at close to a run.

I was attending Southwestern Oregon Community College. Chemistry class was held in some old Navy buildings near the North Bend Airport. If I was fast, I could make the drive to Myrtle Point in thirty-seven minutes. If I could punch in on the time clock by thirty-seven minutes after the hour, I would get paid from half past the hour. To a young college student paying his way through school, that meant over an extra hour each week.

I threw my books in the back seat beside my lunch box and work clothes as I jumped in the little Corvair and sped out of the parking lot. The class was released early, and I had a couple of minutes to spare as I pulled onto Highway 101 and heading south.

I made the turn off of 101 onto Highway 42 and increased my speed. I had a few more miles of a four-lane highway, and there were seldom any police on this section. Glancing at my watch, I was still several minutes ahead of schedule.

As I approached the highway's merge section as it narrowed to two lanes, I slowed my speed and looked in the rearview mirror. Here came a state cop with his lights on. Where had he been hiding?

I pulled over and got out of the car to greet the cop.

"Do you know the speed limit on this highway?" the state cop asked as I handed him my driver's license.

"I know it's fifty-five," I said.

"Do you have oversized tires on this car?" he asked as he leaned down to look at my tires.

"I know I was going fast," I said. "You see, I go to college in North Bend, and I work at the cheese factory in Myrtle Point. I was in a hurry because if I punch the time clock at two-thirty-seven, I get paid from two-thirty."

"You wouldn't be pulling my leg, would you?" the cop asked.

"No, my books and my work clothes are right there in the back seat," I said.

He looked in the back seat. "Okay, it looks like you are telling the truth. We need more kids who work for what they have. But you need to slow things down a bit. I work this section of the highway often, and a ticket will eat up that extra hour a week."

"Thank you, sir. I will slow it down."

I had learned early in life to take your medicine when you got caught in the wrong. I started down the highway at a legal speed—no need to hurry now after losing those minutes with the cop.

I punched the time clock at the Safeway Cheese Factory at two-forty-five and headed to the break room to change clothes. I noticed a strong odor from the production area but didn't think much about it.

I pulled on my boots and headed out to get to work. This was my fourth year of working after school and summers at the cheese factory. It was an excellent job, and I could pay my college expense and maintain a car with no problem.

I pushed through the swinging doors onto the main production floor, and a rancid odor hit me. I stood for a moment, trying to assess the situation.

"What smells so bad?" I asked old Paul Davis, who was waiting with his forklift to retrieve a cheese pallet.

"The pasteurizer broke this morning," Paul said. "Nothing to do but to make the cheese today with unpasteurized milk. Gives you an idea what cheese was like a hundred years ago."

"What are we going to do with it?" I asked.

"We have a truck coming in the morning. It is all going to a plant in San Francisco. They will use it to make pasteurized processed cheese."

"Looks like it is going to be a fun afternoon," I said.

"Yes, I think George has your vat just about ready for you," Paul said, pointing down the row of five large cheese vats.

I walked down and signed in on the vat sheet and said hi to George Gasner as he was heading back to the lab. George was the head cheesemaker, and he managed the vats until the hard work was to begin.

George filled the vat with six thousand pounds of milk, heated it to the prescribed temperature with the steam jacket in the vat while running two large mechanical agitators. He added twenty gallons of starter culture. After a timed interval, he would add the rennet to coagulate the milk. After cutting the soft curd, he would cook this vat before turning it over to the cheesemaker for the cheddaring of the cheese.

I stopped the agitators and removed the paddles, allowing the soft curd to settle to the bottom of this sizeable twenty-four-foot-long vat. As it dropped to the vat floor, I hooked up the drainage pipe and started draining the whey from the vat. When half the whey was removed, I began to form the soft curd into two large mats using a stainless steel rake, one on each side of the vat with a ditch down the middle. These mats were twenty feet long, thirty inches wide, and six inches deep. After they were allowed to settle and become solid mats, I would cut them into loaves about six inches wide. Once cut, these loaves were turned over and heated with the steam jacket to make them more solid.

Then the real work began. The speed was determined by the acidity of the cheese. We checked the acidity at every step. Adding heat would speed the developing acidity. At the start of the process, the acid test would be around a pH of six point five. And the ending pH would be close to five point three.

After the loaves were turned over, they were cut into two pieces and stacked on themselves. This gives a row that is two high on each side of the vat. These were then turned, flipping the top half loaf and then placing the bottom loaf on top of it. This progressed down the line on each side of the vat.

During the next step, with the aid of another cheesemaker, the loaves on the left side were thrown over to the right side, and the stacks were now four high.

Based on time, heat, and acidity, the rows are turned and stacked five high and then six high. The loaves started out six inches by six inches by fifteen inches after the second cut. They are now twelve inches wide, two inches thick, and thirty inches long.

These loaves are now run through a mill that chops them into the familiar cheese curds. These are salted and heated again and then scooped into molds. When pressed for a couple of hours under hydraulic pressure, they yield forty-pound blocks of cheese.

These fifty blocks are then removed from the molds, wrapped and heat-sealed, then boxed and moved to cold storage for aging. By the time this two thousand pounds of cheese is loaded on a pallet, it has been handled by a cheesemaker ten times. In one vat, the cheesemakers moved twenty-thousand pounds of cheese.

It will be nice to get back to a functional pasteurizer tomorrow and see this stinky cheese shipped to the processed cheese plant.

This is a link to some pictures of a small scale cheddar cheese making process:

https://en.wikipedia.org/wiki/Manufacture_of_cheddar_cheese

This is a link to a 1962 article in the Myrtle Point Herald newspaper on the Safeway Cheese Factory:

https://myrtlepoint.advantage-preservation.com/viewer/?k=gasner%20cheesemaker&i=f&d=01011960-12311990&m=between&ord=k1&fn=myrtle_point_herald_usa_oregon_myrtle_point_19620628_english_8&df=1&dt=2

I Presume?

T he auditorium class quieted down as the professor took the stage. This was an entirely new experience for me. This class filled the auditorium, maybe five hundred students.

The professor was a large man, and he looked like he could have been a linebacker in his college days. Not fat, just tall and well built, and very muscular.

He picked up a piece of chalk and, in a giant cursive script, he wrote, 'I presume?' on the board. Then he returned to the podium.

"For those who don't know me and have not figured it out yet, my name is Doctor Livingstone."

The fall of 1964 found me searching for some spark of inspiration to get my education back on track. I had been admitted to Colorado State University, and I was determined to pursue admission to veterinary school.

Just how I ended up in Dr. Livingstone's botany class was a bit of a mystery to me, even at the time. It was a science course and could have been in the pre-veterinary requirements at the time. Or possibly, an astute advisor recognized that Dr. Livingstone could be helpful for this farm boy.

Dr. Livingstone's lectures were as intriguing as was his initial introduction. I always preferred to sit in the back of the class, and I initially picked a seat near the back and closest to the exit, and I had a full view of the auditorium. When Dr. Livingstone was speaking, he held the full attention of the entire class.

Graduate students conducted the lab classes of about thirty students, but seeing Dr. Livingstone dropping into the lab was not unusual.

This system had pluses and minuses. For one thing, it allowed for a personal relationship with the graduate student. But with that relationship, I would learn that the lab class had an assigned row of seats to use and that attendance would be taken. That wasn't too bad, but I lost my perch in the back of the auditorium.

In one of our Thursday afternoon lab classes, Dr. Livingstone stood behind our small group as we were discussing the microscope slide we were working on that day. As was typical for me, I stumbled over a few scientific words.

Dr. Livingstone corrected my attempts at pronunciation and helped the four of us complete the exercise. Then I noticed he went and talked with the graduate student and checked the grade book.

As the class was cleaning up and I put my books into my pack, Dr. Livingstone came over and sat beside me.

"Mr. Larsen, you're a pretty good student, at least in this class," Dr. Livingstone said. "Do you always have trouble with these long words?"

"I just have to hear the word a few times before I can get all the syllables to come out right," I said.

"I will give you a couple of tips that helped me a lot when I was your age," Dr. Livingstone said. "I had a lot of problems also. Maybe I am a bit dyslexic, I don't know, but I just had problems with the big words. It doesn't matter what you call it in your mind. You just need to learn to spell it correctly. And then, when you do have to pronounce it, you should do so with utter self-confidence. You will find, if you do that confidently, after a short time, everyone around you will be using your pronunciation."

It was sometime later before I wondered what it was that prompted the doctor to spend those few minutes with me. But it was advice that I follow to this day, and there are still words that I stumble over.

My stay at Colorado State in 1964 was brief. My classroom performance was less than stellar. This was primarily due to the lack of maturity to apply myself to necessary classes that did not interest me. The fact that Colorado sold three-point-two beer to eighteen-year-olds could have had some influence on my school work.

I experienced the best in professors in Dr. Livingstone. And I watched the worst professor in my educational experience in my History of Western Civilization class, but that is a different story. Friday night dinner with my roommates was always five hamburgers, purchased for a dollar, something new to me. My PE class was swimming, and it took several weeks for me to adjust to the altitude. I spent way too much money that term, but it was fun. And then there was a brief encounter with a wild preacher's daughter. All life lessons, some better than others.

It took me seven years before I returned to Colorado State University. I was admitted to the College of Veterinary Medicine in the fall of 1971.

There are lessons to be learned here, and they don't involve the preacher's daughter. I have always been concerned about all the advanced placement available for students coming out of high school today. It is hard to argue against because of the high cost of higher education today. But suppose you are placed above some classes. In that case, you may lose the opportunity for a great professor, like Dr. Livingstone, to influence the rest of your life. And perseverance pays off. Not everyone is made to fit the mold educators plan out for kids; some of us have to find our own way.

Howard Daniel Vandenacre

There was still a slight chill in the August morning air as we waited in front of the Coos Bay post office, a little unsure of what was to happen next.

Then the doors swung open, and Mrs. Baxter emerged with her entourage of four middle-aged men, all dressed in ill-fitting suits.

Mrs. Baxter, whose hair was dyed a slightly reddish color with grey roots showing, was the chairwoman of the local draft board. She had a stack of manila folders in her hands.

She came to an abrupt stop directly in front of me. She extended her hands and pushed the stack of folders into my belly. I took the folders.

"You're are in charge of this crew," Mrs. Baxter said as she wrinkled her pointy nose. "These folders contain everybody's information, meal tickets and bus tickets home. Don't lose these folders, or you will not be very popular. When you arrive, you check into the YMCA, across the street from the bus station. After breakfast tomorrow, you report to the testing station, just down the street from the YMCA."

"Wait a minute," I said. "Who elected me to be in charge?" I was surprised that she knew who I was. We were not wearing name tags and were not otherwise identified.

"Young man, you are the oldest one here, and that makes you the leader," Mrs. Baxter said. "And you know what that means. You pass this physical, and I will see you again, very soon."

With that, we loaded onto the waiting Greyhound bus. Mrs. Baxter stepped aboard the bus and handed the driver a packet with our tickets for the ride to Portland.

For me, the last half of 1965 was sort of a hectic blur. In mid-May, I received my "Greetings" from Uncle Sam. I had dropped out of school for the spring quarter to work full time. This would ensure I would have adequate funds for a year at Oregon State in the fall. The greetings sort of disrupted those plans.

On the appointed day, I reported to the Post Office in Coos Bay for a bus ride to Portland for the first of a couple of physicals and a lot of testing. At twenty years and four months of age, I was the oldest in this group of some thirty young men. We were on the leading edge of the military's build-up for Vietnam.

Of course, I passed the physical with flying colors. After considering my options, I elected to enlist to have some semblance of control over my fate in the Army. I traded a couple of extra years for that control and enlisted in the Army Security Agency.

In the middle of September, I took another bus ride to Portland, another physical exam, and more testing. Then they herded us into a room and administered the oath. We were now in the Army.

I boarded my first commercial plane for a short flight to San Francisco. I had a window seat, and we landed on the runway that extends out into the bay.

"There is nothing but water under us," I said to the guy sitting next to me.

The water got closer and closer. I was ready to jump before the runway suddenly appeared.

By the time we were checked in at the airport, it was dark. We had a middle-of-the-night bus ride to Fort Ord, located on Monterey Bay.

At this time, Fort Ord was still battling a meningitis epidemic. Forty of us were assigned to the fifth platoon of Company A, Second Battalion. We were restricted to our platoon area. We had limited contact with the other four platoons in the Company. For eight weeks of basic training, the forty of us lived and trained together. We learned a lot, about the Army, about ourselves, and about each other.

The Company consisted of two hundred men. We were divided into five platoons of forty men each. Each platoon had four squads of ten men each. When we marched, the fifth platoon was at the rear of the Company. The squads were aligned by height. I lacked the genetics for growing tall. I was the shortest in my squad, so I marched at the very end of the Company.

During this period of a rapid build-up of manpower, the Army was desperate for bodies. Almost anybody would do and the mix in our group of forty guys illustrated just how desperate they were.

Of the forty guys in the platoon, at least a half dozen suffered from dyslexia. They had reading problems and so tested poorly when it came to aptitude testing. Most of them were more intelligent than their papers told.

The guy that I felt the most empathy for was in the third squad. Howard Daniel Vandenacre was a big, strong farm boy from Montana. Close to six feet tall, he was well-muscled from hard work on the farm. His close-cropped hair from his Army haircut went well with the peach fuzz on his face. Despite his baby face appearance, he was one of the more muscular guys in the platoon.

Howard was one of those with dyslexia. He was normal in his conversations and a lot of functions, especially in physical training. But give him a task that required hand-to-eye coordination, and it would take forever for him to learn it.

And his voice was distinctive. To say it was high-pitched would be an understatement. It was almost a squeak.

It was this squeaky voice that first had the drill instructors (DIs) on his case. "Sound off like you have a pair!" they would shout into his face.

Howard's reply would be a slightly louder squeak, "Yes, sergeant!"

The first inspection was meant to be a learning experience. That is what it was for most of the platoon. Everyone seemed to have something wrong; how the bed was made, how the footlocker was arranged, or how the uniform was hung in the standing locker.

For Howard, it was a disaster. He had nothing correct. His footlocker was a mess. The DI threw it across the bay, almost hitting the guys standing across the aisle, scattering the contents everywhere.

After that inspection, several of us helped Howard daily. We helped make his bed in the mornings, clean his rifle and roll his socks in the evenings.

"I can make my bunk, and I can clean my rifle," Howard said the second morning after the inspection. "But I need a lot of help with my footlocker. I just can't roll my socks."

Rolling his socks the Army way was a significant challenge for Howard. I think it took him a full six weeks before he could roll his socks without help.

His voice was just part of him. We were no help there. But all the abuse from the DI did not alter his cheerful nature.

Howard slept through every training film we attended. He would be sound asleep, but his head never wavered. The DIs were all over anybody whose head bobbed.

"How do you manage to keep your head straight up when you sleep in these films?" I asked Howard.

"That is easy," Howard said. "I sat in front of Dad in church. Dad would bat me on the head if he thought I was sleeping."

Howard had the work ethic that came from his upbringing. If there was work to be done, he was there, often with a few other farm boys and me in the platoon. In combat training that required strength or athletic ability, he would excel. He was always there to lend someone a hand. He would carry the pack of some of the small guys when they needed a break or help them through a trench filled with water or over an obstacle. Always with a smile, and I never once heard him complain.

About the sixth week of basic, we were given training with gas warfare and the use of the gas mask. Howard had trouble getting his mask on most of the time and probably suffered a little more than most of us.

The final exam, so to speak, was an obstacle course of sorts. The platoon left a starting line, climbed through a large trench, and crawled under about thirty yards of barbed wire.

Somewhere in the middle of the barbed wire, they would hit the group with tear gas. Then we were to turn onto our backs, put on the gas mask, and continue through the wire on our backs. There was no way that Howard would be able to get his mask on under that wire.

After we were out of the wire, the assembly area was a large tree at the top of the hill. We would be out of the gas at that location.

I stood beside Howard at the starting line.

"I figure that if we go fast, we can be through that wire before most of these guys are out of the trench," I said. "You stay up with me, and we won't have to worry about the gas stuff. We should be up at the tree when they use it."

The horn blew, and we were off like a shot. I hit the bottom of the trench and made the top of the far bank with one bounce. I glanced back as I started to crawl under the wire. No sign of Howard. I started my crawl under the wire, going as fast as I could. When I stood up at the far end and looked back, Howard was just getting out from under the wire. We ran up to the big tree together and were joined by Archer, another guy who had it figured out.

"You weren't behind me at the start of the wire. How did you catch up?" I asked Howard.

"I got held up a little at the start. I dropped the magazine out of my rifle," Howard replied. "I figured I was in trouble being behind everybody, so I just jumped the trench."

I just shook my head. That had to have been quite a jump. I wished I had seen it. About then, I noticed the DI coming our way. He came up and sat down beside Howard.

"I have been doing this training for almost two years now," he said. "I have never seen anybody even attempt to jump that trench. That was one hell of a leap, Private. Good job."

Howard beamed and broke out in a broad smile. That was the only time I witnessed the DI giving Howard any positive feedback. We laid back and watched the rest of the platoon struggle getting through the wire with tear gas streaming over them.

As we prepared for the graduation ceremony at the end of basic training, I felt a sense of pride when I checked on Howard. His uniform was neat, and his brass was all on correctly. He had progressed a lot in these eight weeks, probably more than the rest of us.

"I have never graduated from anything before," Howard said. "I am sort of nervous. I wish my mother could be here."

Graduation was short, then everyone was given their orders for the next training assignment. The last I saw of Howard, he was standing on the company street as I boarded a bus to the airport.

Time passes, and old Army buddies fade into that distant corner of your thoughts that are seldom visited. It was many years later when I started to wonder what had become of Howard. The search did not take long.

Today, if you are looking for Howard, you will find him on Panel 18E - Line 27.

For those who are not familiar with the address, it is on the Vietnam Memorial Wall.

Howard Daniel Vandenacre
DOB Nov 18, 1946 Conrad, Montana
 PFC E3 9th Infantry Division
 Tour began Dec 1, 1966, Casualty was on Apr 14, 1967
In Long An, South Vietnam
Multiple Fragmentation Wounds
Panel 18E - Line 27
newspapers.com link: https://www.newspapers.com/image/
353890648/?terms=vandenacre&match=1

US Army, Basic Training, 1965

I looked out the window as the plane made its final approach to land at San Francisco International Airport. The water was getting closer by the second. This was the first commercial aircraft I had been on, and I had no concerns until now. The water was getting very close now. I wondered if I should say something to somebody. I was sure we were going to ditch into the bay. At the very last moment, land and the runway flashed into view. I took a deep breath and settled back into my seat as the wheels contacted the runway.

There were about forty of us, new recruits for the Army. We had only a vague idea of what the next few weeks would bring us as we unloaded from the plane and boarded a bus waiting on the tarmac. Now a road trip to Fort Ord, wherever that was located.

It was still daylight when we landed but dark when we pulled into the receiving station at Fort Ord. The drill instructors were quick to make examples of the jokers in the crowd. There was no consideration for dinner. There was a hasty orientation, and then we were herded into our temporary barracks for the night. There was some quick organization of the platoon for the night. Fireguard assignments were issued, and responsibilities were outlined. Then it was lights out.

The next day started early. Formation out front and squad assignments were given out. The platoon and squad leaders were assigned. Then a whirlwind started. An early breakfast, uniform, and equipment were issued, and everything civilian was mailed home. Then we ran through the barbershop. No big deal for most of us, but some of the guys lost a lot of hair.

After lunch, we started testing. For me, the Army tests were a snap. They were virtually all multiple choice questions with easily eliminated two or four possible answers. If I didn't know the answer, I could make a good educated guess. I would finish their hour test in fifteen to twenty minutes. This gave me lots of time to lie on the lawn, ponder the coming days and the next test.

We pulled KP in the receiving station mess hall on the third day. I decided then that I might not be the best, the fastest, or the biggest, but nobody was going to work harder than me at anything I was going to do while in the Army. The mess sergeant gave us a little pep talk at the end of the day, and he thought we were an exceptional group.

They loaded us and our gear into the back of a few trucks on Sunday morning. The next stop was home for the next eight weeks. Our company was located in the last barracks in a long double row of three-story concrete barracks in the second battalion. We would become the 5th platoon in the company.

Fort Ord was still in the recovery phase of a major epidemic of spinal meningitis. There were a lot of rules and restrictions that we would live with. Most of those probably served to eliminate some of the previous rigors of basic training. We were restricted to the company area, and platoons could not mingle. These forty guys were going to be my world for the next eight weeks.

There were a bunch of guys from Montana and a bunch of us from Oregon, with a few others mixed in from other areas. Most of us were well versed in the outdoors. But some of the kids had never been out of the city. There was one older guy who had been in the Army before and back for a second try. Other than him, everyone was young. I was twenty with a couple of years of college under my belt, and I was one of the older ones. I would guess at least twenty, if not more, were eighteen. At least one was seventeen. Probably half were drafted.

We settled into our barracks. Our platoon bay was on the ground floor. My squad occupied the first set of bunks on the right as you entered the large bay. Bunks were well spaced, and heads were alternated, the top guy with his head opposite the guy on the bottom bunk. The next bunk was opposite the preceding bunk. This gave everyone the largest amount of breathing space possible. Windows were open; all windows when it was warm, every other window as it cooled down a little.

We made up the fifth platoon, forty men in each platoon, two hundred men in the company. I was in the first squad. The squad was aligned in formation by height. Being the shortest man in the squad, when we marched, I was at the end of the line for the company. We would march down the street; I had two hundred men in front of me. I would learn, this was a very favorable position to be in. We were seldom looked at, back at the end of the company.

Jim was the kid that slept on the bottom bunk below me. Jim was a good kid, a little slow and absolutely dyslectic. I always considered myself somewhat dyslectic. I always had to double-check numbers I wrote down because I would often transpose them, and spelling was a constant challenge.

But Jim literally did not know his right from his left. When we marched, Jim marched just in front of me. When the company made a turn, we would watch two hundred men in front of us, turning right. As we approached the spot to turn, Jim would start bouncing, bobbing his head. We had a right turn coming. I would say in a low voice, "turn to the right." We would get to the point, and Jim would turn to the left, every time. Then stop and run to get back in position before he was descended upon by two or three drill instructors. The left turns were worse because he would run into the guy next to him.

We had long marches, several miles, to the rifle range. Most of this distance was on loose sand, which proved very tiring.

These marches were led by the executive officer. Lieutenant Garcia was a small, stout man from Cuba. He had been in the Bay of Pigs invasion before joining the US Army.

Being in the back of the company, we would pass a canteen around. Smitty and I would tell jokes and laugh, and we had several rows in front of us laughing a little.

We were never bothered by the drill instructors. But one day, when we were marching back to the company facility, Lieutenant Garcia had dropped out to the side of the company and was watching us pass a canteen around as we marched past him.

He was none too happy, to put it mildly. Everyone in front of us was suddenly marching like they didn't know anything was wrong. Lieutenant Garcia pulled Smitty, Jim, and me out of the ranks and really chewed us out. We had to dump the water out of our canteens. This went on for several long minutes while the company continued to march.

When he was done chewing on us, he pointed to the company, now disappearing over a slight rise, hundreds of yards in the distance.

"You three, run until you are back in position," Lieutenant Garcia barked. "Run and do not stop."

We ran, and the lieutenant was right on our rear. The loose sand made the run seem like a mile. We finally caught up to the company just as it reached the paved road.

"Don't let me catch you jokers again," Lieutenant Garcia said as he continued to run to the head of the column.

Once we were dismissed and were back in the barracks, everyone wanted to know what had happened. I just wanted to get cleaned up for dinner so I could get to bed. I was planning to wait until morning to clean my rifle since I was generally one of the first ones up in the platoon.

Our DI caught up with me as I was leaving the mess hall after dinner. This surprised me a little, as he was usually not around after dinner.

"Larsen, you guys need to make sure your rifles are cleaned, and your beds and footlockers are ready for an inspection in the morning," the sergeant said. "I understand that Lieutenant Garcia plans to check in on you three in the morning. It will be a surprise inspection, and he will be surprised if you are ready for it."

It was late that evening when I had everything done. I had cleaned my rifle and helped Jim with his rifle, and Smitty was doing okay with his stuff. We were the last ones to crawl into bed just before lights out.

"I almost think I should sleep on the floor tonight," Jim said. "I hate to mess up my bed."

"I will wake you up when I get up, and we will have plenty of time to be ready," I said. "You need to get some sleep tonight. Tomorrow won't be any easier than today."

***

Lieutenant Garcia entered the platoon bay with our DI right at the stroke of seven in the morning. He casually inspected the first few bunks until he came to Jim and me. He went through our footlockers with a fine-tooth comb. And then he bounced a quarter on our bunks. He smiled and nodded his head at me.

"Which rifle is yours, Private Larsen?" Lieutenant Garcia asked.

I retrieved my rifle from the rack in the middle of the room.

"Is your rifle always this clean, Larsen?" he asked.

"Yes, sir," I replied.

Then he had Jim get his rifle. I think he was sure he could find an issue with Jim's rifle. He had to know that Jim was dyslexic.

"Did you clean this rifle yourself, Private?" Lieutenant Garcia asked.

"I did most of it, sir," Jim replied. "Larsen gave me a few pointers."

Lieutenant Garcia again nodded his head at me and smiled.

After looking at our rifles, he went right over to Smitty's bunk and put him through the same routine.

Satisfied, Lieutenant Garcia left. The DI was all smiles. A favorable inspection always reflected well on his leadership. The rest of the platoon was relieved that it was over.

Our conduct at the end of the company formation became a little more in line with standard military discipline for the rest of basic training.

KP, Basic Training, Fall 1965

I was up and through the showers and lacing my boots when the fireguard came into the bay to wake up the KP crew. We had to be in the kitchen by 5:00 a.m. I was in the kitchen waiting for the cooks and the rest of the KP crew a good 15 minutes early.

Most of the guys hated the shift that ran until 7:00 p.m. I had decided that nobody was going to work harder than me while I was in the Army, and this was just another day. And just like a day at work, time passes faster if you are working rather than sitting around watching the clock.

The assistant cook was the first to arrive, and he was surprised to see me already there. We started getting set up to cook breakfast. It was interesting to be mixing pancakes for 200 guys, and the scrambled eggs were mixed from powder.

By the time the cook came through the door, we had the bacon ready to go into the oven. The oven was hot, and the griddle was fired up. Just about all he had to do was to start cooking.

"Are you the whole crew today?" the mess sergeant asked me. His voice was gruff, and his frown wrinkled his entire forehead. He wore a little white sock-like cap to cover his bald head.

"I was up early, Sergeant," I said. "The others should be along any time now."

When the others did arrive, the mess sergeant barked out instructions with practiced repetition. The milk dispenser needed to be filled, and the juice set out. Coffee needed to be made. He was assigning chores as fast as he could, and the assistant cook was trying to give instructions fast enough to keep up. It was a system that was used to make guys useful, even though many of them had never been in a kitchen.

"Who wants to mix the pancake batter?" the cook asked.

"Larsen had that mixed before you got here," the assistant said. "And the eggs are mixed, and the bacon is ready for the oven."

"The cook looked at me and scowled. "Have you been a cook?"

"No, Sergeant, I was just here early and needed to keep busy," I said.

Breakfast went off with no problems. We were each assigned to serving positions or other chores like keeping the milk dispenser full or moving dishes from the collection area to the dishwasher.

When breakfast was over, we started cleaning up, getting ready for lunch, and making desserts for tomorrow's dinner. The cook was pretty good at keeping everyone busy and ruled with a loud voice and a frown.

"Larsen, you wash the vegetable steamer," the cook says as he points to the sizable stainless steel steamer that was anchored to the floor. This was a large tank, maybe fifty gallons.

I jumped right to it. Having made cheese in Myrtle Point for four summers, if there was something I knew, it was how to scrub stainless steel. I didn't wait for any instructions.

I dumped a couple of handfuls of powdered detergent into the steamer and started filling it with water. With a large scrub brush, I mixed the soap with the water and turned on a little steam to warm the water. About that time, I felt the presence of the cook, more than seeing him. He was standing at my left shoulder.

"What the hell have you done?" he boomed into my ear. "Did you put soap into my steamer?" He continued before I could answer. "Nobody puts soap in my steamer."

I looked at him, and then I looked back at the steamer. Everybody in the kitchen was watching now.

"How long have you used this without washing it?" I asked. I knew I probably had made a grave error by talking back to this guy. Still, I probably had him over the barrel because it was supposed to be washed.

The cook looked at me, red-faced, eyes narrowed, and breathing hard. Then he looked at the steamer.

"If they taste soap in their peas tonight, I will have your ass, Larsen," he bellowed.

"I have washed more stainless steel than you will ever see in your life," I said.

He stood and looked at me for what seemed like minutes. I was expecting to catch his full wrath. Finally, he took a deep breath and relaxed his facial expression. "We will let them decide," he said, pointing out to the dining hall. Then he turned away and got back to other tasks.

I scrubbed and scrubbed on that steamer. Swirling the brush around, I was hanging half over the rim into the tank. By the time I was done, sweat was dripping off my eyebrows and my nose. I drained the tank and rinsed it several times. During this whole process, I could see both the cook and the assistant cook watching me. Plus, the other guys on KP.

When I was done, the cook came over and looked at the steamer. It glistened compared to its old self. He nodded in approval.

"Now, if you're so good at scrubbing, you can scrub all the garbage cans," the cook said.

I am sure he thought this was a punishment. It sort of reminded me of the rabbit story when Br'er Rabbit begs not to be thrown into the brier patch. Every fall, I would scrub hundreds of milk cans, cleaning them for winter storage. A few garbage cans were nothing.

I was outside, enjoying working in the sunshine. I had water flying and cans spinning as I washed the cans and set them out to dry in the sun. I noticed the cook watching from time to time. I think he was a little upset that I was enjoying myself.

Then one of the other guys in the platoon, who was cleaning the storeroom, came out with a bunch of empty bags and cardboard. He handed them down to me to put in the dumpster. I took the load and tossed them in the dumpster.

"I have one more load," he said. "You can take a break for a minute while I grab it."

I grabbed the bags, and this time they were cumbersome and heavy.

He smiled, "Payback for the ass-chewing," he said. "Put the heavy one in one of those clean garbage cans, and we will pick it up tonight."

I looked at the heavy bag. It contained a whole bunch of bananas, stem and all, enough for the entire platoon.

Dinner went without a hitch. Nobody complained about soap in the peas. We cleaned up and were thanked by the cook.

"You guys have been a good bunch," the cook said. "I think you will do well in this man's Army."

It was nice to get back to the barracks and get through the shower. I was in clean clothes when the guy who had stolen the bananas came by and motioned toward the door.

It was close to dark, and the two of us exited the rear door and ran across the backyard. We grabbed the bag of bananas from the garbage can, turned, and ran back across the yard with the bag carried between us.

We felt like we just put one over on the cook. We had bananas for the whole platoon. We burst through the back door and almost ran over Sergeant Lopez.

Sergeant Lopez was the DI for the fourth platoon. He had lost his wife to the current meningitis epidemic at Fort Ord, and he lived in the company barracks. His room was right by the back door.

Here we are, standing at attention against the wall with a bag of stolen bananas between us. We both thought we were dead.

Sergeant Lopez said, "Ah, what have we here?" He peeks into the bag.

We knew we were dead now.

Lopez smiles, looked down the hall, and shook his head. "I didn't see a thing," he said as he turned and heads for his room.

The whole platoon had two or three bananas each. The trip back to the dumpster with the peelings was just as scary.

Our opinion of Sergeant Lopez changed that night.

The Game

I held my three cards firmly and a little cupped, so the three aces were out of view to the other players and the crowd of half-dressed GIs watching the game. It was Saturday evening in mid-October, and a poker game was the best entertainment available to our platoon. We were in the middle of basic training at Fort Ord.

This was 1965, and we were still under restrictions due to the recent epidemic of spinal meningitis. These thirty-nine other guys were my circle of friends for the duration of the eight weeks of basic training.

I waited anxiously for my draw of two cards. There were six of us in this game. We probably had half the platoon watching, all in various states of dress and undress. Boxers were standard attire in the barracks in the evenings. Boxers and a tee-shirt were almost Sunday-go-to-meeting dress. There were a few guys still in their fatigues. I watched as the other players called for their cards. Only Tangerman, a younger kid, sitting across the makeshift table, a couple of footlockers pushed together, drew two cards.

I slowly picked up my two cards, one at a time. I turned the first card over and stuck it in my hand, a king. I took a deep breath and picked up the next card. It was an ace. I am sitting here with four aces and a king, the only hand that can beat me is a straight flush. It is highly unlikely that Tangerman would draw two cards to a straight flush.

I watch as the bet goes around the table, one guy, to the right of the dealer, bets, then Tangerman raises. The next guy folds, the next guy sees the bet. I am trying to decide if I want to raise now. The rules of this game say we are limited to two raises. All of us playing are in the same boat. We need some money to last until payday. We have tried to construct a game that will be fun but where nobody will be hurt. I go ahead and raise the bet.

The group of guys behind Tangerman is excited, which means he hit his draw. The dealer folds, as does the next guy. So there are three of us still in the hand and my guess is the other guy will fold.

Then Tangerman makes a fatal error in judgment. He asks if we can suspend the rules. Could it be that he has a straight flush? I can't believe that.

I agree. "Bet away," I say.

Tangerman raises my bet again. The third guy folds. There are a few guys behind me now, wanting to see my hand. I see Tangerman's bet, and I raise him back. I relax a little and show my hand to the guys behind me. Both groups of guys are going crazy now. There is enough tension in the platoon that you could cut it with a knife. Virtually the entire platoon is watching the game now. Tangerman's group has more than twenty guys, more than mine, and much more vocal.

Tangerman sees my bet and only has a few dollars left in front of him. He fingers his dollars as he considers his final raise.

"We have over a week before payday," I say, "you might want to hang onto a few dollars."

Tangerman looks at the pot, there must be close to thirty dollars in the pot, a half month's pay for us. He looks at his remaining three dollars.

106

"Okay, I call you," he says.

With a sigh, I lay my cards on the table. Tangerman's group erupts in a colossal moan.

"Damn," Tangerman says as he lays his hand on the table. Four queens and a king.

The game is over after that. Tangerman is tapped out, and there is no way the excitement can be matched. I scrape in the pile of bills.

Everyone is dispersing to their bunk area, and as we are repositioning all the footlockers, I grab Tangerman by his elbow.

"If you run short before payday, you let me know," I say. "This game wasn't supposed to leave anybody broke."

"Thanks," he says.

That is the only poker game I played in the Army. After basic training, there was either too much work to do or too much fun to be had elsewhere.

***

Much later in life, in Sweet Home, I would play an occasional friendly game with a group of guys. Most games were casual, everybody had more money to lose than the guys had during basic training, but it was more of a social gathering than a serious card game.

I had been playing in a weekly group with five or six guys for a couple of months. I considered myself lucky if I broke even. I think once or twice I came home with an extra twenty dollars, but never anything more than that. Usually, the host would have some finger food on the table, and there was maybe a beer or two on the table.

I got a call one afternoon to castrate a group of young bulls. This was a purebred Black Angus herd, and this was a group of twelve young bulls who didn't make the grade for the bull sale. These bulls were all approaching a year of age, or they were just over a year.

This was a pretty routine call, but the candidates for bedroom guards were a little older than the usual crowd.

The first bull was waiting in the chute when we pulled up to the corral. I used my standard castration technique. I had Hope pull the tail up over the back to create a good tail pinch on the spinal nerves. I would grasp the scrotum above the testicles and squeeze them into the bottom of the scrotum, make a quick incision down each side of the scrotum and squeeze the testicle out of the scrotum. I would grab each testicle and stretch it down until I could feel the cremaster muscle tear. That done, with a clamp on the cord above the testicle, I would remove the testicle with the emasculator, holding firm pressure on the emasculator to ensure a solid crush on the vessels. In small bulls, I would remove both testicles together. Bulls this size, I removed each testicle individually.

With the first set of testicles in my hand, I looked at Debbie.

"Do you want these," I asked.

"Are you kidding?" she asked.

"I don't know, they tell me they are pretty good eating," I said.

"If you want them, you are welcome to them."

"Hope, grab me a few OB sleeves," I said. "I happen to have a poker game tomorrow evening. These might make pretty good hors d'oeuvres."

We worked through the remaining bulls similarly. By the time I was done, both OB sleeves were full of prime testicles. I tied the sleeves at the top, and we packed up our stuff.

"You will find that they will all be singing soprano from now on," I said. "Thanks for the leftovers."

I had no recipe to follow in cooking these things. I figured I would just imagine the end product and work backward. These were probably a little larger testicles than what one might see in a bar in Colorado. Mountain oysters were a fall delicacy in many Rocky Mountain areas. Each testicle was over three inches long and approaching two inches in diameter.

I removed the loose tunic from each testicle, and then with a sharp knife I sliced the epididymis from the testicles. I then sliced them into rounds, about the thickness one would slice a potato for frying.

With them all sliced, I dipped them in milk, dredged them through a beaten egg, and then flour. Then, each round was fried to a golden brown. Sandy always says I cook things at too high a temperature, so I was careful to use medium heat. A little salt and pepper finished the process.

When they came out of the frying pan, I let them cool on paper towels and then carefully stacked them on a platter. When finished, it was a pretty impressive plate of mountain oysters, if I do say so myself. I covered them with plastic wrap and put them in the refrigerator overnight.

I took the platter to the office the next day because I was going to be at the clinic until I left for the poker game. The girls in the office were impressed with the appearance of the platter and wanted to taste one.

Hope took a bite and immediately ran to the bathroom. She was embarrassed when she came back. When she bit into the sample, she had gotten a small tubule stuck between her teeth. Needless to say, that ended the sampling at the office.

I arrived early at the poker game, but there were a couple of guys there already. I set the platter on the table, a little off-center but where it was within reach of everybody. I removed the wrap and didn't say anything about it.

The group arrived, and we settled into the game. As the evening wore on, guys started picking away at the platter. It wasn't long, and the plate was nearly empty.

"What are these things?" Jerry finally asked, holding up one of the rounds. "They are pretty good. Who brought them?"

I never said a word and worked hard to maintain my best poker face.

Finally, Gil chuckled and pointed to me. "Larsen brought them," he said as he continued to laugh.

Of course, the whole table thought they were poisoned for sure.

I quickly fessed up to the truth, "They are just mountain oysters. And they are as fresh as you can get anywhere."

Just Don't Eat the Apple Pie

There were a bunch of guys milling around outside of the barracks waiting for the Company Clerk to call the company to formation. This was G Company of the Second Battalion at Fort Devens, US Army Security Agency Training School. I had been at Fort Devens for over eight months now. Three of those months had been waiting for school. Now I was in school, but I was in night school because of the significant buildup of troops for Vietnam. That allowed them to double their output.

We were billeted in the old WWII portion of the base. The barracks had been pulled out of mothballs and made livable. There were a lot of us living in the second battalion. Con 4 was a large central mess hall that fed everyone in the battalion, probably close to fifteen hundred troops. Tonight would be my first and only shift of KP at Con 4. We were a night school group, so we got the KP night shift.

The clerk climbed up on his elevated platform and blew his whistle. Company G was made up of about two hundred men in five platoons, very similar to the makeup of the basic training

110

companies. With all the platoons formed up, the clerk called the company to attention and read off the day's orders. Then we were dismissed and fell into our class groups to march to school.

We marched nearly a mile to school in these smaller formations made up of our respective class groups. Today, I and almost forty other guys, marched in a different direction, to Con 4.

The night shift was actually the best. We had to clean up after dinner, but it was just cooking and getting ready to cook for the next day after that clean up was done. Bags and bags of potatoes needed to be peeled. The kitchen needed to be set up for cooking breakfast.

The better part of the early evening, the entire crew cleaned the dining room and set it up for breakfast. Then we took our assignments for the middle part of the night. Peeling potatoes seemed to me to be the best gig. You were out back of the kitchen, almost outside on a warm summer night. And nobody to bother you.

Potatoes were dumped in a tumbler that removed the majority of the peelings. We just had to dig out the eyes and anything that was missed by the tumbler. There were four of us sitting around, going through one bag after another. How many potatoes do fifteen hundred guys eat in a day? I don't know, but we worked at it for several hours.

When the potatoes were all peeled, we went back into the kitchen to see what the next chore would be.

"Apple pie," the cook said. "You guys always like the apple pie your mothers made. But your mother never made apple pie for fifteen hundred guys."

"This might be fun to watch," I said to Fred. Fred was one of the guys who peeled potatoes with me. I had never seen him before tonight, and I figured I would never see him again after tonight.

"A couple of you guys go get that wok and bring it over to the table with all the apples," the cook said.

"I don't know what a wok is," I said to Fred.

"He pointed over to the far corner," Fred said. "Let's go grab it."

My first exposure to a wok was interesting. This wok was about six feet across and nearly three feet deep. It rested on a metal cart with four small wheels. We got behind it and pushed it and the cart over to where the cook was waiting.

The apple filling was in gallon cans. We started opening the cans and dumping them in the wok. I can't say how many gallons were used, but the wok was filled to six inches from the top.

The cook sprinkled several cans of spices over the top of the apples, and a couple of guys started to mix the spices into the mass of apples with large wooden paddles. This was somewhat of a fun event with a dozen guys involved. Most of the crew had been working on the pie crusts while we had been peeling potatoes.

"Okay," the cook said. "Let's wheel this over to the pie crust."

The pie crusts were in large flat pans, laid out on several tables over in the next room. About four guys grabbed the wok and started pushing it toward the tables with the pans of crust. Once they got it moving, the speed increased.

As the cart came to the doorway, it hit the ribbing on the floor, connecting the tiles between the rooms. The little wheels of the cart carrying the wok stopped when they hit this rib. The wok did not stop.

The wok continued, and the cart stopped. The wok made it halfway out of the cart, rested a brief moment at the midpoint of the rounded bottom, then flipped over. All of the apples hit the floor, and the wok landed upside down on the pile.

My first thought was that I was glad I had not been pushing the cart. I thought the cook was going to explode. He took a deep breath like he was going to let someone have it. Then he relaxed and took command of the situation.

He looked around the room and looked at the mess on the floor and the empty pie crusts. Then his focus came to rest on a shovel near the rear door.

"Larsen," he said. "You go wash that shovel. We will clean up this wok."

I couldn't believe it. The cook was going to shovel that stuff back into the wok. I took the shovel to the big sink and started scrubbing. After a couple of scrubbings with a large brush, I started scrubbing with a steel wool pad. Finally, I thought I could probably use it to fry an egg on if I had to.

"Larsen, you don't have to be able to eat off the thing," the cook said. "We are ready for it."

The crew shoveled the apple filling off the floor back into the wok. Then they moved the wok over to the pie crusts and continued to make the pies.

The evening went along fine after that. The floor in the kitchen looked cleaner than it had in months. And there was no trace of apple pie filling on the floor.

The morning crew arrived, and we were discharged to return to our barracks. I got back to the barracks about the time that my classmates were returning from school. There was a little chatter in the barracks as everyone settled into their bunks.

"How was KP, Larsen?" Mac asked.

"It was okay," I said. "Just don't eat the apple pie."

A Day at the Track

The late afternoon sky looked very threatening. The clouds were black and billowing up to great heights. Nobody was looking forward to marching to our night classes in the rain.

The Company G corporal was having difficulty getting the company to line up. About the time he was on his elevated stand and called the company to attention, there was a large 'crack' as a bolt of lightning struck a telephone pole in the middle of the company street. The corporal hollered "Dismissed" after half the company was back in the barracks. We will be a little late for class tonight. I had never seen lightning like this. Massachusetts was a strange land for a farm boy from Oregon. Maybe now I could understand how Ben Franklin was interested in his electricity experiments.

As the sky cleared, our class started off on the mile-long march to school. We were in the Terminal Intercept Equipment Class for the Army Security Agency at Fort Devens, Massachusetts. Tonight was to be the end of the first section of the course of study. The class would divide tonight, some going into tactical equipment and the rest into strategic equipment. Next week we would move to the secure compound for the remainder of our training on classified equipment.

As everyone was sorting out their status at the end of class, the instructor came over to me.

"You finished this first section at the top of the class," he said. "So you get this three-day pass for the weekend."

"This is the weekend before payday," I said. "Is it possible for me to take it next weekend? I will have more money in my pocket at that time."

"I'm sorry," the instructor said. "This is how the program is set up. Tomorrow night we don't do any real instruction. It is mostly just getting everyone lined up with the changes going on next week."

So Friday morning, I took my pass and walked to the bus depot in Ayer. It was nearly three miles, but I was in great shape. My funds were limited. I would have to pinch pennies the whole weekend.

I purchased a round-trip bus ticket to Boston. I would at least be able to get home. The Friday morning bus was almost empty, very different from the chaos of the Saturday morning bus rides. I sat in the back and stretched my legs out. I would have to walk again when I got to Boston. I planned to stay at the YMCA; you could get a room for five dollars.

The weather in Boston was great. Still enough of Spring remained that there were blossoms on many of the trees in the Commons. The streets were not busy in the mid-morning, so my walk was an enjoyable one. My mood changed when I got to the YMCA.

"There are no rooms available tonight," the clerk said. "I can reserve you a room for tomorrow night, but I can only offer you a cot on the gym floor for tonight. The cot comes with the use of the gym shower. It will be a full gym tonight. We generally have a couple hundred sailors sleeping there on Friday night."

"The fee is a dollar and a half for the cot and five dollars for the room," the clerk said. From his mannerism, I am sure he repeated that speech many times during the day. "You can use one of those lockers over against the gym wall for your bag if you would like."

I paid the six and a half dollars and looked at my wallet. It was a good thing that I had eaten a large breakfast at the mess hall this morning because I could skip lunch today. Dinner

115

tonight and Saturday night, maybe a beer or two and a couple other meals, it was looking pretty thin. I would probably be riding the subway or spending time in the USO for the only entertainment I could afford.

That just about summed up my Friday. I purchased a handful of subway tokens and then walked as far as I could down the Commons.

The USO was not far from the Commons. Friday noon, and I was about the only one there. There were a few donuts and some crackers available. I ate a couple of donuts, filled a pocket with the crackers, and headed for the elevated subway stop.

Two sailors were waiting for the subway. They were in the same boat I was in. Payday came the first of the month, and for a private first-class, that meant a hundred and ten dollars. By the last weekend, there was generally not much available. We boarded the subway together. These guys were typical sailors, thinking they had the best deal the military had to offer.

"What do you guys do?" I asked as the subway pulled out, heading toward Harvard.

"We are on our last liberty before going to the Bahamas for a shakedown cruise. Once there, the captain says we get liberty every night for two weeks," the talkative one answered.

"Shakedown cruise? That sounds like you are getting ready for a big trip or something," I said.

"Yes, we are on an ice breaker. We are heading for the Arctic Ocean and will be there for six months," the sailor stated.

"By the end of six months, two weeks of liberty will be a distant memory," I said.

They were a little quiet after that and exited on the next stop. I rode the subway to the end of the line, got off, and caught the first car heading back to Boston. I had a few dollars to spend on a hamburger and maybe a beer in the Combat Zone. It won't be much of a Friday night on my budget.

The Combat Zone seemed more hype than anything, just a bunch of drunken sailors getting ripped off. It didn't occur to me that this would be the same bunch that I would be sharing the gym floor with in a couple of hours. I entered a bar and stood up to the bar. The barmaid was prompt, checked my ID, and wanted to know what I wanted.

"How much for a beer?" I asked.

"You have to buy two," she said. "Two beers cost six dollars."

"That's too rich for my wallet," I said.

I went across the street and had a cheap hamburger for dinner. From the restaurant window, I could do a little people watching. Sort of felt sorry for the sailors.

I walked back to the YMCA. It was across the street from the Boston Gardens. I had not noticed that on my first trip there. I was not impressed. It did not look like it did in all the pictures. It was sort of dark and dingy.

There were cots set up covering most of the gym floor. I picked up my blanket, pillow, and sheets from the janitor manning the storeroom.

"We are going to have a gym full of drunken sailors tonight," the janitor said. "You want to pick a cot in the middle, so you will miss out on the commotion of the late arrivals. And make sure you hit the showers early because the hot water doesn't last too long. The sailors all seem to be used to cold showers."

He was correct on every count. I picked a cot in the middle of the room, and I could hear guys coming in all night long. The good thing was I was one of the first in the shower. I got my change of clothes from my bag and decided to leave the bag in the locker until I could get into my room. I made a short walk to a little restaurant I had noticed last night. It would cost a couple bucks more than the YMCA breakfast, but I had just about had enough of the sailors.

My Saturday was not much different from Friday. I rode the subway, walked the Commons, and dropped by the USO. The USO had some sandwiches on Saturday, and it was packed with sailors. I headed back to the YMCA in the afternoon and checked into my room. Not much, but private and quiet. I took a little nap. I would have to find a place for dinner and beer when I woke up.

I ate breakfast at the same little restaurant and bought a newspaper to read on Sunday morning. Maybe I could figure out something to do. After breakfast, I sat on a park bench with a bunch of old men. One guy was watching me pretty close. As I read the paper, an ad jumped out at me. Suffolk Downs was racing horses today. That was great, I thought, as I counted my assets.

I had my bus ticket home, two subway tokens, and two dollars and fifty cents. Not much to go to the races on, but that is what I am going to do. As I stood up, the old man raised a hand to me.

"If you are done with that paper, can I have it?' he asked.

I tossed him the paper and headed for the subway. I knew nothing about horse racing, but I knew animals, and I would think I could pick a good horse once in a while.

The subway on the way to the track was packed. I stood the whole way. The subway car was filled with quite a group of characters, but not a single sailor among them. When we came to a stop at the track, the entire group poured out of the car.

I had not figured that there would be an admission fee to get into the track. I was down to two dollars in my pocket with the fifty cents admission.

I was glad that I had the one subway token and a bus ticket home. This might be a short adventure.

I scoped everything out. The stewards were just bringing the horses into the paddock for the first race. I went down and watched them close, picked my horse, and headed to the two-dollar show window.

With my last two dollars gone, I went out and watched the race.

My horse won. I was relieved that I wasn't broke yet. I went to the window and collected five dollars and forty cents. That was easy, I thought.

The following four races were all the same. I watched the horses in the paddock, picked my horse, and bet two dollars for the horse to show. In each race, my horse won. By now, I was not rich, but I had nearly thirty dollars in my pocket. I went and bought a hot dog and a beer and headed over to the paddock for the sixth race. Confident now that I was a master at picking winning horses, I changed strategy a little.

In the paddock was the best horse I had seen today. A big black horse with long legs, he stood a good two hands above the other horses. Without any hesitation, I went to the ten-dollar window and bet him to win. I was going to be rich after this race.

M horse took off and left the field in his dust. On the backstretch, he was probably leading by twenty lengths. I was excited, counting my money now. He came around the last corner, and his legs began to flail. He acted like he was having trouble staying on his feet. His lead evaporated as first one horse, and then another passed him like he was standing still. Finally, the race was over. He did get across the finish line, dead last; so much for my new betting strategy.

For the remaining five races that day, I returned to my two-dollar bet to show. Each of the following five horses I picked won.

This day at the races, I picked ten out of eleven winners. I left the track with seventy-eight dollars, almost a small fortune for a GI in training.

I was very content on the bus ride back to Ayer. It was dark when I arrived. Unlike Friday, a large group of guys got off the bus and headed for the base. There was even a bus to the main gate waiting for us.

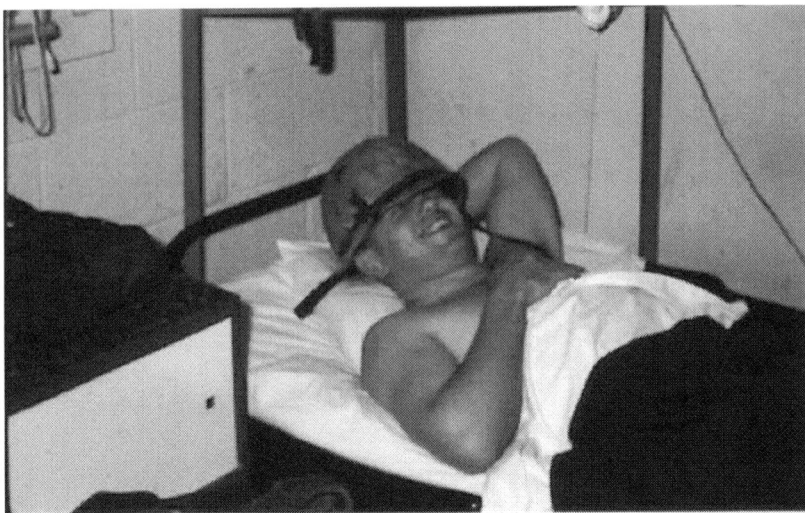

South Korea, Winter 1966 to 1967

The Korean winter was brutal to this farm boy from the Pacific Northwest. I was used to a little wet snow that would last a day or two. And freezing temperatures slipped below the twenty-degree mark on the thermometer only on rare occasions.

Actually, my time in Korea was a piece of cake. I was a member of the 177th US Army Security Agency Operations Company. We were located in Camp Humphreys, probably an hour south of Seoul.

Our unit was responsible for most of the electronic intelligence involving those infiltrators. But we were insulated from the actual conflict. The conflict was accountable for losing over one hundred American servicemen during my thirteen months in the country. That was a small number compared to the losses in Vietnam during the same period.

I lived in a concrete block building that was uninsulated. For the first couple of months, I was the only inhabitant of a two-man room on the second floor of the barracks that housed the second trick. My room was on the end of the building, on the west end.

By Army standards, life was easy. We had a houseboy that did all work. For five dollars a month, plus what the Army paid him, he polished my shoes, made my bunk, cleaned the room, and took care of my laundry. He also was a fifth-degree blackbelt in karate, so he added a bit of security to the barracks while we were at work.

It was probably in late November when a new guy, Clarence, moved into my room. Clarence was a great guy, and we got along well. He tried to teach me some of the finer arts of photography, but I was a lost cause. Most of the pictures I have of that time came from Clarence.

Clarence was from Maui. If I thought I suffered from the winter temperatures, Clarence really had reason to complain.

Clarence related the story of the day he joined the Army, nearly a year before my enlistment. When he enlisted, the Army gathered a planeload of new recruits from Hawaii and flew them to San Francisco. They would do their basic training at Fort Ord, just south of San Francisco at Monterey.

"When I grew up, the coldest temperature I experienced on Maui was fifty-four degrees," Clarence said. "When we stepped off the plane in San Francisco, it was raining and thirty-seven degrees. We all thought we were going to die. Fort Ord in November is not a fun place for a bunch of Hawaiian kids."

Korea was far more severe than Fort Ord ever thought of being. Camp Humphreys was located on a coastal flat close to the shore of the Yellow Sea. We were buffeted with a strong west wind that came off the Yellow Sea straight from China for most of the winter.

Those winds would turn my room on the west end of the block barracks into a virtual icebox. If I made sure the heat was set high enough, I was relatively comfortable with my bunk against the room's interior wall. We called the outside wall the freezer wall.

When Clarence arrived, it was about the time we were issued winter gear; wool pants and wool fatigue shirt, coupled with insulated liners for our field jackets and headgear with ear flaps, life was a little better. The brass even allowed us to purchase black-market hoods for our field jackets. These were lined with fur, and I am pretty sure it was from the dog farms.

Clarence always looked uncomfortable, no matter how bundled up he was at the time. And his bunk was against the outside wall, the freezer wall.

I realized how uncomfortable the weather was for him when I woke up in the middle of the night, and Clarence was pulling his bunk out to the middle of the room, away from the freezer wall. I could sympathize with him, but never to the extent of changing places for our bunks.

Clarence was sent to the 177th because of his unusual MOS (Military Occupational Speciality). We had a van that was set up to intercept faxes. This was in 1966, and I had never heard of fax. This van had been in mothballs for some time, and Clarence was sent to make it operational. Of course, he needed the help of the maintenance crew, which in this case, turned out to be me.

It took Clarence and me nearly a whole week before he pulled the first newspaper-sized fax out of the machine. I was amazed, although I would guess that the technology had been in use for some time by industry.

Clarence's climate issues were destined to get worse before the winter was over. Once the fax van was fully operational at the 177th, Clarence was transferred to another unit near the DMZ.

There the accommodations were more primitive and the weather even more severe.

I was back to being the sole inhabitant of my two-man room. Clarence and I have remained friends for the last fifty-some years, if only by mail and e-mail.

Dumb and Dumber

By the summer of 1967, I had been elevated to Quality Control NCO in our maintenance shop for the 177th USASA Operations Company located at Camp Humphreys, South Korea.

The year I was there is often called the second Korean War. We were besieged by many infiltrators from North Korea that year. Firefights on the DMZ were regular events. In that year, we lost over six hundred UN soldiers. Over one hundred of those were Americans.

The 177th was the hub of the low-frequency radio intercept and direction-finding operations in the country. We had a lot of equipment to maintain, both installed in our operations and mobile vans.

This position removed me from the rotating trick maintenance position and gave me a day job. That was a blessing, but the role also gave me a couple of headaches, namely, in Dumb and Dumber. The two trick workers could also be called Mutt and Jeff. They seemed to do everything together, and their work often had to be redone by someone more competent.

123

Promotions were given out almost automatically in Korea. Nearly everyone in the shop was promoted to Specialist Five when they had two years in the Army. I wondered why these two were still Spec Fours, and they were close to rotating to their next duty station.

"Dumber, I have a job for you," I said as I assigned Dumber to fix a mobile jamming transmitter located down at the motor pool.

"Great," Dumber said. "I will take Dumb with me. We can go to lunch when we are done. That will get us out of the shop for a few hours."

I had a strange foreboding as the two left the operations building, each carrying an armload of equipment. They still managed to laugh and butt shoulders as they went through the exit door.

Starting at ten-thirty in the morning, most of the guys in the shop would have had the job done well before lunch. But actually, having the pair out of the shop for a few hours was a good thing, so I let them work at their own pace.

When Dumb and Dumber returned to the shop, it was nearly two o'clock.

"I thought you two would be back right after lunch," I said.

"We got the transmitter fixed and checked out its operation," Dumb said. "Then, after lunch, we had to go back to the motor pool and get all our equipment. We got back as soon as we could."

Their explanation was marginal, but there was no sense in questioning their time frame. They settled into the afternoon work schedule, and everything was going along fine.

That is, going fine until Chief Warrant Officer Neal, the officer in charge of the shop, stormed across the hall from his office.

"I have the old man on the phone, and he is really pissed," Mr. Neal said. "It seems we have been jamming a local radio station for the last several hours. Do you know anything about this?"

I looked at Dumb and Dumber; no words were needed. They immediately fessed up.

"We fixed that transmitter and rolled it up on this Korean radio station, just to check it out," Dumber said. "I guess we must have forgotten to turn it off when we went to lunch."

Mr. Neal fumed. Steam was coming from his ears.

"You get your ass down there and turn the thing off," he yelled to Dumber.

Then he turned to me. "You should know better than to send that pair to do anything without direct supervision," he said. "That means they don't do anything out of this shop."

So Dumb and Dumber were sent to visit with the commanding officer. They were given an article 15 for lack of detail in the performance of their duties. Article 15, a company-level punishment, just about confirmed that they wouldn't be promoted before leaving Korea.

***

It was a sweltering hot August afternoon when the swing trick took over for the trick on days. Everyone wanted to be in the operations building. It was about the only place with air conditioning in this section of Korea.

I was just leaving the shop when I heard the trick chief handing out assignments for his crew. They had to run the emergency generators today. I cringed when I heard him give the job to Dumb and Dumber.

"You know the situation," I said to the trick chief. "Those two are not to be doing anything outside of the shop without direct supervision."

"The generators are inside the compound," the trick chief said. "They have done this every time we have the assignment."

We had two massive diesel generators for emergency power that were manually started, stabilized, then switched over to run the operations building. The comm center had its own generator that would automatically switch on in a power failure.

We ran the operations building on emergency power for a half-hour every month, just to make sure the generators were operational and that the maintenance crew was familiar with the operation and switch over protocol.

That protocol required the generator to be started and stabilized before switching the site over to emergency power. Although the switch would only cause a blink in power, we would always have the equipment turned off before switching over to the generator.

I left with the rest of the day crew, and we went down the hill to mess hall for dinner. We were through the chow line and had just started to eat when one of the swing trick guys came running into the mess hall.

"You guys are needed back at the shop, stat," the guy said.

"Can we finish dinner?" I asked. The mess hall had Korean servers and cooks, and no shop talk was allowed at any time.

"No, we need all hands on deck immediately," the runner said.

Climbing the hill back to the operations building in the afternoon heat was not the most pleasant exercise method. But the gem at the end was an air-conditioned building, so that made the task bearable.

When we checked in through the security gate, the guard said, "You guys had better hurry."

We walked into a completely dark operations building. The smell of burnt power supplies was overwhelming.

"What happened?" I asked the trick chief.

Mr. Neal almost ran over me as he rushed through the door of the operations building.

"What happened?" Mr. Neal asked.

"Every light bulb in the building is burned out," the trick chief said. "Even the light bulbs in the comm center. Apparently, their lights are not hooked into their emergency power supply. And almost every piece of equipment has a blown power supply."

"That doesn't answer the question," Mr. Neal said. "I want to know what happened."

"Apparently, when Dumb and Dumber switched the site to emergency power, they hadn't stabilized the generator. It dieseled on them, and it must have put three or four hundred volts of power into the building. They hadn't told anybody they were making the switch, so all the equipment was still turned on and operating. Most of the power supplies are toast, as you can smell."

"I want those two out of operations," Mr. Neal said to the trick chief. "They can pull weeds for the old man until they rotate out of here. And you knew they were not to do anything out of the shop. You are going to have some explaining to do."

"They only have a couple of weeks before they rotate out of here," the trick chief said.

"God, I hope they aren't getting sent to Vietnam," Mr. Neal said. "They will get a lot of guys killed down there if they pull a stunt like this. It is bad enough here. How long until we can get things back online, Larsen?"

"If we get some lightbulbs working, we can get some stations working in a couple of hours," I said. "We are going to be limited on the supply end."

"You let the operations officer select the stations he wants up first," Mr. Neal said. "I will start working on the supply issues. We are probably going to have to bend a few of those Army rules."

And so it began, nearly forty-eight hours of work before the operations were fully functional again. Then a few hours of sleep and a big party to celebrate the fix.

Dumb and Dumber were just gone. I have no idea what became of them, but I would guess they were shipped out to Seoul.

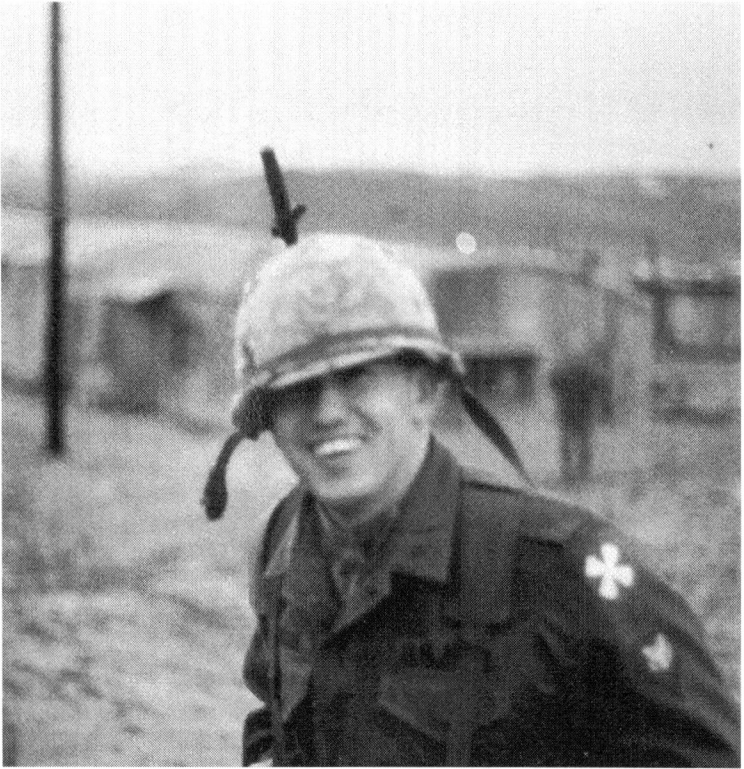

My Christmases in the Army

T he phone rang on a snowy Christmas Eve in 1965.
   "Company D, Private Drake speaking, can I help you?"
Bill answered. Bill and I were pulling CQ (charge of quarters)
duty for Company D, a duty company for troops waiting for
school at Fort Devens.

   We were a couple of lucky ones; we were permanent CQs.
We were given private squad rooms in the old World War II
barracks that housed an overload of troops in the considerable
build-up of Vietnam forces. We worked in twenty-four hour
shifts, with forty-eight hours off.

   "Yes, I know a couple of guys who would be interested," Bill
said.

"What are you getting us into now," I asked? I was not expecting an answer, but Bill was always quick to volunteer my services.

"We can meet you at Battalion Headquarters by 8:15. We don't get relieved until 8:00, but we should be able to make that schedule."

Bill hung up the phone and looked at me with a big smile on his face.

"We have a Christmas dinner to go to tomorrow," Bill said. "We have to be in Class A uniforms and meet the Battalion CQ at Headquarters by 8:15."

"Where are we going?" I asked.

"Does it matter? It is going to be better than eating Christmas dinner at the mess hall and sleeping for most of the day."

Bill and I took turns going to the barracks, showering, and changing into our Class A uniform at six in the morning. When we were relieved by the next CQ crew, we walked through the snow the half a dozen blocks to Battalion Headquarters.

I imagined that we looked somewhat like Mutt and Jeff. Bill was six-four and had a heavy black shadow on his face even though he had shaved a couple of hours before. And I was trying to match his stride, and I had to stretch to measure five-eight.

The Battalion CQ was a Specialist four who had been in the Army for several years. He was waiting at the doorstep and fell in with us.

"We meet them at the main gate in fifteen minutes," Stan said.

Bill and I were mismatched on height, but we were both in good shape and trim. Stan was taller than me and somewhat well-rounded.

"The main gate is over a mile," Bill said as he lengthened his stride. I was used to matching his long stride, Stan sort of looked like a young kid who had to take four steps and then run four steps to keep pace.

By the time we reached the main gate, the snow was probably close to four inches deep. Mr. Terhune was waiting across the street in his VW van, and he had a couple of preteen boys with him. Getting into the warm van was a welcome relief.

We drove to their house in Groton, some four miles distant. The Terhunes had four kids, and the oldest was their daughter, a freshman in high school, and three younger boys. We had dinner, which Bill jumped right into the kitchen to help prepare. Then we spent the afternoon and evening telling stories and enjoying the company.

Having just pulled twenty-four hours of duty, a full day of eating, and storytelling, I was asleep before my head hit the pillow that night. But it was a Christmas to remember, and the Terhunes remained friends and a place to escape to for the entire year we were at Devens.

***

Christmas in Korea was a different event but just as memorable. I arrived in Korea in the middle of September 1966, and I was well adjusted to the country by Christmas. I was stationed south of Seoul with the 177th USASA Company. I spent a lot of my free time at the orphanage we supported in An Song.

A group of us spent Christmas Eve at the orphanage. Following dinner, the group of the primary school kids continued my lessons in Korean. The little girls were very serious about this instruction. They would frown when the boys were hysterical over my pronunciation of even the simplest words.

We did a Santa for the kids with toys purchased by the guys at the 177th. The kids all went to midnight mass, so it was late when they got to bed.

On Christmas morning, we loaded everyone up and took them to Camp Humphreys for Christmas dinner with the entire Company. Before dinner, all the staff and the older kids had the opportunity to take showers in the barracks. That was probably the best present we could give them. Then dinner in the mess hall and entertainment in the NCO club. All the kids were well worn out when we loaded them onto the trucks for the trip home.

The next morning the young kids were hanging all over me. It was apparent the kids didn't want us to go. The staff was still in a state of euphoria from their day at the company compound. But we loaded up in the trucks for the drive back to the

Company. I opened the window and shouted goodbye to the kids in Korean.

"*Annyeonghi gyeseyo*," I said. The boys almost rolled on the ground, but the girls laughed and waved.

The drive back to base seemed longer than usual as we rolled down a dusty dirt road lined with dry rice paddies. My mind did drift back home with only a twinge of homesickness.

***

My experience in Germany was different still. I arrived in Germany in the middle of December 1967. Even though I had friends from Fort Devens there, I really had no time to settle into an off-duty routine before Christmas. My first Christmas in Germany was spent on the base at Rothwesten. Christmas dinner at the mess hall was well done and accompanied by some German carolers. The evening I spent at the NCO club, again filled with entertainment. It was less than ideal, but it was a pretty good day.

***

Christmas in 1968 found me in *Schöningen*, a small village on the East German border. I was stationed at Wobeck, a significant border electronic listening post, with about seventy of us stationed there. Christmas here was super. The town went all out on their decorations and festivities, and there was a Christmas spirit everywhere.

We had a major Christmas Eve party at our 'Swing Club' in the *Bahnhof* Hotel. The club was not supposed to make a profit, so it had to give away a lot of booze to make sure the books came out even for the year. Needless to say, there were a few drunk GIs.

A couple of us were invited to Christmas dinner at Howey and Holley's house. Wives were a recent addition at *Schöningen*. Until recently, only men without dependents were stationed there. Holley was the best cook that I had seen since my mother.

Howey was very drunk at the end of the Swing Club party, and we had to help Holley get him into the car.

They lived in *Wolsdorf*, a small village a few miles out of *Schöningen*. They had an upstairs apartment in a new house, still under construction. It was built on a hillside, and there were three stories with a high porch to the entry on the middle level. The steps and porch were new and not completely finished. There was no railing on the steps or porch.

When we arrived at one in the afternoon for dinner, Holley was slow to answer the door, and she looked like she was running on empty.

"Are you okay?" I asked. "You look like you have been cooking all night.

"I feel like it. We had quite a time at the party last night," Holley said. "And my night was just starting when we left."

"You know, we can find a place to eat in town," I said. "You don't have to wear yourself out to feed us."

"I should have had you guys help me get Howey home last night," Holley said. "Let me tell you the story."

"When we got to the house, it was not too hard for me to get him out of the car. And I sort of kept him against the wall as we struggled up the steps to the porch. We made it up here with no problem. I stood Howey up on the porch, then I turned around and unlocked the front door. When I turned back around, he was gone. There he was, ten feet below, spread eagle in the snow and mud."

"Is he okay?" Kurt asked. "That is a long way to fall."

"He was too drunk to get hurt. But that was just the start of it. I had to get him up out of the snow and mud, back up the stairs, and then up the stairs to the apartment."

"It looks like you made it," I said.

"Yes, I made it, but there was a trail of snow and mud all the way. There was mud on the wall going up the stairs. You know how the Germans are. They would kick us out of here for such a mess. So there I am, in the middle of the night, mopping the porch and washing the wall. It seemed like I no more than finished, and it was time to get the turkey into the oven. It was certainly a Christmas Eve that I won't forget in a long time."

About this time, Howey makes his entrance from the bedroom. He was fresh out of the shower but still feeling the effects of the party. We greeted him, but Holley didn't have much to say to him.

The dinner was excellent, as was expected from a cook like Holley. But with Holley shooting visual darts at Howey all through dinner, there was more than a bit of chill in the air.

Kurt and I made a pretty quick exit following dinner.

That Last Glass of Milk

D ad came through the kitchen door with a bucket of milk fresh from the morning's milking. The kitchen was the center of life in our modest farmhouse. The kitchen was not only the source of food, but it held the wood stove, which was the only source of heat in the house. Mom ruled the family from the kitchen.

All life entered through the kitchen door, the back door to the house. The front door was used only to access the front porch on rare occasions or during the summer when we boys would sleep on the old bed on the front porch.

Mom kept two large pans of milk on the bottom shelf in the refrigerator. She would allow the cream to rise to the top twenty-four hours before skimming the heavy layer of cream off the top of the milk. Living on a Jersey dairy, the raw milk contained about seven percent butterfat. We always had an ample supply of cream. It was used for whipped cream, for topping on desserts like pies or berries, and any excess was churned into butter.

With three growing boys in the house, plus Mom and Dad and a sister, we would go through at least two gallons of milk in a day. We laid down a lot of calcium in our bones. It was rare for anything other than milk to be served at mealtime.

I grew up on raw milk. But that was a different time. In those days, a calf was born on the farm, grew up, and had calves on the same farm. It was a rare event for an outside cow to be brought into the herd. Herds were routinely tested for brucellosis and TB. In such a closed herd environment where the milking was done by family members, and it was handled properly, the risk to the family from raw milk was very slim.

That is not the case today. Routine testing is no longer done because those diseases are rare. Other organisms are transmitted in raw milk, usually from poor sanitation or handling. Some microorganisms can be present in raw milk coming from undetected mastitis in a cow.

Closed herds are as rare as the small family farm. When I was growing up, a herd of fifty or sixty milk cows was a large herd. All the cows had names, and I could recognize each cow by her udder. Today, a small herd is four hundred or five hundred cows, with large herds numbering in the thousands. Milkers are hired regularly, often with a questionable experience base. Diseases in the milking cow may or may not be detected on a timely basis. Raw milk scares me today.

When we got a new load of alfalfa hay, the milk's flavor would be different for a time, and it would take us a few days to adjust to that change. Then in the winter, when we would switch back to grass hay, there would be another period of adjustment.

When I joined the Army, one of the most surprising things was the variety of beverages offered at mealtime. I always chose to drink milk, not because I didn't enjoy the other drinks, but because that was what one drank with a meal.

When I went to Korea, things were a little different. The Army shipped milk to Korea as a powder. They had a large plant in Seoul that reconstituted it. Then it was distributed to all the mess facilities in the country.

I almost gagged on my first glass of milk in Korea. The reconstituted milk was terrible. Worse than the milk from the worst truckload of alfalfa at home. But it is hard to change a farm boy's habits. I gagged the stuff down, and after a few days, my taste was adjusted, and it was fine. I drank milk the entire thirteen months I was in Korea. With some of the long hours I was on duty, I also learned to drink coffee. But that was only on duty, never with a meal.

Then comes one of those moments that changes one's life forever. It happened at the Seattle Airport. Our flight back to the States was a long one. We had thirteen hours of flight time and crossed the international dateline. We arrived in Seattle at ten in the morning on the same day that we had left Korea at two in the afternoon.

A group of us from the same unit were on the plane. We sat down for breakfast at the Seattle Airport while we waited for our flights back home. I ordered milk. After drinking the Army's reconstituted milk for thirteen months, this real stuff was awful. I couldn't gag it down. So I had coffee instead.

That inability to handle milk continued through my leave time at home. Then I headed to Germany to finish my enlistment. In Germany, I was stationed in a small town, *Schöningen*, and lived away from the regular Army installations. I guess there was milk available, but I drank either coffee or beer with my meals.

That last glass of milk at the Seattle airport was the last glass of milk that I ever drank or tried to drink.

Fort Dix Transfer Company, December 1967

I set my B-4 bag down on the walkway while I adjusted my collar and straightened my tie. I buttoned my coat. My uniform didn't fit well after gaining fifteen pounds on a forty-five day leave at home following Korea. With a deep breath, I climbed the steps and entered the orderly room. There was a whole crew working on records in the back of the room. Only the First Sergeant was at the front desk.

The First Sergeant was older and looked like he ate nails for lunch. He was about my height, five-eight, thin, and his rough complexion told of a life of hardship and many hours in the sun.

"Boy, am I glad to see you, Larsen," the First Sergeant said. He was practiced reading name tags.

"Good morning, Sergeant," I said. "I am here to report for duty and transfer to Germany." I extended my hand with my orders. "You act like you knew I was coming."

"I knew an E-5 would walk through that door sooner or later," the First Sergeant said. "I have an important job for you today. I want you to go get settled into the barracks and change into your fatigues. As an E-5 working for me today, you get a squad room in the barracks. Do you have a combination lock for the door?"

"Thank you, that will make my stay better," I said. "And yes, I have a couple of locks in my bag."

"You can lock your room, and your stuff will be secure," the First Sergeant said. "Once you have changed, you hurry back over here, and we will discuss your job."

This company was housed in a group of older World War II buildings. They were neat and well maintained but older. Having a squad room would provide me some privacy. I had not lived in an open bay in a barracks since my early days in the Army.

This company gathered troops for transport to Germany. They would assemble a planeload of soldiers over several days, then make sure everyone got on the plane. Hopefully, my stay here will be a short one.

With my fatigues and combat boots on and a field jacket to give me some protection from the New Jersey December air's chill, I headed back to the First Sergeant.

"Larsen, you are going over to the stockade and process Private Jones out of there and bring him back to me," the First Sergeant said. "This kid is a deserter, he is a piece of scum, but my job is to put him on the plane tomorrow."

The First Sergeant hands me a folder of paperwork and then reaches into the cabinet behind him and hands me a .45 with a belt and holster.

"You put this on and sign for it over at the orderly desk," the First Sergeant said.

I buckled the .45 on my hip, adjusted the fit, and found the paperwork to sign on the orderly's desk. I picked up the folder and turned to head out the door.

"Do you want directions to the stockade?" the First Sergeant asked.

"Yes, I guess that would be something I should know," I said.

"You walk out this door and turn right. The stockade is down that street about a half-mile. You can't miss it," the First Sergeant said.

I turned and started for the door again.

"And Larsen, this jerk has run before. If he runs, you shoot him," the First Sergeant said. "That is why you have that forty-five. Do you understand?"

"Yes, Sergeant, I understand," I replied as I walked out into the December air.

The walk to the stockade was just what I needed after the overnight flight I had from Portland. I am sure that my face was flushed when I stepped through the door to the orderly room at the stockade. I was one of several NCOs there to pick up an inmate. I handed my paperwork through the screened enclosure to the sergeant on duty.

One of the other guys noticed the Eighth Army patch on my field jacket and commented.

"How lucky does a guy get in this man's army?" he asked. "Coming from Korea and going to Germany, how does that happen in today's Army?"

"I guess I was in the right place at the right time," I said. "I just asked for the assignment, and some clerk must have felt like doing a good deed that day. It is the clerks in personnel that run this Army."

"For an E-5, you seem to have this Army figured out," the guy said.

"First Sergeant Scagliotti told me that when I was at Fort Devens," I said.

The rest of the day was consumed with processing Private Jones out of the stockade. I had planned to sign a paper or two and take him back to the First Sergeant—no such luck. The out-processing was part of making these guys hope they were never returning to one of these places.

Private Jones was assigned a drill instructor to help him out -process. A checklist filled an entire page, and the DI was on his ass the whole time. Private Jones was not allowed to walk anywhere. He had to run the whole time. From one station to the next, usually separated by a couple of buildings, we would run.

Pick up his personal items, pack his clothes in his duffle bag, then carry the duffle bag and run to the next building.

Finally, we were back in the stockade orderly room, and I finally had to sign for his release. I had begun to worry that I would miss dinner, but there was just one signature here, and we started out the door.

The sergeant in the orderly cage reminded me as I opened the door. "Larsen, this scum has run before. If he runs, you shoot him," the sergeant said.

Private Jones was a little guy. Size-wise, he reminded me a bit of Don Miller, my friend who was killed in Vietnam in April. As we walked away from the stockade, he began to talk, and I don't think he ever stopped.

"They are going to send me to Germany to be in an infantry unit," Jones said. "Look at me. I am too small to be in the infantry."

"I would say you are pretty darn lucky," I said. "You could be going to Vietnam to be in an infantry unit."

And on and on, it continued. The half-mile walk to the First Sergeant's office seemed like three miles. We were finally there, and I opened the door and shuffled Jones into the office.

"Good job, Larsen," the First Sergeant said. "Now, you take Jones over to the mess hall and get dinner. You are both probably hungry."

So, here I go, over to the mess hall with this little jerk who won't shut up. We go through and fill our dinner trays. I realize how hungry I am. I had only a few bites at the airport when I got off the plane early this morning.

After dinner, we return to the First Sergeant's office.

"Okay, Larsen, you two are going to be on the same plane tomorrow," the First Sergeant said. "Why don't you keep track of him tonight? I will give you a set of handcuffs so you can cuff him to his bunk."

"Now come on, Sergeant," I said. "I think I have done enough. I am not going to sleep with this little chatterbox."

"Okay, I will get somebody else to keep track of him tonight," the First Sergeant said. "You have done more than could be expected. You turn in that forty-five to the orderly desk, and I will see you tomorrow at roll call."

The orderly gave me my travel orders when I turned in the forty-five. The flight was not leaving until late afternoon, and the roll call was at two in the afternoon. I was duty-free tomorrow morning. I could eat an early breakfast and rest in my room until lunch. Then I should be rested for the overnight flight to Germany.

Roll call was held in a large multipurpose room across the street from the First Sergeant's office. They had us pretty much lined up by rank in four columns. The room was packed.

The Duty Sergeant would call a name from the list and wait for a "Yo!" When they came to Private Jones, there was no reply. The Duty Sergeant paused, then called the name again, still no response.

As he called the name a third time, the First Sergeant came up and stood beside me. "Larsen, that little bastard ran again," he said. "I should have made you keep track of him."

"I'm not sure he would have been worth the bullet," I said. "I sure wouldn't want him in my squad if there was any fighting to be done."

"I know," the First Sergeant said. "But he needs to spend some time in that stockade before they wash him out of this man's Army."

After roll call, we loaded on a bus to the airport.

It was dark when the plane finally took off. What an ordeal it was, getting to that point. After the final roll call, we boarded a bus to the airport on a neighboring Air Force base. Then they parked us in a holding area with maybe just enough seats for everyone. After loading the plane, it must have been another hour before we started to taxi to the runway. The take-off was fine, and then they announced that we would make a stop in Bangor, Maine. After that stop, just as I suspected, they came by and tossed me a warm ham and cheese sandwich and a coke. I doubted there would be anything else. I could almost hear my Dad's words, "It would be a damn sight tougher if you didn't have it."

After eating the sandwich and downing the coke, I returned the can and wrapper to the bag held at the aisle. I loosened my belt, pulled down the knot in my tie, leaned the seat back, and drifted off to sleep. There would be nothing to see on a night crossing of the Atlantic.

It was daylight when we touched down for another stop at an Air Force base in England. We could get up and stretch our legs a little. The line at the bathroom was long. We could not deplane, but the doors were open, and a gangplank rolled up to the plane. We could stand on the platform at the top of the gangplank. The English air was also chilly and crisp but was better than the air inside that plane full of troops.

The flight on to Frankfurt seemed short. The reception center was in total chaos. In Korea, they called out for all the ASA troops right after calling for colonels and above. Here there was no such benefit. After working my way up to the desk, the clerk handed me a train ticket to *Kassel* and said that a bus to the *Bahnhof* leaves every thirty minutes from right out front.

"What the hell is the *Bahnhof*?" I asked.

"Train station." That was the only reply I got. I guess I would be on my own to get to *Kassel* and Rothwesten.

And so my eighteen months of duty in Germany started.

Rothwesten, West Germany, December 1967

The train lurched to a stop. Then, with a couple of jerks, it started backing up. I rubbed my eyes as I woke from a sound sleep. Straightening my uniform, I peered out the window. It was dark outside as we backed into the lighted station at Kassel, West Germany. I remained seated until the train came to a complete stop. It was a jarring stop, and I was glad I was not standing.

The night air of early December in northern Germany had a bite to it. I wished that I had not shipped my trench coat in my trunk. I could see my breath as I walked toward the main station. Hopefully, there will be a courier meeting this train, I thought.

143

But when I reached the central platform, there was no evidence of any army guys. I stood and looked around, wondering what my next step would be. I knew not one word of German but figured I could at least get a cab that would know the way to Rothwesten.

I must have looked a little lost. A well-dressed older gentleman stopped before me as he was heading to the train. Pointing to the far corner of the platform, in perfect English, he says, "Most of the GIs read the information on the bulletin board over there, in the corner."

There was not a lot of information on the board. Basically, it said if a courier was going to be at the train, they would meet you here. Not seeing one, your best option would be to catch a cab. You could call the base for a ride, but that may take some time. I stepped outside and walked down to a short line of cabs. The driver quickly loaded my bags into the trunk. Getting in, I realized I only had dollars, no Deutsch Marks.

I asked, "Do you take dollars?"

"Rothwesten?" he asked, "ten dollar."

I handed him fifteen dollars, and he was happy. Off we went.

The cab did a quick u-turn at the main gate and stopped. The driver jumped out and had my bags on the ground before I got to the rear of the car. He stood there, briefly. I was not sure if he had forgotten the extra five dollars I gave him at the start.

I stepped up to the MP booth and handed my orders to the guy on duty.

"ASA Company A is about a mile down this road and a couple of blocks to the right," he said, pointing in the direction of the road.

I took a deep breath, picked up my bags, and started toward the road.

"Wait a minute," the MP shouted, "We will run you down there."

I was relieved as I threw my bags into the back of the jeep and jumped into the front seat. The streets were empty, and the guy drove too fast to suit me. He would give a GI a ticket for this kind of speed.

Rothwesten was an old German Army Air Force base, about five miles out of Kassel on a high hill. The buildings were arranged in long rows around the edge of the hill. The buildings were long, three stories high, and made of stone. The old landing strips were now filled with antennas at the top of the hill. The operations building was also on the old airstrip.

Rothwesten was on top of this hill on the southeastern side of Kassel. It was apparently disguised well enough that it avoided being bombed during the war. The city of Kassel was heavily bombed. Early in the war, mainly at the request of the citizens, they had shot over a hundred and thirty British POWs. There was a saying within the bomber crews when they started bombing Berlin, "Save a bomb for Kassel." Most of the planes, virtually all British planes, would drop any bombs they had left when they passed back over Kassel.

The young MP pulled up in front of Company A barracks. "This is it," he says, pointing to the main door of the large building. "The mess hall is in the next building there. It is probably too late to get anything to eat. They hire Germans to run the place, and they don't cater to us GIs."

I took my bags, thanked the MP and walked up the steps, and pushed through the door into a chaotic orderly room. There were at least a dozen guys doing anything but something official. Finally, the CQ noticed me standing at the counter, and I handed him a copy of my orders.

"I will put these on the First Sergeant's desk," he said. "He won't be in until Monday. In the meantime, you can find a bunk in the maintenance section on the second floor, at the very far end of the hall," he said, pointing in the direction I was to go.

Almost home, I thought, as I climbed the stairs and started down the hall. Halfway down the long hallway, around the corner, walks Bill Smouse. Bill and I were close friends at Fort Devens. He was dressed to go out on the town.

"Aw, who is this but Dave Larsen!" Bill says with an outstretched hand. "Let's stow your bags, change your clothes, and go downtown to celebrate your arrival."

Bill leads me down the hall to the last room. "I'm sorry that you have to take this bunk. Your roommate is the biggest jerk in the shop, but this is the only bunk. You change out of that uniform, and I will run down to supply to grab your bedding."

It felt good to get out of my Class As. I was just pulling on my shoes when Bill returned with my bedding. My bags and bedding were neatly stacked on the bed. It would have been a good idea to make the bed because I might not be in very good shape later tonight. But Bill was anxious to go, so off we went.

Bill had an old VW bug. It didn't look like much, but it ran. We hit a small *Gasthaus* that the maintenance shop frequented. My first German beer impressed me, especially the liter mug they used to serve it. I was introduced to more people than I could possibly keep track of, and Bill was trying to make up with his girlfriend in the middle of the celebration.

Later we went to a large bar in downtown Kassel. The main memory I have of that place was the restroom. The urinal was a tiled wall with a drain on the floor. You just stood up to the wall and made sure your toes were out of the way.

Friday night, we slept downtown at an apartment of a married couple Bill knew. The husband also worked in the maintenance shop. No spare bedrooms, we slept on the floor.

Bill was a guy who drank pretty heavy. We probably all drank more than we should, but Bill always seemed to overdo it. We woke early before anyone was up. Bill got up and pulled a bottle of cognac off the shelf. He poured a large glass and offered me a glass.

"No thanks, way too early for me," I said.

We said thanks for the floor and made some small talk when the couple finally got up.

"I wonder if we could borrow your floor again tonight?" Bill asked. "It sort of depends on how things go during the day."

"You're always welcome here, Bill," the guy's wife said. "As long as you replace that cognac bottle."

We headed back to the small *Gasthaus* for breakfast. German breakfast was not much, a small piece of sausage, an egg, and a hunk of bread. The coffee was excellent but strong, and it was definitely stronger than the coffee I was used to drinking.

We spent most of the day at the *Gasthaus*. The girls started filtering in well before noon. Bill was well known, and I was sort of a novelty.

Bill drank the whole day, and I stayed with coffee until evening. I was not sure how he would drive up the hill to Rothwesten, and we would probably end up on the floor again.

Most of the girls were at least somewhat linked to various GIs. They all looked pretty good, and with little effort, I thought I could fit in somewhere.

When we finally got back to base on Sunday morning, there was quite a stir in the orderly room. They were making a big deal about my absence. Nobody knew what had become of me. Was I was lost or injured. All they knew was my stuff was untouched on the bunk upstairs. Apparently, my roommate was the source of the concern. Up at the room, he was really worked up.

"The First Sergeant will have your ass in the morning," he said.

Bill was correct about this guy. He was quick to tell me that he was the best man in the shop. Then he filled me in on the organization of the maintenance department. Since my clearance papers were still in transit and the barracks were no place to discuss classified information, he was the one who should be in front of the First Sergeant.

When I got back from breakfast on Monday morning, there was a note that the First Sergeant wanted to see me ASAP.

Sergeant Ziggler was a short, heavy-set man who reminded me of Sergeant Scagliotti at Fort Devens. He mainly seemed bothered that he had to deal with petty concerns on Monday morning.

"Smouse and I are old friends from Fort Devens," I explained. "We never thought there would be a problem with me going out. If you did your job in Korea, you were free to go without worrying about a pass."

"Well, things are a little different here," Sergeant Ziggler said. "But I can let it slide under the circumstances. Your personnel file preceded you, and you are highly recommended. You just need to play the game a little here."

"What about my clearance papers?" I asked.

"They usually follow in a day or two. They come under separate cover. I will let you know when they come. In the meantime, coming from Korea, you can Dx your uniform. So that is something you can do today. Turn in anything you want, your entire uniform if you want."

"What are my chances of getting a jeep to run down to supply to pick up the stuff I had shipped. I shipped a trunk and my duffle bag," I asked.

"You don't ask for much, do you," he said. "I bring you down here to chew your ass, and you end up driving off in my jeep," he said as he handed me the keys. "Do you know where you are going?"

"I have no idea."

"When you get your supply papers, stop by here, and I will send one of these clerks with you. Then you can use the jeep to Dx your stuff. Just have it back here before noon."

It turned out to be a good Monday. I think I will like Sergeant Z as he was called.

Rothwesten Operations

Tuesday morning was a little busy. I had borrowed Sergeant Z's jeep again to get my new uniform taken care of as far as new patches and the like sewn on and laundered. By this evening, I should start to look like a soldier again. When I brought the jeep back at noon, I stopped at the orderly room with an armload of new laundry.

"Any word on my clearance papers?" I asked. "I'm pretty anxious to get to work."

"Nothing yet, Sergeant Z has been trying to build a fire in personnel for you. I think he sort of likes you," the clerk said.

With nothing to do, the afternoon was a real drag. The swing shift guys were just starting to stir. I would be bored to death if those papers don't come through pretty soon.

Just about this time, my roommate comes through the door. He is a little excited and starts throwing things into a bag like he is going away for a few days.

"What's up?" I ask.

"They have serious problems at one of the direction finding (DF) sites. The new TRD-23 is down, and the maintenance guy

149

there can't get it fixed. Anyway, they are sending me up there to take care of things," he says.

"I can tell you how to fix the thing. We had the same problems in Korea a few months ago, and I spent a couple of weeks with the factory team," I say.

"No need; I am perfectly competent. I will have it up within the first hour that I am there."

Smouse was right. This guy was a real jackass. If I give him any information, it will be just enough to hang himself. He heads out the door with his bag.

"I expect to be back by tomorrow night," he says as he heads down the hall.

Wednesday morning, when I checked, Sergeant Z had my papers and badge. He hands me the envelope and I am all smiles.

"I have called the operations gate, and they are expecting you. So is Sergeant Moyer. He is maintenance NCOIC, a good man," Sergeant Z says. "I'll have the clerk run you out there as soon as you're ready. It's not too far to walk, but I know you're ready to get to work."

Sergeant Z had coached the MP at the operations gate well. He took my papers and glanced at the badge. "You drop that here when you leave, and we keep it on the board," he said.

Smouse was sitting at a large desk in the middle of the maintenance shop. He had worked himself into the desk job. He jumped up and showed me around the shop and took me on a tour of the operations building. Other than Smouse, there was nobody I knew. When we got back to the shop, he introduced me to Sergeant Moyer.

Sergeant Moyer was about average height and in good shape. His short dark hair was starting to get sparse on top. He seemed a little preoccupied and not very talkative.

I told Sergeant Moyer that I had a lot of factory-trained experience on the TRD-23 and could help them with any problems they might have. He assured me that they had their best man on the job, and it should be fixed in no time.

"If you don't have any power transistors in supply, you should be getting some on order, 2N174. I suggest you order as many as they will allow you to order," I said.

"Here, we handle orders by the book. We are not authorized to order supplies that we have not documented that we have a need for them," Moyer says. "You will find that we follow the book around here."

That was all he had to say. Time would show him that he needed to bend those rules once in a while.

Smouse showed me my workbench and handed me a toolbox. He shrugged his shoulders and tilted his head toward Moyer, "He is all right most of the time. But times like this are why I work at that desk. The DF network is down, and it will be his ass if it is not up and running in a short time."

I sat on my stool and thought, here I am at work with nothing to do. Just about that time, a tall, thin Sp4 entered the shop and came over to my desk. He looked young to me, and I wasn't twenty-three yet.

"Hi, I'm Jim Simpson from the DF center. We heard that you came from Korea, and I know that they are very functional in DF and Radio Fingerprinting. We wondered if we could get you to look at our RFP unit. It has been down for about two years now."

"I'm Dave Larsen," I said as I extended my hand. "What the hell are you talking about? How could that unit be down for two years?"

"Nobody here seems to know how to work on it," he replied.

"Let's get a look. I took care of the unit at the 177th. It is complex, but everything comes together if you go about it systematically."

After looking things over, I glanced at him and shook my head. "It might take me two or three hours, but we should be up and running by mid-afternoon." Jim just looked at me blankly. I wasn't sure if that meant he had heard that line before.

Since this had sat for two years, the first step was to go through and check all the tubes. Hopefully, supply would have replacements. After Moyer's comments earlier, I was a little concerned about that part of the project.

After all the tubes were checked and the bad ones replaced, I started through the alignment. In Korea, I usually had the next in line working with me. Being new in the shop and working on something they had neglected for two years, I had no new guy to be an understudy. That required a lot of extra steps when I started alignment on the CRT deflections. I finally talked with Jim, and he came and helped out a little, so I didn't have to run from the back to the front all the time.

Working through the lunch hour brought some attention from Mr. McCann. He was the chief warrant officer who was the DF Operations officer. He had been sitting and watching the process for the last hour. It was about 2:30 when I had Jim pull up a signal and turn on the camera. I was worried that the high-speed camera might also be a problem if it had sat for two years without being used.

The signal came up, the camera ran, and everything looked good. Now we just had to wait until Jim developed the film. I sat back and relaxed for a minute. Mr. McCann looked at his watch.

"When did you start on this?" he asked.

"I don't know. It must have been 11:30 or so this morning. I had to test all the tubes and get replacements from supply, which took a while. Usually, this alignment only takes an hour or an hour and a half," I said.

Jim was excited when he returned with the film. He stood stripping through ten feet of the paper film before handing it to Mr. McCann.

"How come you can come in here on the first morning and fix this unit when that shop has not been able to get it to run for the last two years?" Mr. McCann asked.

"Beats me, pretty standard stuff in my view. In Korea, we limited the people who could work on the unit to one man, like myself, and a new kid who would work into my place. Too many hands in the soup makes bad soup."

"Don't you worry. This is your baby from here on out!" Mr. McCann said.

I picked up my tools and closed the back of the unit. Jim was getting a crew together. They had a lot of work to do to catch up on stuff they had missed for the last couple of years.

When I got back to the shop, Mr. McCann was at Moyer's desk.

"Larsen has just fixed the RFP unit. He has done in two hours what your entire shop has failed to do in the last two years. I want Larsen to be the only maintenance man to touch that unit, period. Do you understand?" McCann said in a loud enough voice that the entire shop could hear.

Moyer was not too happy but busied himself at his desk. Maybe half an hour later, the phone rings. It's my roommate from the detachment. He tells Moyer that he has problems figuring out just what the problem is with the TRD-23, and he thought he might benefit from talking with me. Moyer calls me over to his desk and hands me the phone.

He starts running down the list of his checks. He is way out in left field, but I listen as he goes on and on.

"Have you checked the two power transistors in the rotor power supply?" I ask, almost as if it is an afterthought.

"I have checked them three times, and they are fine," he replies.

"They have an emitter to collector short, and they need to be replaced," I said.

A long silence. "I have checked them three times, and they are fine," he says again.

"I don't have anything else to help you," I say as I hand the phone to Moyer.

He tells Moyer he will be a few days longer than expected. When Moyer hangs up the phone, I tell him he had better get some transistors on order.

Smouse almost snickers. After the dust settles, he drops by my bench and says he thinks I am causing more havoc in the shop than it has seen in a long time. Moyer comes over and says he is assigning me to the swing shift starting tonight. I think he wanted me out of his hair. It was going to be a long day. Moyer sent me to dinner early so I would be set for the shift starting at four.

The first night they sent me with a couple of guys to do maintenance on a transmitter at a nearby Air Force detachment. These guys were excited about the job. "This is an excellent way to spend the evening without having to do much," Jim said. "This is a radar station located on another hilltop."

"I don't know much about transmitters," I said. But these two assured me it would be a good trip.

I can't say that much was accomplished. These guys checked some gauges and made sure the thing was running. Then we sat

153

around and shot the breeze with the Air Force guys, played some pool, and drank some beer. We started back to Rothwesten about eleven, planning to get back just in time for shift change. It had started to snow while we were there, and it was snowing hard when we walked to the car.

We drove down the hill, the snow was not quite a white-out, but it was really coming down. The guy driving was straining to see, knowing that the main road was coming up anytime. Suddenly, there was the road, and we were speeding across it. We bounced across the shoulder and were in the middle of a snow-covered plowed field.

"Whatever you do, don't stop, or we will never get going again," I shouted from the back seat.

We drove in a wide circle and came back to where we could see a gate to the road. We drove through the open gate and right back onto the road. I would not have believed it would be possible. We laughed all the way back to Rothwesten. Actually, we were pretty lucky the field was there.

When I reported to the shop the next night, Mr. McCann and Sergeant Moyer were waiting to talk to me. The new TRD-23 at Munster was down and had been for several days now. It was desperately needed as the entire DF network was nonfunctional without it.

"How much do you know about this problem?" Mr. McCann asked, not giving Moyer a chance to say a word.

"I can fix it in a few hours if I can come up with the correct transistors. I have been suggesting that we get them on order for several days now. I spent several weeks with the factory team in Korea. I can train the on-site maintenance man to handle the problem," I replied.

"I want him up there tomorrow!" McCann said to Moyer as he turned and left the room.

"You better go and get packed and get some rest," Moyer said. "We will see you at eight in the morning. Bring your bags and be ready to go.

I arrived at the shop the next morning with my bag in hand. My roommate was there. He was pulled home overnight. He still couldn't believe that he was unable to fix the problem. I didn't have anything more to say to him.

Trip to Münster

I set my stuff on Smouse's desk and watched as Moyer had guys scurrying about gathering every possible piece of test equipment that I may need. They had a car delivered from the motor pool, and all this stuff was packed out and loaded into the car.

Since I didn't have a European driver's license yet, I would need a driver.

Moyer looked around and finally asked Smouse who they could spare.

Smouse looked at the shop schedule carefully. "Looks like the best option will be Geib."

So Geib was my driver. If anybody in the Army ever looked like Zero in Beetle Bailey, it was Geib. How he ever got into the shop was beyond me. Geib was tall and thin, walked slightly stooped over, and his glasses were like the bottom of coke bottles. When he talked, he squinted his eyes and wrinkled his nose.

Smouse spoke to me in a hushed tone. "Geib never does anything right. Good luck, you're going to need it."

155

We loaded into the car. Moyer was giving Geib some last-minute instructions about driving in the snow. There was still snow on the ground, but the roads were clear. The trip started off well. Actually, I enjoyed the ride. Geib seemed to know where he was going. However, he constantly leaned over the steering wheel and squinted as if he needed a better view. He kept up a constant chatter. He was excited about the extra money he would be getting for TDY (temporary duty) pay. The heater was going full blast, and it was still a little chilly in the car. But the countryside was fascinating.

By noon it had started to snow a little. Geib held his face closer to the windshield to see better. We were pretty close to Paderborn, probably just a few more miles to go, and I thought that would be a good place to find lunch.

As we met an oncoming car, there was a sudden flash with a cracking sound as the windshield shattered into a million fragments. I had seen car windows do this before in freezing weather, and I believe it was a spontaneous event. Geib was sure the other car had thrown something at us.

Geib was able to stop. We broke a small six-inch hole in front of Geib so he could see.

"All you have to do is get us to Paderborn, and we can call back to the shop and get another car," I assured him.

It was slow going, but we pulled into Paderborn sometime later. I was looking for a good place to stop when we came to a German Army MP station.

"Pull in here," I instructed Geib. He was reluctant, but I often dealt with the Korean Army in Korea and found them more than willing to help. I figured these guys would be just as helpful.

They were very willing to help. We called the shop from the main office. Moyer had a little trouble getting the story straight but finally arranged to have a van from the detachment come and pick up us and the equipment. They would send the motor pool to pick up the car.

The Germans were very helpful and wanted to be good hosts. They assured me that the car was very secure in their parking lot. As it turned out, the commander of the MP station had gotten married that day, and they were having a big party upstairs in the *Cantina*. They said we were welcome to wait in the main office, but we were also most welcome to come upstairs and join them in their celebration. I declined the invitation, saying we needed to watch the car. They pointed out that it would be several hours before anyone arrived from Rothwesten or Münster.

Finally, after repeated invitations, we agreed to join the party. The duty sergeant assured us he would watch the car, and since it was after five, I thought it would be okay. We headed up to the third floor and entered the small *Cantina*. The place is packed, and the atmosphere is electric.

A couple of beers are pushed into our hands. We are pushed to a table in the middle of the room. Everyone wants to talk with us and practice their English. I speak not one word of German, and Geib, who has been in the country for over a year, doesn't speak much more than me.

One beer follows another. I return downstairs to double-check our situation.

The duty sergeant gives me a thumbs up. The car is okay, and no word from anybody else. Back upstairs, the party continues. There is not much to eat. Some sausage and cheese and a hard roll are all I can come up with.

After what must have been a couple of hours, the van arrives from the detachment. The driver, the maintenance man, happens to be MacDonald, a classmate from Fort Devens.

Another reunion, one more reason to celebrate. Mac has no trouble settling into the party. The guys from the motor pool don't arrive until after eight in the evening. We transfer our stuff from the car to the van. The motor pool guy tells MacDonald that we should stay the night here, but we head to the detachment anyway.

The ride to Münster was exciting, but we made it while most of the crew were still awake. Maybe twelve or fifteen guys, the detachment was housed in a large German farmhouse. It didn't take long for us to get into the spare room and hit the sack.

I was in shape for partying, and nothing was unusual about last night by my standards. I was up for the trip to breakfast at a small *Gasthaus* in town and then on to work. Geib wasn't up to the schedule, and we let him sleep. His job was done anyway.

On the way to the site, I started going over the problem with MacDonald.

"The problem is really a simple one," I explained. "It is in the power supply for the antenna rotor. There are two large power transistors that burn out. The number is 2N174, I believe. All we have to do is come up with a couple of those, and we're done. The problem is I doubt if they are in the supply channel. I tried to get Moyer to get them on order, and he would not do it."

"We checked those transistors, and they are fine," MacDonald said.

"The problem is an emitter to collector short," I said. "We can't detect that short the way we check transistors."

We immediately tore open the rotor power supply and removed the transistors when we got to the site. The typical burned braided wire on the emitter side told me all I needed to know. We called the shop, and sure enough, there were no 2N174s in stock.

Moyer was surprised to hear from us so early. He had already heard about the party. "It will take several days to get those transistors to the site," Moyer said.

"You get several pairs on order with an ASAP on the order. If this site is down, the others will be soon to follow," I instructed Moyer. "We will probably be able to get started with some from the German economy, I would say black market in Korea."

Mac knew of a little German TV repair shop that also served as a supply for a large group of ham radio operators. We made a quick trip to town and came up with a half dozen transistors with a bit of bartering. These didn't have the braided wire attached to the poles, but they would serve their purpose until the supply channel was full.

We had the site operational before noon. Mr. McCann was on the phone to thank me shortly after it returned to service. I told him that we had about three pairs of transistors that would work in a stop-gap manner.

"Each of the transistors that we have will last about three days, four days at the most," I said. "That gives you nine to twelve days of function before we are out of transistors. So you had better get on Moyer's ass to get the right ones into supply. I tried to get him to order them earlier, and he was going to go by the book, and there are none in-house now. This site will not run if you guys go by the book," I say.

The Army had strict rules on supply inventory. You could only stock so much of any one item. The figure was based on the need for that item in the previous six months. If you had an inspection and were found to be overstocked, there was some hell to be raised. You could get around this in a couple of ways. One was to order an item more often than you actually used it. The other way was to hide the overage (in your pocket if necessary). Moyer knew this stuff as well as I. He just liked to follow the book. I wanted to keep the equipment running.

It took a couple of days before Geib and I were retrieved. MacDonald was eager to learn everything I had to teach him, and we used our time well to cover the entire unit. The evenings were used to celebrate us as visitors, and these guys could party just as well as the Germans at the MP station.

When we returned to Rothwesten, our glory was short-lived. The story of the windshield and the party at the German MP station had been entirely blown out of proportion. The maintenance officer, a second lieutenant who knew nothing about maintenance, wanted to see us right away.

He really raked Geib and me over the coals. How dare we drink on TDY? How dare we jeopardize the equipment in the car? He didn't give a damn if I was the only one that could fix some of this equipment. Our asses were his, or we could go see the company commander for an Article 15. He restricted us to the base for thirty days. I was really pissed.

Christmas came and went. I was restricted to base, so dinner at the mess hall and an evening spent at the NCO club watching a bunch of lifers and their wives get drunk and call it a celebration.

The next day the Army issued a directive that said that any soldier volunteering for duty in Vietnam would go. Commanders were not allowed to prevent that transfer.

I read this directive posted on the orderly room bulletin board on the evening of Tuesday, December 26. The next morning, the 27th, I marched into the first sergeant's office and filed a DD1049 (request for transfer) for Vietnam. He took it with a wry smile on his face.

When I told Smouse what I had done, he was so inspired he filed one also. He said I had things in such turmoil he didn't know what would happen. Nothing had ever happened in the shop like this before.

In the afternoon of the 27th, I was working at the bench doing a routine tune-up on an R390 receiver. Colonel Paris, the Field Station Commander, walked into the shop. Colonel Paris was very tall, probably in his early fifties, with slightly graying hair that was sparse on top. Judging from everyone's reaction, this was just something that never happened. He spoke briefly with Sergeant Moyer and then walked over, pulled up a stool, and sat down at my bench, facing me in a very relaxed manner with one foot on the rung of the stool.

"I guess I owe you a real thank you. Mr. McCann tells me you have done more for the mission of this station in a couple of days than anyone else has done in the last couple of years. So thank you," he says.

"Thank you, Sir," I replied. "I just happened to be lucky enough to arrive at the right time."

"Thanks anyway, and keep up the good work," he said as he left my bench. He walked around the shop, stopped again, talked with Moyer, and left.

A couple of hours later, near the end of the day, Moyer came over to talk with me.

"Colonel Paris wants to know what it will take to get you to withdraw that 1049," he says.

"I don't like it here, not one bit. I will withdraw it if you send me to a detachment," I said.

"Well, we have you scheduled for a detachment as soon as a spot becomes available."

"Not good enough," I said, knowing I had him over a barrel. "You send me to a detachment this week, or the request stands."

"Okay," he said, "go pack your bags. I'll send you to Wobeck tomorrow. And by the way, the old man was going to recommend that your transfer request be denied."

"I am sure that he read the same directive that I read," I said as I started to clear my bench.

The outcome of those few days at Rothwesten took a few more weeks to completely unfold.

I went to Wobeck, and we arrived late at night on December 28. I checked into the *Bahnhof* Hotel in *Schöningen*, West Germany. *Schöningen* was a small village located right on the border of East Germany. The site, Wobeck, was located a couple of miles up the hill in The Elm, an ancient elm forest full of local lore of witches and goblins.

TDY pay for the site started on my arrival, an extra sixteen dollars a day. Smouse let his transfer request stand, and he went to Vietnam.

MacDonald was pulled from his detachment for poor behavior displayed on my visit. Geib was in the dog house deeper than ever.

My biggest allies, the DF and RFP operators, were back to poor maintenance. My presence was short-lived, but they had a new starting point and an understanding of what they should be expecting from the maintenance shop. Moyer knew he would have to keep someone on top of things a little more.

It took a while, but Moyer was replaced by Sergeant Z. The shop was run more efficiently, and I had someone I could work with from this distant shop.

I was in bed shortly after my check-in. Morning came early, and the bathroom was at the end of the hall. The clerk said if you wanted hot water for a shower, I needed to be the first one there.

It was a brisk shower in the morning as most of the hot water was gone. By the time I got downstairs for breakfast, most of the maintenance crew were there to meet me.

This was the start of a whole new chapter in the Army.

Power Line Splice in Yellow Snow

The winter of 1968 in West Germany was cold, with multiple ice storms and plenty of snow. I had just been promoted to noncommissioned officer in charge of the maintenance shop of a remote Army Security Agency site at Wobeck.

Located in the middle of an ancient elm forest outside of the village of *Schöningen*, this site had been operational for ten to twelve years. It was responsible for the electronic intelligence of the Soviet and East German Armies across the border.

We had a small maintenance crew, and most of our work was done on the day shift. Eight-hour days were rare, and we often had one to two guys on night duty. This winter, Marsden was working at night. On this particular night, I had stayed to help with a problem on one of the main operations stations.

The site operations were housed in a couple of old Quonset huts. Stuffed with sophisticated equipment, these huts drew a lot of electricity.

Marsden and I were working on this station, and there was a sudden drop in power. Lights dimmed, some equipment clicked off, and there was an odd sound that we didn't identify at the moment. This was a brief event, maybe a second or two at the most, and then everything was back to normal.

Marsden and I exchanged a puzzled glance. We waited a moment, but when everything returned to normal, we returned to work.

A few minutes later, it happened again. This time we could isolate the source of the sound. It came from where all the power input panels were located in the far corner of the operations bay.

Marsden and I went over and opened the panel. Everything appeared normal. When it happened again, the sound was that of an electrical arcing. And it was right at our feet.

"That has to be in the power input cable," Marsden said.

We stepped out the back door into the cold. There were about six inches of snow on the ground. We moved around the corner to where we were outside the wall holding the electrical panels.

We were struck with a strong, unpleasant odor.

"What is that odor?" Marsden asked.

I sniffed again, "Piss," I said. "Burnt piss."

The arc happened again as we were standing there. We could almost see the arc this time. It was just under the surface of the snow.

"It has to be the main power cable," I said. "Let's get a shovel and see what we can find. We have to fix it tonight, or it will start frying equipment."

"What the heck is going on?" Marsden asked. He was speaking more to himself than to me.

"It looks like guys are stepping out the back door, and instead of taking a hike to the outhouse, thirty yards across the snow, they are just stepping around the corner and pissing here."

Once we found a shovel, we started to carefully dig into the problem.

"Keep your hands on the wooden handle," I said.

With some careful digging, we uncovered the large buried power cable coming into the building. And then we found the problem. There was a splice in the cable just as it entered the building.

"Why would they put a splice in that cable?" I asked.

"My guess is they had some German contractors doing the electrical work, and they couldn't go inside. So they ran the cable to this point, and the Army guys spliced it to the cable on the inside," Marsden said.

I wiggled the cable with the shovel, and we were showered with sparks as the lines arced between themselves. Looking close, we could see that the tape between the lines had broken down with the moisture of the snow and the piss. The lines started arcing. We would have to redo the splice tonight.

"These jokers have no idea how lucky they are to be alive," Marsden said. "Can you imagine the jolt if a stream of urine was hit with one of those arcs?"

"We are going to have to shut the site down for a brief time," I told the NCO in charge. "We are going to have to repair the main power cable coming into the building."

"There is no other option?" Sergeant Duke asked.

"We can't do it without turning off the power out front at the generator shed."

"Okay, give us a few minutes to wind things down and make sure the comm center is not in the middle of a transmission."

"Do you think I should call Lieutenant Lee?" I asked.

"No, if it is only going to be a few minutes, there is no need."

We turned the power off, and then, with the aid of a few flashlights, we were able to clean up the cable and wrap the individual wires with rubber tape. These wires were the size of my thumb. When we had the individual wires wrapped, we covered the entire splice with rubber tape and electrical tape.

Everything worked fine when we turned the power back on. The site was down for less than twenty minutes.

"Sergeant Duke, we are up and running," I said. "All you have to do is make sure everyone uses the outhouse instead of pissing around the corner of the hut. And make sure they know how lucky they are to be alive if they were the ones doing it."

"Let's leave this open so we can recheck it in the daylight," I said to Marsden. "I would guess the powers that be will want to make any final decisions about what to do."

"They can discuss it all they want," Marsden said. "But short of replacing the whole cable, there is not much else to be done."

"Now, the only thing we have to worry about is finding enough water around here to wash up. I think I am going to enjoy the shower tonight."

A Wrong Turn

In August of 1968, I became the non-commissioned officer in charge (NCOIC) of the electronic maintenance shop at a small border detachment near *Schöningen*, West Germany. The detachment was called Wobeck, named after a tiny village nearby.

Wobeck was located in the middle of an ancient elm forest on a small hill overlooking the East German border. We were in the Army, but our mission was directed by the National Security Agency. Our mission was electronic eavesdropping on the East German and Russian armies between Berlin and us.

The NCOIC position was about the only thing Army that went on in our shop. We all knew we had a job to do, and everyone worked to get things done. There wasn't much of a need for a command structure. It was my head on the block if something went wrong or if the powers that be wanted to chew someone out. I had less than a year left in the Army, so it wasn't a big concern for me.

The one thing it did require was a trip to our headquarters in Rothwesten every month. That was about a two-hour drive, and you had to play Army a bit while there.

166

I would usually make the trip as quick as possible, accomplish what needed to be done, sneak out the back gate, and head home.

The route out of the back gate was a narrow road through a hillside pasture with many twists and turns. At the bottom of the hill, you drove through the tiny village of *Knickhagen*. It was a slower route, but it cut out many miles of the trip back to *Schöningen*, and avoided the city traffic of Kassel.

I was by myself on a trip to Rothwesten in the middle of December. I had spent a couple of hours with my boss, Sergeant Ziggler, at the maintenance shop. Then, with Christmas approaching, I had a more extensive shopping list at the PX. I was ready to get back to *Schöningen* when it was done.

I never gave a thought to the time of the year or the recent snowfall when I made the turn to take the back road out of Rothwesten. This road was not gated, so there were no MPs to caution me. I started down the narrow road.

After a hundred yards, I realized I had made a serious error. I touched the brake. The little Volkswagen beetle skidded on the icy pavement. There was no stopping now, and there was no hope of turning around on this narrow strip of pavement.

Thankfully, I was in second gear. So down the hill, I went, gathering speed as I went. Taking turns on the icy pavement at speeds far above what we drove this road in summer weather conditions proved to be an exciting event.

Finally, I had one more sharp corner, and then I would be in the middle of the village. There is little relief in that fact. I could see a whole gaggle of village kids playing in the middle of the street. They probably had not seen a car come down this hill in weeks. I honked the horn to get their attention. Then I laid on the horn.

The kids scattered to the sides of the broad icy street. Standing there holding their sleds, they watched this crazy Army guy in a VW go screeching past them, hoping he could hit some dry pavement before he got to the main road.

As I exited the village, the ice on the pavement disappeared. I slowed the car and took a deep breath. That had been quite a ride, and it made the remainder of the trip home to *Schöningen* seem like a piece of cake.

Events of August 20 to 23, 1968

August 20 was an unusually warm day for northern West Germany. Our operations building and the attached maintenance shop had our small air conditioners running full blast. They were only needed on rare occasions here, but some of the equipment was temperature-sensitive, and on these rare hot days we needed some air conditioning. I had just assumed the position of NCOIC (Non-Commissioned Officer In Charge) of the maintenance section at Wobeck, a small Army Security Agency outpost for monitoring the East German and Russian Armies. Wobeck was considered the best "ears" in Europe. Wobeck, situated on the East German border, was located in an isolated clearing in the ancient elm forest on a hill outside Schöningen, West Germany.

The day had been an uneventful Tuesday and everyone on the day shift was dreading leaving for the day because there was no air conditioning in Schöningen. As we were getting ready to leave, Jim said he thought we should go to Braunschweig for dinner and some beer. I didn't require any arm twisting. *Braunschweig* was the nearest large town to us, maybe twenty-five miles south and west. We visited reasonably often.

Our first stop was a large Chinese restaurant in the center of town. Not only a good restaurant but one with air conditioning.

After dinner, we took a brief stroll down the nearby *Strass*. The *Strass* was a gated street lined with old apartment-like buildings on each side, where girls of the trade could peddle their virtues in a controlled environment, behind display windows, in all states of dress and undress. It was pure old fashioned prostitution and didn't interest me a great deal. But window shopping was fun and killed some time.

Then we visited a popular little bar down the street. The bartenders were a set of twin girls from Norway. These two girls were lots of fun and sought after by more than a couple of GIs. They probably would have to stretch with their heels off the floor to be called five feet. Paola was thin and spoke the best English. Pina was just a little plump.

Pina spotted us as we picked a table, and brought us a couple of beers. We watched the crowd thin out as we drank the stout German beer. It wasn't long before I saw Pina throw her apron into the hamper behind the bar, Paola followed. They were quite the matched pair; short, blond with pixie-style haircuts, wearing matching light green dresses. Their aprons had obscured just how short their dresses were.

We sat and talked for a time. Pina was trying to tell me something.

"Pina is trying to tell you that we are planning to go home to Norway for two weeks over Christmas," Paola said. "She thinks it would be an excellent trip for you. You could meet our family and see your home country."

"I'll have to see if I can work that out," I replied.

On the drive back to *Schöningen*, Jim made a lot of small talk. As usual, I was mostly quiet. Finally, out of the blue, Jim said, "That trip thing is sort of scary."

"Damn scary to me," I replied.

It was getting close to three when I finally crawled into bed. I looked at the clock and told myself seven-thirty. The entire time in the Army, I never used an alarm clock. I could say to myself what time to wake up, and I would bound out of bed within a minute or two of that time. I had learned that I could pull a twenty-four-hour shift with five hours of sleep. Tonight should be four and a half hours, tomorrow should be an easy day, I will be fine.

Bam, Bam, Bam! Somebody is at the door, I thought. I looked at the clock, it was four-thirty.

"What?" I yelled.

"This is Marsden, we need you on-site, stat! All hell is breaking loose," he said.

Marsden was my right hand in the shop. He had asked to work at night just last week. Marsden was very involved with a local girl and was trying to match her schedule a little better. He didn't get along with people well and thought he could work better at night. Marsden had thinning red hair and an average build. His uniform was always just a little sloppy, just his way of letting everyone know he would do his job, but he would not play Army games. From Ohio, we often argued over how he considered Ohio as being the west.

I got up, pulled on a pair of pants, and opened the door.

"Things are really going crazy at the site. Russia has just invaded Czechoslovakia," Marsden said in a hushed voice. He seemed short of breath. "It looks like we are going to be sending about half the site down to the Czech border. We have about three weeks of work to do in the next forty-eight hours, and everyone is yelling at me over the phone. I need you to handle things."

"I'll be ready in a couple of minutes," I said as I started pulling on my combat boots.

"I will get Jim up and meet you up at the site," Marsden said as he started to leave.

"Let him sleep," I said, "someone is going to need to be awake tonight."

I was not the only one headed to the site early. There was a small caravan of cars headed into the elm forest at a few minutes before five. There was an extra MP at the guard shack, and they had my badge ready when I finally got up to the gate. I had trouble finding a parking spot. It seemed like everybody was on site.

When I stepped through the door, the whole place was in chaos. The first sergeant walked past in a rapid stride. He tapped me on my chest and said, "In my office now! I have your list!" he said. "Or book," he added with a smile.

And a book it was. Marsden was correct; three weeks' work, and we had only hours. This was going to be fun. The top of the list was the MLQ-24. This was a mobile radar intercept and electronic intelligence unit. The only problem was it has been on blocks and connected to our tower antennas for at least five years. Now we had to reconnect the mobile antennas, and make sure the cabin was watertight when the holes were patched from the tower antenna cables. I doubt that the motor pool has kept up with the maintenance schedule on the truck. And the tires have not touched the ground in years.

Blackwell, our motor pool guy, came through the shop door about then. A tall thin kid from Arkansas with dark hair and dark eyes. You couldn't see his complexion because he was always covered with grease, oil, and a light coating of dust.

"We need the MLQ-24 truck on the ground and ready to run to the Czech border by the end of the day," I stated flatly. "Do you think the tires are okay?"

"They changed the tires last year. The rest of it should be in pretty good shape. You get it unhooked, and I will have it ready to go before dark."

We had guys working on the tower cables and on the installation of replacement stations in operations. That equipment had not been used in a couple of years.

Most of the maintenance crew were coming through the door, having been called up early.

"We have some busy hours ahead of us. Jim is sleeping in this morning so he can be the sharp one at the end of the stretch. He is not going to miss out on any of the workloads," I explained. "As of right now, nobody leaves the site until this tick sheet is complete. We are sending a lot of this site to the Czech border, and three guys from this shop go with it, maybe for three weeks, maybe for the rest of your tour."

We had a good group of guys, and we completed the task within the allotted time. When our convoy drove out of the gate, most of us started melting. I had been on-site for many hours on less than two hours sleep. Marsden had worked the night before this stretch. Jim fared well and handled most of the administration details at the end when my eyes would hardly focus.

As our contribution for the three guys from the shop, I was able to get the home base to accept Geib, who was assigned temporarily to Wobeck; Blackwell, the motor pool guy whose time was nearly up; and a new guy, who had not arrived yet, as our three guys to go.

That left most of the crew relieved that their lives were not going to be disrupted. All I could think about was sleep. My concerns over the Christmas trip to Norway were a distant memory at this point.

Die Schwarze Katze

It was getting late, and the snow has been falling all evening. There was still a sizable group at the club but the reality of the evening coming to a close was upon us.

"I think we should caravan out to *Bad Helmstedt*," Ed announced.

I looked at the label on my nearly empty wine bottle, Die *Schwarze Katze*. The Black Cat wine had become a popular label this winter. This January, we had endured more snow than expected for *Schöningen*, West Germany.

"Are you going to come with us, Dave?" Ed asked.

"No, I am going to be lucky to get my car home," I said.

Ed continued to badger the crowd. Guys with cars were agreeing, and available seats were being consumed rather quickly. In a short time, five cars were agreeing to the caravan. Five vehicles and all the seats were taken.

"Dave, we need you to go, or Jim and I won't have a ride," Huffine said.

"No, I have had too much of thi"s stuff tonight," holding up the empty bottle of Black Cat wine. And the snow has not let up at all," I said.

But the pressure continued, and I finally agreed to go. *Bad Helmstedt* was a small resort community that sat right on the East German border on the north side of Helmstedt. There was a large *Gasthaus* that always welcomed a bunch of GIs. There were usually a couple of old ladies of the evening working there. That was what interested some of the guys.

Stepping out of the *Bahnhof* Hotel, the cold reality of the evening's weather hit me square in the face. It was cold, and the snow was still falling. Harder now than it was earlier. There were over six inches on the ground.

My car was parked up the street a little, and we had to hurry to catch up to the caravan as it was leaving *Schöningen*. With the rear-mounted engine, the VW did pretty well in the snow.

As we were headed downhill a little, I passed the other cars in the caravan to take the lead position, waving at everyone as we passed. On the slight corner, coming into the small village of Esbeck, the VW went into a vicious spin.

With a little struggle, I was able to get the car under control and we came to a stop, but we were in the opposite lane, facing the oncoming traffic. One more maneuver to miss the cars trying to stop, and that swerve started another spin that ended in a thud. We would have been fine except for the apple tree.

My memories are sketchy for the time following the accident. The guys pulled me out of the car, I guess. I remember lying in the snow with Brian talking with me to keep me awake. Brian and I had been in Korea together.

I remember the ambulance but not the ride.

They rolled me around the x-ray table at the Helmstedt Hospital, and then I woke up in the morning in a hospital bed. Speaking excellent English, my nurse gave me the news; seven broken ribs and three fractured vertebrae, plus a good knock on the head.

Then she gave me an injection in my thigh.

"Morphine, to keep you comfortable," she said.

I could quickly feel the euphoria expanding from my thigh, and for the next ten days, I drifted in and out of full consciousness. I had a flood of visitors, guys from the shop, their wives, and my landlady.

Holley brought me a tuna sandwich, which was just about my sole ration for my stay there. Others brought all sorts of goodies, mainly apples and oranges.

After the fourth or fifth day, an orderly came in with a wheelchair commode and wrestled me out of bed. I seem to remember teaching him some new words in English. Following that ordeal, they took me down to see the doctor. He put a girdle around my chest to make it more comfortable.

"We are going to try to go through the night without a shot tonight," my nurse said.

"Okay," I said.

This was about the eighth day, and I felt more comfortable, but other than the commode episode, I had not been out of bed.

I laid there, looking at the ceiling, wondering what I would do to entertain myself. I thought about it a little time and then rang for the nurse.

"I think I am pretty painful," I said. "I think I need a shot."

It only took her a minute to return with the injection. As I lay there feeling the glow grow out of my thigh, I realized that I was not painful. I just wanted that shot. That was the last one I took.

On the tenth day, the Army came and rescued me. They loaded me into an ambulance, and we drove nearly three hours to Frankfurt.

This Army hospital was massive. The doctor on duty checked me in, and the first thing he did was remove the girdle the German doctor had put on me. Then they put me on the fifth floor in the surgical ward.

This was a large ward, maybe twenty guys and one orderly on duty. Far different from my private room in the German hospital. I was encouraged to get up and around a little, which I did as needed.

On the first morning of rounds, a group of six doctors sat at my bedside discussing me and my case. Their conclusion was that I needed to go to physical therapy and they could teach me to walk. They gave the slip to the orderly.

"I can't find a wheelchair," the orderly said. "Do you think you can walk to physical therapy?"

"Sure, where is it located?"

"It's on the ground floor, clear at the other end of the hospital."

He handed me the slip of paper, and I was off.

Going down five flights of stairs was a bit of a challenge, but there was a rail to help keep me upright. Then this hospital was longer than a city block, and the hallway seemed like it would never end. But finally, I was at the large double doors that said Physical Therapy.

I pushed through the doors and stood in amazement, watching the zoo-like scene in front of me. There were guys everywhere doing all sorts of things. I have no idea how many, maybe fifty guys. There were two captains, physical therapists, ladies.

I stood there with my note in my hand for almost ten minutes. Finally, one of the physical therapists noticed me and came over.

"What are you here for?" she asked in a gruff voice.

I didn't say anything, I just handed her my note.

She read the note.

"Teach how to walk," she said more to herself than to me. She looked around behind me and out to the other side of the door.

"How did you get down here?" she asked.

"I walked," I said.

She looked at the note again and handed it back to me.

"Get the hell out of here," she said.

I left. I guess I had all the physical therapy I needed.

After a long week, the group of doctors on their morning rounds decided I could return to duty. I got dressed and went down to the supply room to gather my belongings.

"What the hell," the supply clerk said as he brought out a bag of rotten apples and oranges. "Did you get hit by a car coming out of the grocery store?"

"I think you can throw those away," I said.

I caught a bus to the train depot and arrived in *Schöningen* at about midnight. I was lucky that the courier from the site was there to pick up his pouch. He gave me a ride to my apartment, but I was unable to pick the lock. And not wishing to wake my landlady, I ended up sleeping on a friend's apartment floor.

I was still a little stiff but close to normal. It was another couple of weeks before I felt healed.

Two and half years later, when Sandy and I moved to Colorado to start veterinary school, I sneezed. I felt two ribs pop. Hurt like hell.

A German Ice Storm

The winter of 1968 and '69 in northern Germany was throwing everything it could at us. I had been maintenance NCOIC since the middle of the summer. This site had been a madhouse following the Russian invasion of Czechoslovakia.

Snow and ice seem to be coming every week. If it wasn't snowing, it was an ice storm. The weather didn't slow us down much. It just made life a lot more complicated.

"The direction-finding guys are having some problems with the new transmitter they set up for them," I said to Jamie and Ron. "Why don't you guys check it out and see if you can get them up and running."

"We looked at it a bit ago and couldn't get it to load to the antenna," Jamie said. "With this ice storm, that antenna the Rothwesten crew installed is probably shorted out."

"That is sure a possibility, but the big wigs at the Rock are starting to holler, so we need to make sure everything else is in good working order. Let's start by checking all the tubes and running all your checkpoints. Then it doesn't load, we can say with confidence that it is the antenna. At the hundred-foot level on that tower, there is probably an inch of ice. I don't think we want to be climbing that any time soon. I will put a request in for the antenna crew to come to check it out as soon as you guys say everything else is working fine."

***

"Larsen, this is Sergeant Z. What the hell is up with that DF transmitter?" Sergeant Z asked on the phone. " T h a t n e w officer in charge of that section is a real ass, and he is all over me."

"I have a crew out working on it now," I said. "It looks like it is the antenna. We are in the middle of an ice storm here, you know. There is close to an inch of ice covering the tower at the hundred-foot level. Jamie thinks the antenna is shorted out, but I am having them go over the transmitter, checking all the tubes and everything before we call for the antenna crew."

"I don't think there is much of a chance you are going to get the antenna crew up there in this weather," Sergeant Z said. "CWO Anderson is going to insist that you send someone up that tower. You can bet on that."

When I hung up the phone, everyone in the shop looked at me for some kind of word. We were used to working independently, and I was a big fan of the previous OIC of the DF operations. Having someone question our work and my decisions was new to us.

Jamie and Ron came back into the shop.

"The transmitter is fine," Jamie said. "We checked every tube and went through the entire checklist. It has to be the antenna."

"Okay, I will call Sergeant Z at the Rock," I said. "He didn't think that we had a chance of getting the antenna crew up here during this ice storm. But don't worry, I am not going to send any of you up that tower. It is too dangerous for the antenna crew to be on the road, but it is fine to send us up an ice-covered tower. That sort of lets you know where we stand in the line of importance."

"Sergeant Z," I said into the phone. "The transmitter is fine. That means the antenna is the problem. I would suggest you let

Mr. Anderson know that he should get the antenna crew up here. I don't have anyone who is trained or certified to climb a tower covered in ice."

"They told me that you liked to live dangerously," Sergeant Z said. "I will tell the man, but I am sure that he will be on the phone or more likely on the secure radio in a short time. You be careful. This man will think nothing of nailing you to the wall."

***

It was not long, and Brian from the DF station was in the shop.

"I have Mr. Anderson on the secure horn," Brian said. "He wants to talk with you, Dave. He sounds pissed. He is new, you know. Our guys at the Rock tell us he is a real jerk."

I picked up the microphone at the DF station and clicked the transmit button.

"Larsen here, over," I said.

"Larsen, this is Chief Warrant Officer Anderson. I am OIC of the direction finding mission at this Field Station. I have a transmitter under your supervision that is not working. What's up with that? Over."

"I just had a crew go over that transmitter with a fine-tooth comb. The transmitter is fine. It has to be the antenna that your antenna crew installed that is the problem. I have a request with Sergeant Z for that crew to return and fix their work. Over."

"The antenna crew is not going to be doing any traveling in this weather. I want you to send someone up that tower and do the fixing. Over."

"There is an inch of ice on that tower at the hundred-foot level. I don't have anyone qualified to climb such a tower. Over."

"Listen, Larsen, this is a direct order. You send someone up that tower and fix that antenna. Over."

"Like I said, I don't have anyone qualified to climb that tower. I will do it myself. Over and out."

Most of the operations had stopped as they listened to the conversation.

"Wow, what an ass," Brian said.

Brian and I had been in Korea together before coming to Wobeck. The Army Security Agency was a relatively small unit in the Army, and such continuity was almost standard.

"One day, I will get back at him," I said.

I returned to the shop and strapped on a climbing belt and a tool pouch.

"What's the story?" Jamie asked as I was looking in the drawer for a ball-peen hammer.

"I am going up the tower and fix the antenna," I said as I started out the door.

This tower was an AB-105 tower. That is a steel tower, triangular in design and about a hundred forty feet in height. The transmitter's antenna was at the hundred-foot level.

I banged the tower with my hammer, knocking off all the ice I could reach. The ice was not too thick at ground level, less than one-half inch.

I secured my belt to the highest rung I could reach and started my slow climb. After going a few rungs, I started knocking off some more ice. I moved my belt up a few rungs and continued my climb.

I was about twenty feet up the tower when Jamie came out of the operations building. He had a climbing belt and tool pouch on.

"Wait up," Jamie said. "I am going up with you."

I waited as Jamie started his climb.

"You need to belt up as you climb," I said. "It makes things a little slower, but this tower is slick."

It didn't take long, and Jamie was up beside me. I knocked off all the ice I could reach and handed Jamie the hammer to clear his path.

"I don't think we are equipped for this kind of work," Jamie said. "My feet are cold already, and we're not halfway to the antenna yet."

We continued our climb together, going up in three-foot sections, knocking ice off and changing our belt attachment at each stop. I have no idea how long the climb took, but it did not seem long, and we were at the antenna.

I spent some time knocking off all the ice from the antenna that I could reach. At this level, the ice was thick. Maybe not an inch, but then nobody was measuring. I handed the hammer to Jamie, and he knocked off the remaining ice on his side of the antenna.

"I think we got lucky," I said.

"You find something?" Jamie asked.

"The screw clamping this side of the antenna must have slipped," I said. "Either that or the antenna crew was just sloppy in their work. This screw is across the two beams of the antenna, shorting them out completely. It should be a snap to fix."

We loosened the screws on each side of the antenna clamp and repositioned it, then tightened the screws again.

"That should do it," I said. "It would be nice if we had some wood spacers, but that will have to wait. Let's see if we can get some attention and have them load this antenna and give us a thumbs up before we start down."

"That would be a good idea," Jamie said. "I really don't want to climb this antenna tower again any time soon."

We hailed Ron, who was watching from the door of the operations building. He quickly ran to the transmitter van and had them try the transmitter. A minute later, he stepped out and gave us a thumbs up. We started our slow climb down the tower, going about three feet at a time before changing our belt hookup. At least we didn't have to knock any ice off.

"I can't feel my feet," Jamie said as we started walking to the operations building.

"Stomp around on them a bit and then get in by the heater," I said.

"Do you want me to get Mr. Anderson on the horn?" Brian asked.

"No, I don't think I have anything to say to that man unless he addresses me directly," I said. "I trust that he will get the word that things are up and running."

***

The transmitter continued to do its job flawlessly, and my relationship with Mr. Anderson never improved. But I survived the remaining six or seven months of my enlistment.

Almost a year and a half later, both Jamie and Ron dropped in on me in Corvallis for a brief visit. They both were in Portland visiting family, and they decided that Corvallis was not that far away.

We had a good visit. I think it was during finals week, so we drank coffee. Jamie was still complaining about his feet.

A Change of Pace

L t. Bernard came into the maintenance shop with a piece of paper in his hands. Glancing up from the work we were doing, we could see that something was official in that letter.

For the last ten months, I had been the NCOIC (non-commissioned officer in charge) of maintenance at Wobeck, the small Army Security Agency on the border with East Germany. I had been promoted to specialist-six shortly after taking charge of the shop. The Army was less than impressed with the fact that I was not planning to re-enlist, and I didn't play the role of a real NCO.

"I have something for you, Larsen," Lt. Bernard said as he held out the paper for me. "Here are your orders for your early out. It looks like you will be leaving us in a couple of weeks."

I had applied for admission to Oregon State University, and I applied for an early release from the Army at the same time. With this approval, my discharge date changed from September 15 to June 15, 1969.

I wore a short-timer's chain through the buttonhole on my fatigue shirt. There were several of us in the shop with a similar chain. We would clip a ball and smash it on the floor with a hammer every morning. Now I cut ninety balls off my chain, and with the help of a couple of others, we smashed them all.

The following two weeks were a whirlwind of activity as I prepared for departure. I had to fit my worldly belongings into an army duffle, B-4, and overnight bags. That meant I had to make a trip to Kassel to our main base to turn in as much of my uniform as they would allow. Other stuff I gave away. I withdrew money from my savings account in Kassel. That was eleven thousand dollars, all the benefit from seventeen months of TDY pay at Wobeck. I wanted to take it all in a check, but the banker said I should take some cash because I would have trouble cashing a cashier's check.

After a late-night party on the thirteenth, my friends Marsden and Elka picked me up in Marsden's Porsche, and we took a fast trip to Frankfurt. I processed out of Europe and caught my flight to New Jersey. I arrived at Fort Dix close to midnight and slept in an unmade bunk.

On Sunday morning on June 15, being an NCO, I was charged with supervising the lower ranking guys to pick up things on the company street before breakfast. After breakfast, we processed out of the Army. The master sergeant overseeing uniform returns chewed me out for all the items I turned in before leaving Germany. I just smiled and said, "Yes, sergeant."

After discharge, I caught a bus to the airport. Registration at Oregon State started the morning of Thursday, June 19. I had a lot to do in the next few days. Travel across the country, secure transportation, find a place to live, and make it to registration.

Air travel was not bad. If you were in uniform, you could fly for half price on a standby basis in those days. I caught a flight to

Chicago with no problem, and I had checked my large luggage to Portland. Getting on a plane to Portland was a little more complicated, but I arrived in Portland in the early evening.

I figured I could rent a car and drive to Myrtle Point and make plans from there. I made my way through the airport to the Hertz Car Rental booth.

"I would like to rent a car for a few days," I said to the young lady at the counter.

"Fine, will you be returning the car to this site?" she asked.

"It would be better if I could return to Coos Bay or Corvallis," I said.

"Do you have any preference for the type of car?" she asked.

"Just one with wheels," I said.

"Okay, I think we can manage to get you a car with wheels," she said. "Can I see your credit card?"

"What's a credit card?" I asked. This was 1969, and I had been in the Army for the last four years, most of that time overseas. I had no idea what she talking about.

"That is a card that allows us to charge your account for the rental," she said.

"I have the cash to pay for the car," I said.

"We require a credit card," she said.

"I have a military ID card," I said.

"I'm sorry, you can't rent a car without a credit card," she said.

That ended that conversation. I took a cab to a downtown hotel, ate dinner, and went to bed.

In the morning, I bought a car. The bank wouldn't cash my check, but the car dealer took the check but would wait for it to clear before giving me change.

I drove to Myrtle Point to say hi to the folks. My brother was going to be at Oregon State for summer school. They invited me to share their two-bedroom apartment. They had three kids, ages seven, four, and one, and I would share a bedroom with the kids.

I don't precisely remember the rental agreement. I probably paid about two-thirds of the rent and bought most of the groceries. But it gave me the summer to find my living arrangements for the following year or two.

We got moved in, and I made it to registration. I had declared a major in zoology when I applied to school. I gave the lady at the desk my name, and she went to stacks of files behind her.

"Here you are," she said as she handed me my papers. "You can sign up for your classes inside the coliseum."

"Can I change my major?" I asked.

"That is no problem. I can do it right here," she said as she took my papers back. "What would you like me to put down for your major?"

"Let's change it to pre-veterinary medicine," I said.

"Done," she said as she handed my papers back to me.

Registration was easy this time. I took one course, one year of organic chemistry, in the eleven-week summer session.

Talk about a change of pace in my life. Less than a week earlier, I was drinking beer in a German *Gasthaus* and carousing until the wee hours of the morning. Now I was thrust into the middle of family life and studying organic chemistry at a rapid rate.

It had been four years since I sat in a chemistry class. The visiting professor from Idaho had the entire course on slides. We had several hours of class every morning to cover the course material. During the second day, one guy raised his hand.

"Can you go back to that last slide? I didn't get it all," he asked the professor.

"Get yourself a camera, Buddy," the professor said. "We don't have time to wait for anybody."

I was approached by a couple of guys in the class to join a study group. I joined. There were four or five of us guys and a couple of girls. I quickly found the organic chemistry just required good recall. I didn't need to study with my memory, but I stayed with the group anyway.

After a few weeks of school, I was bored enough that I needed something else to do with my time.

"I think I will get a job this afternoon," I told Kathy as she was cleaning up the kitchen following lunch.

"Those are probably pretty hard to come by in this town," Kathy said.

I took the phone book and wrote down the addresses of the power company, the telephone company, and the TV cable company. I walked into the Consumer Power office first and was granted an immediate interview. They liked my resume and would offer me an apprenticeship, but they had no part-time jobs. Next, I walked into the TV cable company. It was just down the street from the power company.

"Are you the guy that the employment agency sent?" Karen asked.

"No, but I'm here, and this is my resume," I said. "I am not looking for full-time work. I just got out of the Army, and I'm in school right now. I can pretty much work afternoons this summer, and I can work full time during the break between summer and fall term, and it will just depend on my schedule next fall."

It took a few minutes and a short interview, but I was hired. I could start tomorrow afternoon.

With a job and school, summer went fast. I did a little fishing with my nephew, Aaron.

And I survived the chemistry class with good grades. The TV cable job lasted for over an entire year. I found a trailer house to purchase and lived in it for the two years I was at OSU.

The Value of a Valid Complaint

Vertebrate Embryology class in the Zoology Department of the School of Science at Oregon State University was a required course for virtually all preprofessional students in 1969. That means that anyone hoping to get into medical school, dental school, or veterinary school was required to take this class. A good grade, preferably an A, was an unspoken requirement.

In the years before 1969, the series, which included two quarters of Vertebrate Anatomy, was required. This was the first year that the requirement was reduced to just the embryology class.

These classes were taught by Dr. Hilliman. He was feared by most students in the class. He virtually held their futures in his hand and could scratch their dreams with a stroke of a pen. Rumor had it that he had just failed one of his Ph.D. candidates who had been studying under him for five years.

189

The lectures were held in a large auditorium in the Zoology building. I don't know how many people were in the class, but the arena was packed. I would suspect there were nearly six hundred students in the lecture, then the class was broken into laboratory groups. Graduate students would conduct the weekly lab classes, and my lab class had about thirty students.

Historically, one of the main features of the fall term was a massive spelling test. This test included anatomy names and phrases extracted from all three classes in the vertebrate anatomy and embryology series.

This was the setting when Dr. Hilliman addressed the packed auditorium about the upcoming spelling test.

"This test will be from the list of words that will be handed out in your lab class this week," Dr. Hilliman said. "This word list is derived from words in this class and the two anatomy classes. This test is heavily weighted in my grade book."

I was thunderstruck. How could he justify testing over classes that are no longer required? I waited for the uproar from the class.

Not a word was said. The entire auditorium was silent, not even a moan. There was nobody brave enough to question this man.

I was mere weeks from the days when I gave presentations to visiting generals and NSA bigwigs in the general staff meetings at Wobeck. Those men actually held men's lives in their hands. Those men had actual power. This professor was nothing compared to those men.

I took a deep breath and stood up. An audible gasp rose from the depths of the auditorium. Dr. Hilliman actually looked shocked as he looked at me. Someone was actually standing to address him. But he did not say a word to acknowledge my standing in the middle of this huddled mass of students.

Finally, I spoke in a firm, loud voice so all could hear.

"Dr. Hilliman, I am David Larsen," I said. "I know this is a historical test, but this year, the requirement for the two anatomy classes has been dropped from the preprofessional requirements. The majority of students in this class today will not be required to take those classes. I think it is grossly unfair to be tested over material that we will not be required to take."

When I was finished, I continued to stand. Dr. Hilliman seemed to glare at me, but he was too distant for me to appreciate that glare.

"Sit down," Bob, a premed student sitting beside me, said as he tugged at my shirt. "You're dead, you know."

Full minutes passed as Dr. Hilliman contemplated how to address this lone student who dared to stand and question the very conduct of his class. Did this fool not know his stature, the power he wielded over this group of wannabes? There was a hushed silence in the auditorium as everyone waited for the explosion.

"I have given this test every fall for over thirty years," Dr. Hilliman finally said. "In that time, not one student has stood up and complained about this test. How dare you question my intentions."

"I know the history of this test," I said. "But this is the first year of the change in requirements. I say again, most of this class will not be required to take the two anatomy classes included in this test. And I do not think that is fair."

"The test will be conducted in your lab classes in three weeks," Dr. Hilliman said. "Its format will be unchanged."

That sounded like the discussion was over. I knew enough to not push too hard and try to get in the last word. I sat down.

"Why did you give him your name?" Bob said. "He is the most vindictive man on campus. You're dead for sure."

"What is he going to do? Send me to Vietnam?" I said.

Bob looked at me with a question in his eyes.

"That is the standard Army threat," I said. "Do this the way I say, or I will send you to Vietnam."

***

The following week, Dr. Hilliman appeared in my lab class. He came through the door and stood in the corner as the graduate student was finishing some instruction. When she was finished, he came over and pulled up a chair to the table that I shared with Bob. He laid his grade book on the table.

"How are you doing today?" Dr. Hilliman asked.

"I'm doing fine," I said.

"I have been looking at my grade book," Dr. Hilliman said. "You are doing quite well. Not the top of the class, but close."

"I enjoy your class," I said. "That makes it easy."

"You are a little older than most of my students. Can you tell me a little about yourself?"

"There's not much to tell. I grew up in Myrtle Point. I didn't do well in my first couple of years of college. So I spent nearly four years in the Army. That gave me some maturity, some direction in my life, and a sense of responsibility to my fellow man."

"The other day, when I said nobody had ever questioned me in class, I meant it. In all my years of teaching, nobody has stood up in my class like you did."

"Everybody is afraid of you," I said. "You intimidate them."

"You're a good student. A little anatomy test should not be an issue for you."

"But it might be for some of your students," I said. "Like I said in class, it's not fair. The test is not fair, and your intimidation is not fair."

Dr. Hilliman sort of recoiled at that statement.

"What makes you so different?" he asked.

"My experience base is a bit different from a lot of your students," I said. "Fear and intimidation is no way to lead men, or women, for that matter."

***

The test turned out to be no big thing. It was a snap, in fact. It was one of the few things I studied for that fall, and getting an A was the expected result.

Following the test, the lab instructor handed me a note. It was from Dr. Hilliman, with an invite to visit him in his office.

"I have never seen Dr. Hilliman take a personal interest in an undergraduate student," the lab instructor said. "Your standing alone, in the middle of the auditorium the other day, must have made quite an impression on him. Good luck with the meeting."

The meeting in Dr. Hilliman's office turned out to be a meeting with casual conversation. Dr. Hilliman wanted to know more about my history and my plans.

"And I want to thank you for your comments about the leadership of men and women," Dr. Hilliman said. "I have given it some thought, and I may make some changes."

***

Dr. Hilliman remained a good friend and advisor in my remaining two years at Oregon State. Unlike his reputation, I found him a cheerleader for my progress and an excellent reference for my applications for veterinary school.

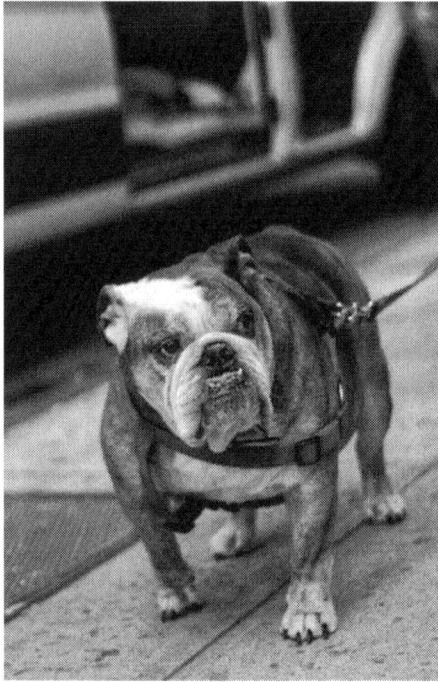

They Look Like Their Owners

It was a lovely Saturday in the spring of 1971. I was close to graduating from Oregon State University with a degree in Zoology. I had just been accepted to school at Colorado State University College of Veterinary Medicine.

I lived in the trailer court beside Benton County Fair Grounds, and they were having a dog show this weekend. Sandy was visiting, and we decided that it would be good to go check out the dog show.

"I have never been to a dog show," Sandy said.

"I guess I have never been to one either," I said. "That is unless you count the pet show that I took my dog, Pinto, to when I was four years old. I had given her a haircut with scissors on the front porch."

"How did that turn out?" Sandy asked.

"I won the prize for the most unusual pet," I said. "I remember doing the haircut, and I remember the prize, but I don't remember much about the show itself."

"People say that when you go to one of these dog shows, you can really see people who look like their pets," Sandy said. "Have you ever heard anything about that?"

"I guess I have not been into dog shows," I said. "I haven't heard that, but that might be something we can watch to see if we can find anybody that supports that opinion."

It was a short walk to the fairgrounds. If we could have climbed the fence, it would have been really short. We purchased a couple of tickets, and I stopped to talk with a classmate who was just coming out of the show. After a brief conversation, Sandy and I opened the door to the auditorium.

There, standing in the middle of the breezeway, probably getting ready to take his dogs for a walk, was a man with three English bulldogs pulling on their leashes.

This man was leaning back against the powerful tug from the dogs. The three bulldogs were broad-shouldered and leaning into the leash. They snorted as they looked at us. The man was short, and heavyset, portly would maybe be a good description. His hair was in a crew cut, and his nose was pointed and turned up, giving him a short upper lip that showed his teeth. He snuffed his nose as he leaned back, trying to restrain the dogs.

Sandy grabbed my hand and pulled me into the main auditorium while she stifled a laugh.

"I can't believe it!" Sandy said. "If that doesn't fit the picture, I don't know what will."

We took our seats in the bleachers and took in the view before us. There was just one large show ring. It filled this end of the auditorium.

The back half was filled with people, dogs, kennels, and grooming tables. There was a constant buzz of activity in the back of the auditorium.

Just then, they started showing a group of Afghan hounds. Six or eight dogs and their handlers began circling the ring with the judge in the center. And there she was, Sandy spotted her first.

She was a tall thin young lady. She was attractive, even from this distance. Sandy would call her thin, I would say skinny. Her long blond hair flowed over her shoulders and bounced as she made the wide circle around the judge. At her side was a beautifully groomed Afghan hound. The dog was tall and thin, bordering on skinny, with a long, flowing hair coat that waved and bounced as she kept pace with her handler.

Sandy buried her head in my shoulder. "I can't believe it," she said. "We need to go. This is just too real."

We made a hasty exit. We were on the edge of the bleachers so we could leave without disturbing anyone. We both laughed as we walked back to my trailer.

Whenever anybody asks my opinion about owners looking like their pets, the scene that greeted Sandy and me when we entered the auditorium immediately comes to mind.

Frank William Larsen, 1909 - 1993

Notes on My Father

My father's early life was difficult at its best. He grew into an exceptional father for having grown up without a father. He rarely spoke of his early life. And when he did, he only told stories in small snippets. It took me well over half my life to piece those snippets together into a story.

He was born in Bellingham, Washington, the last of five births for his mother. His father was a Norwegian sea captain who sailed lumber schooners from the Northwest to San Francisco. His father went by Samuel Lars Larsen. That is all I knew of Sam for most of my life.

Sam married my grandmother, Mary Jane (Mollie) Coats, in Bandon, Oregon, in 1903. Sam was forty-three years old, and Mollie was twenty-one and five months pregnant. They lived in Bandon and Coos Bay for several years. Sam was known for his

197

fondness of the bottle. Some would call him a drunk, but a high functioning drunk. He had his master's license before the age of forty.

In October of 1905, Sam was master of the schooner Sacramento when it ran aground on Coos Bay's north spit. The story was he was anchored waiting out a storm. The anchor line broke, and the ship was aground in the morning. The crew was rescued with herculean efforts by the life-saving team. This was four years before my father's birth, so a large debt is owed to those men by many generations of subsequent Larsen kids.

In January 1906, Sam and Mollie arrived in Bellingham, where his three brothers lived. They had their first son and an infant daughter with them. According to the family story, the daughter was smothered in bed that first evening.

Sam never sailed after that. I suspect he was fired following the shipwreck. Maybe he was sobering up rather than waiting out a storm. That is unknown.

In August of 1910, when my father was one year old, his two year old sister died from acute bloody diarrhea. Sam and Mollie separated following that death. Mollie returned to Bandon with the three boys to live with her folks, Thomas and Sarah Coats.

Dad only spoke of his grandfather in Bandon a couple of times. He feared the old Irishman, probably with just cause. Dad set fire to a mattress in the upstairs bedroom when he was three or four, and the old man had to throw the burning mattress out the window. That probably did not endear him to his grandson. Thomas Coats died when Dad was four, and Dad remembered they had him stretched out on the kitchen table, preparing him for burial.

In 1917, Mollie and her mother moved to Southern California. Life was not comfortable there. In early 1920, at the age of ten, Dad and his older brother Merle, who was thirteen, were checked into The Boys and Girls Aid Society of Los Angeles orphanage by their mother. They were there until they turned fourteen, not long for Merle but over three years for Dad.

That Society has evolved into Five Acres (https://5acres.org), an organization offering a full continuum of care for children and families in crisis, serving over 10,000 children and families annually.

When I tracked down Dad's records, the administrator said it was good to hear a success story from that era.

"Those kids had a rough life compared to today's standards, and there are not many success stories," he said.

Dad was released from the orphanage when he was fourteen, and he worked as a caddie. Dad caddied for Oliver Hardy and caddied for one player in a golf tournament at Pebble Beach. His only comment of that event was he had to sleep in the car.

During this time, he developed a love for the movies. He would stand around the theater's entrance until a family came along and then just go through the door with them. Kids were free with paying adults.

He learned to swim well underwater because the pool had tokens on the bottom of the pool. If you found a gold token, you were given free admission the next visit.

His mother remarried when he was sixteen, and he did not get along with his stepfather. So he hitchhiked to Oregon and stayed with his mother's sister, Hattie Rogers, in Coquille. He took the only job available and became a whistle punk for a logging company in the woods.

He returned to California for a time, only to hitchhike again to Oregon. Riding the rails on the second trip, he managed to separate the cars at one point, and the hobos were unhappy because the crew kicked all of them off the train.

On his second trip, he stayed with another of his mother's sisters, Annie Tripp. He returned to high school at Myrtle Point at the age of twenty-one, met my mother, and worked in the woods for a time after graduating. After they were married in 1934, he attended Oregon State for a couple of quarters.

There are few stories of his high school years. He finished in two years, and I find his name on the honor rolls, something I would have never dreamed of growing up. He spoke of stealing Mom from her boyfriend, right in front of him, something I think he looked on with pride.

1934 OSU Rooks, Frank Larsen, fourth row, behind #64. Slats Gill, first row, far left, in suit

At Oregon State, he managed to make the freshman football squad, The Rooks, coached by Slats Gill. He did get his picture taken with the team but quit before the season was over.

"They just use us for fodder for the varsity," he told Mom at the time.

After winter term, they came home, hitchhiking from Corvallis to Myrtle Point.

I heard Dad tell a friend, "We ran out of money, and I knocked up the old lady. I had to quit."

After that, it was work and family. Dad worked in the woods, eventually becoming a donkey puncher, and they lived in logging camps and isolated houses. My sister, Linda, was born in 1935, brothers Larry in 1936, and Gary in 1941. I came along in 1945.

Life was different in western Oregon in the 1930s and 1940s. My brother told of my sister's whittling on a door jam, and when she dropped the knife. It stuck in her eye. Dad had the one car at work, and there was no phone in the house. Mom held my sister with a washcloth over the wound until Dad got home and could get to the doctor.

In January of 1950, Dad purchased a small dairy farm above Broadbent. I am sure this was a significant achievement in his life. We milked cows, and he continued to work in the woods. We were taught work ethics by observation. We would be considered poor by today's standards, but we thought of ourselves as well to do. California cousins would visit, arriving in new cars and leaving with soiled clothes and broad smiles.

Dad would build a fire in the kitchen stove, the only heat in the house, before leaving for work at five. Mom and kids did the morning milking before cleaning up to go to school. Dad would get home and do the evening milking, also with the kids.

Dinner was always a family affair, and you would eat what was on your plate, period. Fried chicken nights were always open warfare over the white meat. Mom became creative in cutting up the one chicken for dinner.

I was home in 1957, when Dad got the call that his mother had died. He cried, the only time I saw that, and he was mad at himself for it. He never had a relationship with his mother. She never did anything for him, never sent a card to any of the kids.

I was the youngest of four kids in our family of three boys and one girl. Everyone argues about which family position is the most favored by the circumstance of birth. I can't resolve that debate, but I believe that I benefited from observing my siblings receiving their lessons on life from our father.

Teenage years are always difficult to live through. My father was always there and supportive. When I was fourteen or fifteen, I challenged him, and I learned in no uncertain terms that I was the lesser man. He came at me like a charging bull, and I learned quickly. And that was that.

He saw that I understood that a job was necessary, and I got one starting my junior year in high school. I made cheese for four years, after school and summers.

"You do the best job you can at whatever you do, and you will do well in life," he told me once. I have taken those words to the bank for many years.

I don't think he agreed with my enlistment in the Army when Vietnam was a threat, but he supported that decision. I learned in the Army that anyone with a farm boy's work ethic was ahead of his peers. Work hard and play hard was my philosophy for those four years.

Dad played very little golf when we were growing up. Money and time were always in short supply. But when they became empty-nesters, he returned to the golf course. He played well, and I never beat the man. I always thought that he would get old enough and I could beat him one day. But one of his long time playing partners died suddenly, and at eighty-one, Dad quit the game, undefeated by his son.

A couple of years later, Dad was dying from liver disease. I believe it was from a botched gall bladder surgery, but that is another story. When the doctor in Eugene said he had done all he could do, Dad said, "I want to go home."

He wanted to die at home, but that was too hard for Mom. Each trip to the hospital left him weaker and weaker. His final few days were spent in a nursing home. And like in birth, death is an event we all must do ourselves.

It took several years for me to fully realize the impact of his passing on me and my life.

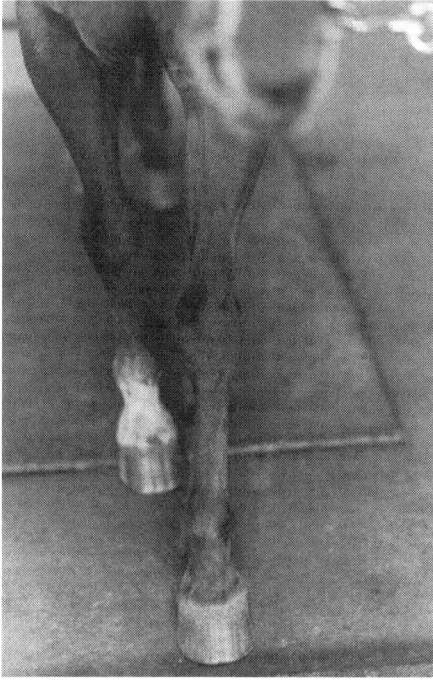

Robert W. Davis, DVM

Preface:

D r. and Mrs. Robert W. Davis Veterinary Anatomy Scholarship (1983)
"For almost four decades, Dr. Robert W. Davis served Colorado State University and the veterinary profession as a professor in the Department of Anatomy. A 1935 graduate of the Colorado A&M's (now Colorado State University) Division of Veterinary Medicine, Dr. Davis had a distinguished career and his contributions to the college, university and veterinary profession were truly remarkable. He was recognized as an outstanding teacher whose enthusiasm and integrity positively affected the lives of many graduates. During its early history, Dr. Davis helped to place the college at the forefront of veterinary medical education. Dr. Davis was inducted into the Glover Gallery of distinguished faculty and alumni in 1990. The Dr. and

Mrs. Robert W. Davis Veterinary Anatomy Scholarship was established by faculty and alumni in their honor."

***

The snow on the ground from last week's storm was almost gone, and we had bright sunshine. Everyone's spirits were improved with this hint of spring in the air.

I found myself spending more time looking out the window than concentrating on the dissection of the horse's leg on the table in front of us. Ben and Chuck, my anatomy lab partners, were busy tracing the digital nerves running down the cannon bone.

Dr. Barr sort of jolted me back to the present when he came up beside me.

"Larsen, Dr. Davis is out in the horse barn and would like to spend some time with you," Dr. Barr said. "He will be waiting for you at the outside stalls, and you can enjoy the sunshine."

Dr. Davis was small in stature, but the muscles in his forearms showed his strength. The vessels on the back of his hands stood out as he extended his hand to shake.

"Dave, I noticed you looked a little bored in the lab," Dr. Davis said. "I thought I would give you a change of pace today."

I was surprised that Dr. Davis had singled me out. We had a class of eighty-four students, and the lab was a beehive of activity.

"It is an old habit," I said. "I just learn at a different pace than a lot of guys. Looking out the window just gives me a little contact with my world."

"Let's look at a real leg on a living horse," Dr. Davis said. "We will try to instill some clinical significance to all this anatomy stuff."

***

Dr. Davis had been a veterinarian in the Army during World War II. He served with General Frank Merrill on his march across the jungles of Burma. He had been one of the veterinarians who cared for the mules used by Merrill's Marauders. If for no other reason, I had great respect for this man.

***

"Are you used to working with horses?" Dr. Davis asked.

"I have been around them most of my life," I said. "But, other than riding, I haven't really worked on any."

"So there are few things we need to go over about working on a horse," Dr. Davis said. "The horse is a powerful animal, and it can cause serious injury to the careless handler. The only way to avoid injury from a horse is to be in the right place at the right time, and the only way you can be sure that will happen is to be at the right all the time."

"That makes sense," I said.

"The horse strikes with his front feet," Dr. Davis said. "He strikes straight forward. If you are in front of him, you are at risk. Work from his shoulder if you can. The same thing can be said about the other end. The horse seldom cow-kicks. He kicks straight back, so work from his hip if you can. We put a horse in stocks at the hospital while working with them. That protects both the horse and the doctor. But you will be in situations where you will be working with an unrestrained horse. You just have to learn to protect yourself."

We got down to the project at hand after that brief instruction. During the next hour, Dr. Davis showed me a roadmap of the horse's leg. His calloused fingertips followed the path of nerves, vessels, tendons, and ligaments. I learned more in that hour than in the preceding weeks of dissection.

"With practice, you will learn to see with your fingertips," Dr. Davis said. "In this profession, where you will be without an x-ray in many cases, seeing with your fingertips becomes vital to your success."

We led the horse out to the paddock and let him run when we were done.

"I would guess you were in the service," Dr. Davis said.

"Why do you say that?" I asked.

"You're older, and you conduct yourself with a bit of military bearing," Dr. Davis said.

"I was in the Army Security Agency," I said. "I was at a couple of listening posts on a couple of borders, no major action. I was in South Korea and West Germany. Interesting times and it allowed me to grow up. Nothing like what you went through."

"That was a long time ago," Dr. Davis said. "You will do well in this profession. It was fun spending some time with you today."

"Yes, I learned more about the horse's leg today than I learned in the lab over the last two weeks," I said. "Thanks a lot for your time."

"The freshman year is the hardest," Dr. Davis said. "There is just so much to learn. It will get better when you get over to the hospital and start working on live animals."

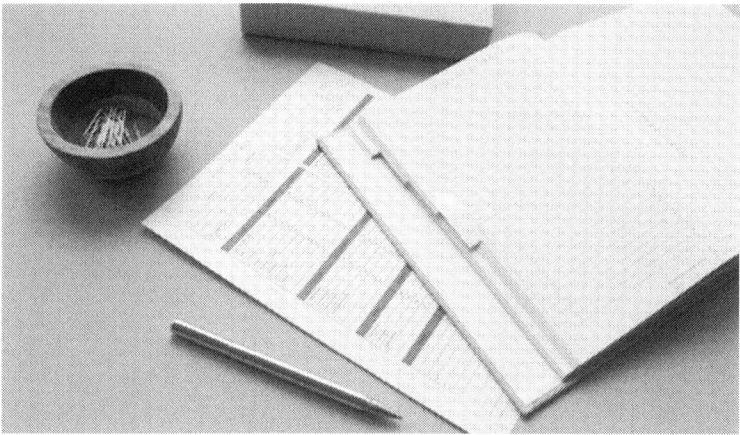

The Budget Book

Some life lessons are quickly learned, others not so much. And then, some lessons come by surprise and are entirely unexpected.

When I started veterinary school, I still had a couple of years left on the GI Bill and several thousand dollars still in the bank from my Army savings. I figured that we could manage the first two years of vet school if we budgeted ourselves carefully and if I could work when I had the time.

When we moved to Fort Collins, Aggie Village, the school's married student housing complex, was full. We had to rent another apartment for the fall quarter. It was not just the apartment, but also some basic furniture. We had sold all our furniture before moving to Colorado and moved with just a U-Haul trailer.

Married student housing provides furnished apartments for a very reasonable rent. Our fall apartment cost a little more, plus we had the added rent expense for the furniture. We were dipping into the savings sooner than we expected.

A budget book caught my eye on one of our first trips to K-Mart to pick up a few household items.

"This is just what we need," I said as I thumbed through the book.

Sandy glanced at it around my shoulder but did not respond. I tossed the thin book into the shopping cart.

As soon as we got back to the apartment, I grabbed the budget book and the checkbook and started filling in the accounts and distributing our meager resources into the various accounts.

"You can't fill that out accurately this fall," Sandy said with a slight frown on her face. "Our living expenses will be a lot higher than when we move into Aggie Village."

"I will fill in the rental expenses as if we were in Aggie Village," I said. "The extra money for this fall will just have to come out of the savings account."

Sandy just left me at the table with the budget book and got Brenda ready for bed. She didn't seem too enthused about my new budget book.

"We really don't know what groceries will cost us around here," Sandy said as she came back to the table. "It will take me a couple of months to find the best stores and the best deals."

"This is just a starting point," I said. "It will give us an idea when expenses are coming and make sure we don't make any extravagant purchases. I have my tuition and books expenses listed, and this fall, I think my final check from the cable company will cover that expense. If I can work over Christmas and spring break, I should be able to come close to covering the tuition expenses."

Sandy made an audible sigh and headed to the kitchen.

I worked late, making sure I had everything entered. I have registration tomorrow, and then classes start the next day. I might not have time for this later.

Sandy finally came back to the table.

"You better get ready for bed," she said. "You might have a busy day tomorrow."

"My guess is there will not be much to the registration process," I said. "There is no selection of classes this fall. We will all be in one big group."

But we went to bed with a little nudge on Sandy's part.

***

I was up and out the door early in the morning. Registration was in the old gymnasium, and it looked like a zoo when I entered. When I finally found the veterinary school table, they handed me a packet, I gave them a check, and that was that. Everything was preordained.

"That was easy," I said to Tom, a fellow freshman I would soon learn was also from Oregon. "I will probably be home before Sandy is dressed."

Sandy was a little surprised when I came home so soon.

"That must not have taken very long," she said.

"I just showed my school ID. They handed me a packet, and I handed them their check," I said. "Pretty simple. After lunch, we can go to the bookstore in the vet school and pick up my books. Then we have the rest of the afternoon off. Maybe we should eat dinner in the park."

"That sounds fun," Sandy said. "I talked to the neighbor lady in the apartment above us, and she said we should enjoy this fall weather, and she said you never know when winter will come."

"Where did you put that budget book?" I asked. "I have a little time, and I can finish it before lunch."

"I put it over in my stuff," Sandy said.

That was a simple statement. Said with little emotion but with a hint of finality. That marked the end of my writing in her book.

In the weeks, months, and years that followed, Sandy kept meticulous records of where every dollar went. But there was never any planning on how much we would spend on anything.

We did avoid any purchases that were out of our financial reach. When we moved into Aggie Village, there was a hookup for a washing machine in the apartment, and that was our first purchase. That way, we only had to use the community dryers.

Next, we purchased a small colored TV made by Motorola. I think the screen was like seventeen inches. It was fine except for the high voltage power supply tube. My Army electronic maintenance skills bailed us out there. It was a straightforward diagnosis and fix. I was horrified when I first opened the back panel. Having worked on some of the most sophisticated electronic equipment in the world, I was not prepared for the consumer electronics of a cheap TV.

We had room in the apartment for an upright freezer, and once that was installed, my folks shipped us some beef to help fill it.

Then we started planning to purchase a small calculator. This was new technology. These small handheld little four-function calculators were expensive at the time. Their cost was out of our reach, and we could not justify spending nearly a quarter's tuition bill for a little calculator.

Then, on Sunday morning, Sandy handed me the newspaper as I finished breakfast.

"Look at this deal," she said.

There was a special price on a calculator. It was made by a subsidiary of Texas Instruments and was on sale for sixty-seven dollars. This was the first time these new small calculators were offered for less than a hundred dollars.

"Can we afford that?" I asked the gal with the budget book.

"I have been setting a little aside every month," Sandy said. "I have most of the money. This is the cheapest we have seen, and I think we should get it."

"That is still a lot of money," I said.

"I just can't keep up with all this bookkeeping doing all the addition and subtraction on paper," Sandy said.

So we went to the store and made the purchase. It was great, handheld. Just hit a few buttons, and it would add a string of numbers with no problem. Sandy was pleased.

We had this calculator for nearly two weeks when Sandy opened the newspaper to the K-Mart ad.

"Oh! Now that makes me mad," she said as she almost threw the paper at me.

There, right in the middle of the full-page ad, was a handheld, four-function calculator on sale for nine dollars and ninety-seven cents. We had just been fleeced for some fifty-seven dollars.

We, or I, learned several lessons. One, Sandy was the one that was going to keep track of our money, period. And two, stores tend to dump products with a sale when they know a competitor is about to undercut their pricing. So don't be so quick to jump at a deal.

All On Number One

We welcomed our first spring in Colorado. The Rocky Mountain winter had been hard for us Oregonians. Spring term gave me a light schedule in school since I already had taken the microbiology course while at Oregon State. And we had a few extra dollars since I was working at the university dairy.

"How do you bet when you go to the dog track?" I asked the janitor, Bob, as I was helping him tidy up after anatomy lab.

"There are a few guys who have a system, and then there are those who pick the dog who takes a dump going to the gate," Bob said. "Actually, the dogs are worse than the horses. I think you have a chance on the horses, but with the dogs, it is all the luck of the draw."

"My wife and I haven't been out since school started," I said. "I have a few extra dollars, and the neighbor lady said she would watch the kids. I thought I would take Sandy to the dog track."

"If you want an evening of fun, and you aren't worried about making a thousand dollars, there are a couple of strategies to use," Bob said. "The one that I think works the best is to pick the top three dogs according to the sheet and bet two dollars to show on each of them. Doing that will give you the best chance of not running out of money. You won't win a lot, but you should win a few dollars."

***

The parking lot at the Loveland dog track was packed, and we had a long walk to the grandstands. A woman from Denver had won seventy-thousand dollars last week, and everyone must think they can repeat the process.

Sandy and I were both a little excited. This was our first date night in some time. We worked our way through the crowd and found a relatively empty section of bleachers that was close to the starting boxes and close to the betting windows.

The first dogs for the first race were just starting their parade as I returned with a couple of glasses of beer. Sandy had been scanning the cheat sheets and had the three dogs for us to bet on all picked out.

Our budget was limited. If we wanted to have anything left over for dinner, we needed to be careful with our betting. Otherwise, we were going to have a short night out.

I took the list and headed to the betting window. There was no line, but the lady in the booth seemed rushed, and I stammered and had trouble getting the information out. She was spitting tickets out faster than I was talking, or so it seemed.

"That will be eighteen dollars," the lady said.

"Eighteen dollars?" I said. "I only wanted to spend six dollars on this race."

"There are no refunds," the lady said. "That will be eighteen dollars." She pushed the pile of tickets out toward me.

I paid her eighteen dollars. That was just about our entire budget for the night. We had set the babysitting money aside but had hoped to have some cash for dinner.

I was quiet as I seated myself on the bench beside Sandy. I carefully looked through the tickets the lady sold me. I had nine tickets, and they were all the same. They were two-dollar tickets for the number one dog to win, and the number one dog was not even on the list that Sandy had given me.

"I'm excited," Sandy said. "And you're sitting there like all gloomy."

"It looks like I sort of messed up at the ticket window," I said.

"What happened?" Sandy asked.

"I'm not sure how I did it," I said. "But I put all our money for the evening on the number one dog."

"The number one dog was not even on my list," Sandy said. "What do you mean by all our money?"

"We have eighteen dollars on the number one dog to win," I said.

"Look at the odds," Sandy said. "The number one dog is way down the list. I guess we had better drink up and get ready to go home."

"We need to watch the race first," I said. "You don't know. They say that those odds don't really mean a thing in the dog races."

They brought the dogs back down the track to load them in the starting boxes. We stood up on the bench to get a better view. The number one dog looked like the biggest dog in the group.

"I don't know, Sandy," I said. "I like the looks of that number one dog."

"Sure you do," Sandy said. "You put all our money on him. You are bound to say he is a good-looking dog."

Sandy grabbed my hand to quiet her excitement as they loaded the dogs into the boxes. The mechanical rabbit was on the inside rail of the track. The doors flew up, the rabbit took off, and the dogs bounded out of the boxes.

The number one dog came out of the box with half a link lead. By the time the pack hit the first corner, the number one dog was clear of the main group. He was almost leaving the other dogs in his dust. Sandy was starting to jump up and down on the bench.

When he entered the final turn, the number one dog was running entirely by himself. I had a flashback to that sixth horse race in Boston where my horse almost came to a standstill and lost just such a lead.

But the number one dog was running strong. Sandy was in danger of breaking the bench now. She was jumping up and down so hard it almost made me jump a bit without even trying.

The number one dog finished the race a full two seconds ahead of the second-place dog. I jumped off the bench and helped Sandy down to the solid ground. We rushed to the ticket window to collect our fortune.

The odds paid out at nine to one, so we collected one hundred sixty-two dollars. That was no minor figure in the spring of 1972 for a struggling college student who got two hundred twelve dollars a month from the GI Bill. We felt rich.

"I don't think we are going to do anything but spend money if we stay here," I said. "The chances of hitting another winner is slim to none. Let's go find a good restaurant and then go to a movie."

"That sounds great to me," Sandy said as we started pushing through the crowd toward the exit.

We found a nice restaurant in downtown Loveland. We had a candlelight dinner with prime rib and all the trimmings, a treat we would not have dreamed of a few hours ago.

As we walked out of dinner, people lined up across the street to go to the movie. The marquee said Sometimes a Great Notion, the story of a logging family set on the Oregon coast. I just glanced at Sandy.

"We have plenty of time," Sandy said. "Judy said she was fine as long we got home before midnight."

So we went to the movie. I would guess we were the only ones in the theater with any real connection to the logging industry in western Oregon or to the setting on the Siletz River.

What a great time we had, and entirely by accident. Or by design, as I liked to kid Sandy. After all, I worked with greyhounds in anatomy lab.

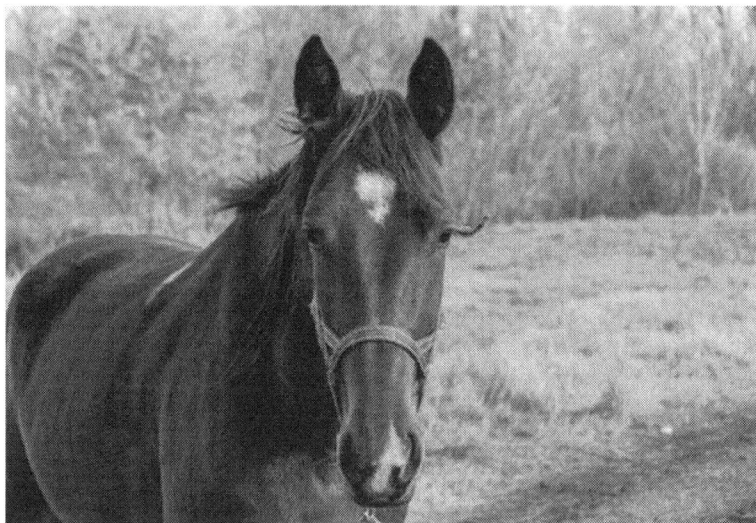

Don't Be Too Smug

I pushed the winch out to the end of the track and jumped up on the truck's bed. I secured a chain around the hocks of the dead horse. With the shackle secure, I connected the hook on the winch cable to the chain, lifted the horse up and pushed it into the necropsy room.

This was the summer of my sophomore year in vet school. I was lucky enough to land this job as a necropsy technician in the Colorado State Veterinary Hospital. Up to this point, it was proving to be a tremendous learning experience.

There was a joke in the profession that had a punch line something like; a veterinarian can eat his mistakes. I was never good at remembering jokes. This summer, I got to see the mistakes and the pathology associated with the profession.

I positioned the dead horse in the middle of the necropsy room and lowered it to the floor. I unhooked the winch and removed the shackles before rolling the winch to the side, out of the way for now.

Dr. Norrdin was on duty as the necropsy pathologist this week. I enjoyed working for him because I got to do most of the necropsy, and he was always challenging my knowledge, usually in a game-like manner.

"Okay, let's look this guy over closely, read the notes and then come up with a possible diagnosis before we start the necropsy," Dr. Norrdin said. "You have to be prepared to defend your suspected diagnosis. Then we will find out who was closest to the actual diagnosis."

This was a young horse, less than four years old, found dead in the paddock this morning. He was never observed to be sick, ever. Looking over him, there was hardly a mark on him. The only thing evident was his front teeth were punched through his upper lip and protruding out of that lip.

Dr. Norrdin quizzed the resident first, the junior technician next, and finally came to me.

"What is your diagnosis, Larsen?" He asked.

"Cardiac tamponade," I said.

"Cardiac tamponade!" Dr. Norrdin remarked. "How in the world do you arrive at that diagnosis from looking at a young, healthy horse?"

"A young, healthy, dead horse," I corrected. "This young heathy horse, who has never been sick a day in his life, was dead when he hit the ground. His death was sudden. We know that, not because he was unexpectedly found dead in the morning, but because his front teeth are punched through his upper lip. He hit the ground nose first. Who has seen a horse, standing in a paddock, fall nose first? This had to be a sudden cardiac event."

"But cardiac tamponade," Dr. Norrdin said, "I have not seen a cardiac tamponade in a horse. You know the saying, when you are in a barn and hear hoofbeats, you look for a horse, not a zebra."

"And, the proof is in the pudding," I said as I stuck my knife into the dead horse's ventral midline on his chest.

"If I am correct, we will know in a minute or two," I said as I sliced open the skin from the end of his sternum to his jaw's angle.

With the junior technician lifting up the right front leg, I severed all the muscle attachment to the ribs, and we reflected the front leg over the horse's back to expose most of the ribs. Then I severed the lower cartilage attachments of the ribs to the sternum. The other technician, standing at the horse's back, pulled up several ribs as I cut the intercostal muscles.

216

There is was, the pericardium, that sack around the heart, distended with blood. I was vindicated, my diagnosis was spot on. Cardiac tamponade occurs when the pericardium fills with fluid, usually blood. That constricts the heart's function. If it is a slow accumulation, it can be recognized and corrected. If it is sudden, it results in sudden death.

"I'll be damned," Dr. Norrdin said. "Now, let's find out just what happened to allow Larsen to win the game."

"Verminous arteritis," I said.

"Now you are really sticking your neck out," Dr. Norrdin said. "But this time, I think you are probably correct."

We opened the pericardium and drained a surprising amount of blood. The heart was small in appearance because it had not been able to fill with blood. And there it was, a hole in the aorta, right where it came out of the heart. This hole, the size of a match stick, would have filled the pericardium with blood in seconds. A very sudden death would have resulted.

"You guys pull the heart and lungs with the aorta attached," Dr. Norrdin said. "Try to keep the aorta intact all the way down to the mesenteric artery."

In the horse, one of the critical intestinal parasites, a large strongyle, Strongylus vulgaris, has a larval stage that causes severe damage and inflammation to the mesenteric artery, the main artery to the gut. This is one of the leading causes of colic in the horse.

We opened the aorta from the heart to the mesenteric artery. There were lesions the entire length of the aorta. The root of the mesenteric artery was swollen and heavily involved with verminous arteritis. This is the standard location of those lesions. The fact that lesions were also located along the entire length of the aorta was an indication of a massive infestation with this dangerous parasite.

"If this horse did not die from this cardiac tamponade, he would have died from severe colic before long," Dr. Norrdin said. "This is as extensive of an arteritis as I have ever seen."

"Do you think the rupture of the aorta was caused by the parasite?" I asked.

217

"Oh, most definitely! This owner needs to get his horses on a rigorous parasite control program, or he will be losing a lot of horses," Dr. Norrdin said.

"And Larsen, don't be too smug," Dr. Norrdin said. "You will never see another case like this in your life. These once-in-a-lifetime cases, just happen, early in your career and later in mine, but only once. Had this been on a test, all of your answers would have been marked wrong. You just had a lucky guess here today."

Of course, Dr. Norrdin was correct. I never saw another case like this. I never read of another case like this. But having seen the damage from uncontrolled parasitic infections, it is much easier to make strong recommendations to horse owners about their parasite control programs.

Always Have Rabies at the Top of Your List

"We have a cow coming in this morning for necropsy," Dr. Norrdin said. "The ambulatory people have been treating this cow all week, and it died this morning."

"It should be a good time for it, we don't have anything in the cooler to work on," I said.

"This cow died with neurological signs," Dr. Norrdin said. "I want you guys to be thoughtful during this necropsy. Especially you, Larsen, when you remove the brain. Do you have any idea what I might be talking about?"

I had talked with a classmate earlier in the week about this cow. He was working on the ambulatory service this summer. Colorado State University had to scramble to keep students in the clinic during the summer months to keep up with the workload.

This cow had been looked at by two different clinicians and their students on multiple occasions. The cow suffered from a progressive neurological deterioration. People had their hands in the cow's mouth and into the back of her throat, trying to ensure there was no foreign body causing some swallowing difficulties.

"What kind of a differential diagnosis list should you be working within your mind when treating a neurological case?" Dr. Norrdin asked.

I had been lax during the summer and was not used to coming up with immediate answers. This job was sort of one to do the manual labor of the necropsy room. It obviously provided a tremendous learning experience but from observation, not rote memory from a textbook.

"I guess viral encephalitis would be on the list, along with secondary bacterial meningitis from any of the respiratory viruses," I said.

"You came close with your first guess," Dr. Norrdin said. "You should always have rabies on your list. It should be at the top of your list, even though you will not see it often these days. The reason is that if you miss that diagnosis and fail to take care of yourself, you end up dead."

"That is probably a good point," I said.

"So be thoughtful, and work with your mouth closed today," Dr. Norrdin said. "Hopefully, that will not be the diagnosis. If it is, we will have a mess. There have been over a dozen guys with their arms down this cow's throat in the past week. The clinicians have really dropped the ball on this case."

When the truck with the dead cow backed up to the loading dock, we shackled the cow's hock and picked her up with the hoist. This allowed us to move her on the track to the middle of the necropsy room floor.

We started the necropsy under the direct supervision of Dr. Norrdin. This was unusual in itself, we seldom had direct supervision at this stage. Dr. Norrdin was very worried about a possible rabies case, and he wanted to make sure everything was carefully documented.

When it came time to remove the head, I moved it to the butcher block in the middle of the room. I had become an expert at removing the brain from all the animals this summer. It was a skill that I would probably seldom use in practice, but I enjoyed being the best at something on the job.

With the skull on the table, I first had to remove the skin and soft tissue on the top half of the head. Then, with a large cleaver, I started shaving the bone from the skull to reveal the brain case.

Once the brain case was exposed, the accuracy of my strokes with the cleaver became more critical. Finally, I would be able to lift the top of the skull cap and expose the brain covered by the meninges—those layers of tissues that become inflamed in meningitis.

There were several specific snips to be made to free the brain. Once this was done, I could lift the intact brain out of the skull and place it on the dissection table. Most of the time, I would slice the brain in a prescribed manner; in half, separating the right and left side. Then slice each side into quarter-inch slices, looking for any abnormalities. This time, Dr. Norrdin took over at this point. He did all the work on the brain and disappeared into the lab with the pieces.

There are several levels of diagnostic testing to confirm rabies as a diagnosis. The diagnosis of rabies is made in several ways. The one that is fastest and considered the most reliable, if present, is finding Negri bodies in the part of the brain called the hippocampus.

By the next day, rabies was a confirmed diagnosis in the cow. Most of us students had received several doses of rabies vaccine during our freshman year of school. Because of that previous vaccination and a positive titer, I only had to have a single booster vaccine. The students who had carelessly had the hands and arms in the cow's mouth during the week preceding her death had to go through a complete series of vaccinations.

That was a lesson well learned. But then, there is just a little more to the story.

***

A long year later, I was in Enumclaw Washington, ready to do a necropsy on a large dairy cow. Standing in the middle of the field, I sharpened my necropsy knife, the same one used to necropsy the rabid cow. As I stood there, the farmer had a whole list of questions. We stood and talked for some time. The entire time during this conversation, I continued to sharpen my knife on the whet stone.

Don't allow anyone to tell you that a sharp knife never cuts you. After standing there sharpening my knife for fifteen minutes, I lifted the hind leg of the dead cow and started the cut through the skin on her belly. This knife slid through the skin like it was butter. My stroke was so smooth, the knife flew through the prescribed cut, continued out into the air, and buried into the muscle of my lower left leg, going into my leg a full inch. Ouch!

I stopped and put a wrap on the wound before proceding with the necropsy. By the time I was done, my left boot was sloshing with blood.

I did make a trip to the doctor's office. We laughed at my careless actions and decided to leave the wound open. Antibiotics and a light wrap should take care of things.

Then I mentioned that I had done a necropsy on a rabid cow with this knife a little over a year ago.

"What do you think?" the doctor asked. "I would think that it would not be a problem at this point in time."

"Well, the knife has been washed since then, but never autoclaved," I said. "I would think that any virus on it would be long since dead."

"I would think so also," said the doctor.

"I am sure I still have a positive titer, just for insurance," I said.

I did live, by the way.

Cowboy Education

During the fall of my junior year in vet school, I worked part time for Monforts of Colorado. At the time I worked for them, they ran two feedlots with about a hundred thousand head of cattle in each lot. My job was to work in the hospital during the weekends. This was an excellent opportunity for me. I was able to see a lot of management of a large feedlot and a lot of feedlot medicine. I also learned that education happens in more places than in the classroom.

The hospital for the Greeley feedlot was small but well laid out. There was a crowding pen that led to the treatment chute. The cattle that stayed for multiple days were held in a series of small holding pens, arranged according to the treatment group they were assigned. Treatment protocols were established by the feedlot veterinarian. As a hospital technician, I just did the daily treatments called for by the established protocol.

For example, the pneumonia protocol (the most common) called for five days in the hospital with IV antibiotics each morning and often some supportive medication if needed. Steers were treated, and the treatment was recorded on their record. They were returned to the treatment pen after they were treated. Any steers with unsatisfactory progress were put into another treatment group, and the protocol was intensified.

Each morning the cowboys would meet in the hospital and get ready for their day. While they drank their coffee, they would assign the pens that each group would check. In the central feedlot, the steers were held in large pens of approximately five hundred head each. Two cowboys would ride through each pen each morning and check for sick or injured steers. During these morning sessions, they would make sure everyone knew if there were questionable steers from the previous day's ride that needed to be double-checked. It was also time for them to kid the young 'doctors' working on the weekends. I was a little older than most of the guys who worked in the hospital, and I could hold my own most of the time.

After the cowboys mounted their horses and started out for their assigned pens, we would start with the daily treatment schedules. Our goal was to get all the hospital treatments completed before the cowboys were back with the new steers for diagnosis and treatment.

During the ride through the pens, if they found any steers needing treatment, they would cut them out of the large pen and put them in a holding pen until they had a group of ten to twelve steers. These steers were then herded to the hospital by a couple of the cowboys. They would help us get them into the crowding pen, and they would relay any particular information to us that would help with the diagnosis. They also took the time to make sure the young doctors were teased a little.

This one morning in November was a bright, cold late fall morning in northern Colorado. It was frigid, and the hospital was the only warm place available to anyone. We had the doors closed, and the electric ceiling heater was turned up full blast.

I was herding the last steer back to the hospital pens when the first group of new steers arrived from the central feedlot. The cowboys herded them into the crowding pen. When I got back to the hospital and warmed myself by standing under the heater blowing warm air, Eli Hernandez already had a steer in the treatment chute. Eli was the lead cowboy. He was a large Hispanic man; he towered over me. I considered him an old man in those days, that means he was probably in his early fifties. His worn face told of his years of working in the sun. His large belly suggested that he drank a beer or two. I am sure his horse was enjoying the morning break.

Eli was anxious for me to look at this steer. "Doc," he said, "what do you think about that mass on this steer?"

This was a test, and I understood that it was a test. Eli was really going to find out what kind of a cow doctor this kid was. I was going to have to make some thoughtful comments. This was a massive swelling on the right side of the abdomen. I had no idea what it could be, maybe a hernia, or could be a tumor. One thing I had been taught was it is okay to admit you don't know something as long as you could illustrate a plan to find out what was wrong.

"I have no idea, Eli. We will probably have to stick a needle into it and get a sample under the microscope," I replied.

Eli listened as he was cleaning his fingernails with his large pocket knife.

"Yeah, Doc, you get your needle ready, I have got to get back to the pens," he said, half chuckling under his breath.

He looked down on me with a broad smile as he turned for the door. As he walked by the chute, he made a quick swipe at the bulging mass on the side of the steer. His knife was obviously very sharp, and it sliced through the skin like butter, opening a large gash in the belly of the steer.

The pus poured out of the swelling like you were pouring milk from a large pail. Eli made one more look back at me as he opened the door. He still had a big smile, but there was no malice in his glance. Just like a professor who had provided a good lesson.

There was limited circulation of air in the hospital when it was buttoned up against the cold outside. The odor was suddenly overwhelming. Steam rose from the growing puddle of pus on the floor. There must have been five gallons of pus on the floor, and it was reaching the drain very slowly. I headed for the garage door that had been closed all morning and pulled it open. The air was cold, but at least you could take a deep breath. Then I grabbed the hose and washed the bulk of the pus down the drain.

That taken care of, I turned to the steer. Eli had probably seen this type of abscess many times before and knew that drainage was the first line of treatment. The gash that he had made was maybe six inches long. That was good. This abscess needed adequate drainage to allow for the healing of the tissues on the inside of the abscess. This could take a couple of weeks.

The problem was the gallon of pus at the bottom of the abscess, below the gash. I shaved the area around the gash and down the abdomen so I could open the abscess at its lowest margin. I scrubbed the area with Betadine Surgical Scrub, then injected some lidocaine into the gash and into the area of the planned opening. That done, I used a scalpel to open the abscess on its ventral margin. This time I caught the pus in a bucket. The smell still filled the room, but it was easier to clean up. The open garage door provided some air circulation. With the drainage complete, I threaded a large Penrose drain through the upper gash and out the lower incision. I tied the drain in a loop so it would stay in place for as long as it was needed.

Next, I flushed the abscess with a bottle of hydrogen peroxide. This made a lot of foam and probably provided some mechanical cleaning. I followed the peroxide with dilute Betadine. The large gash was large enough to allow me to reach my gloved hand and arm into the abscess. I removed several large chunks of consolidated pus and explored the body wall to ensure it was intact. Then I found the culprit, a large splinter lying in the bottom of the abscess. Probably from a fence rail or a feed bunk. This abscess grew so large before it was detected because the steer would act normal until the size of the swelling started to interfere with his function. When looking at five hundred steers, the cowboys look for steers acting less than normal.

Next, I gave a hefty dose of Combiotic, a penicillin/ streptomycin combination, an antibiotic in use at that time. No worry about flies in this weather. This steer would be in the hospital for a week or two.

The diagnosis was an obvious abscess. This would be a common problem for me in the years to come. The size of the thing was what was exceptional. Turns out to be one of those once in a lifetime diagnoses. In over forty years of practice, I have never seen anything to come close to the size of this abscess.

Financial Aid

I looked hard at the man seated behind the desk.

His dark hair was fading into a grizzled gray. His oversized nose had a mass of red pimples. I suspect it was rosacea. The wrinkles in his face were smoothed a bit by its puffiness. His large ears actually added balance to his whole appearance. On somebody else, they would be considered large.

"What did you ask me?" I asked, not believing the question. This was my first experience with a financial aid office. I was getting ready to start my junior year in vet school, and my funds were exhausted.

Before I went into the Army, I could work a summer in the cheese factory and pay for a year of school. So I had no need for any aid in those years. Following the Army, I had four years of the GI Bill. With those payments of around two hundred dollars a month plus some part-time work, I finished twenty-four months at Oregon State without any debt.

The same was true for my first two years in veterinary school. But now, entering my clinic years in vet school, I would not be able to work part time, and the GI Bill was exhausted. I was forced to seek financial aid.

"How much money do your parents make?" the man repeated his question.

I could feel a growing contempt for this man with a rumpled shirt and a belly hanging over his belt. I had worked with generals who were this man's age and who would have little regard for this man.

"Would you look at me," I said. "I'm not one of your twenty-year-old students who still takes his laundry home on weekends. I am twenty-eight years old, and I have a wife and three kids at home. I have six years of college under my belt, and I spent four years in the Army. I have not lived at home for ten years. I have no damn idea how much money my parents make, and I will be damned if I am going to ask them."

"Well, Mr. Larsen, I generally don't talk with students who have six years of school under their belts, and who don't have some school debt, unless their parents have paid for their schooling," the man said.

This guy looked like he had been in the public trough his entire life. He probably had little understanding of how someone actually works for things he accumulates in life. I stiffend my stance in my chair.

"Are you suggesting that I am being less than honest with you?" I asked, and I continued without giving him a chance to answer. "I have virtually worked my entire life. After age ten or twelve, I haven't spent a dime that I didn't earn personally. I resent your insinuation."

"I'm sorry that you took it that way," the man said. "I was just explaining my observation from this desk. I have had a few of you veterans through here, and you guys, as a group, have a level of maturity that I admire."

He's trying to soften me up now, I thought.

"My service was pretty plush compared to some guys in combat in Vietnam," I said. "And a bunch of those guys never came home."

"Yes, I know," the man said. "Look, you and I have sort of gotten off on the wrong foot here. You, obviously, are qualified for financial aid. I will give you a packet of forms to fill out. You get those turned in, and we will send things to your bank for a guaranteed loan. Because you haven't borrowed anything before this time, you are not eligible for grants or scholarships. I will put special processing on your folder, and your bank will have your information in a couple of days after you turn in those forms."

"Thanks for the special consideration," I said as I stood up and picked up the packet from his desk. "My wife will appreciate it, but she was hoping I would get a Pell Grant or something."

"Yes, those grants are nice," the man said. "But one of the requirements is prior school debt or a family with great need. You don't qualify with six years of college paid for. Next year, we will be able to come up with a better package."

"Thanks again," I said as I shook the man's hand. "We will have these papers filled out tonight and turned in tomorrow."

I felt a little better about things as I left the office. At least the guy recognized the error of his ways. Maybe another veteran or two will benefit from my conversation with the man. But Sandy was not going to be happy about not getting a grant.

"What do you mean, we don't qualify?" Sandy asked. "Why don't we qualify for a grant?"

"The guy said if I had paid for six years of school without borrowing any money, I wasn't poor enough for a grant," I explained.

"Well, I don't think that is fair," Sandy said. "If fifty dollars a month from the Oregon GI Bill doesn't qualify a family of five as poor, I don't know what does."

"We only have a couple of years left, and then I can go to work," I said. "Living on borrowed money won't be too bad for that amount of time."

***

The man at the financial aid office was true to his word. I turned in the packet of papers in the morning, and the gal from his office called in the afternoon to say things were approved and sent to the bank.

The loan process was simple. The bank in Oregon sent me some forms to sign, and we were flush with money for the year.

The following year was better with a large Pell Grant. I think I graduated with a debt of around six thousand dollars, chicken scratch compared to the debt students incur today.

Once in the Wilds of Afghanistan

The large poster on the wall with a picture of W. C. Fields caught my eye. "Once in the wilds of Afghanistan, I lost my corkscrew, and we were forced to live on nothing but food and water for several days." He was talking about wine, but it reminded me of my army days when beer was the preferred beverage.

We were gathered around the dinner table in the small country restaurant in the middle of Nebraska. There were six of us, all senior veterinary students, spending a week pulling calves in a progeny test herd of six hundred heifers for a company supplying semen to the cattle industry.

The practice of cross-breeding using bulls of exotic beef breeds was becoming a popular option in the mid-1970s. There were a couple of problems with the practice. One, the bulls involved were selling for extremely high prices, some as much as fifty thousand dollars. And two, with some of these exotic breed bulls, the incidence of dystocia (difficulty calving) was high.

This test herd was utilized to document a calving ease figure for the bulls used to sire the delivered calves. This figure was then used for marketing the bull's semen, giving the rancher more confidence that his cows would have the cross-bred calves without undue complications.

The experience provided to us students was invaluable. We learned from the numerous obstetrical problems and had to help manage this herd of six hundred heifers in an open pasture of nearly forty acres. We also had to meet a client's expectations, something that we had little experience with while in school.

The six of us were given a school car to drive to the ranch. The six students we were replacing jumped in the car with a bit of glee and drove it back to school. On the ranch, we had a pickup to drive to the village for our meals at this small cafe and an old military three-quarter-ton to check the cow herd.

Divided into three shifts, we were responsible for checking the herd of heifers every two hours, twenty-four hours a day. We kept track of the heifers and the time of their labor. We tagged calves and recorded data on their births. And we moved to the barn any heifer having difficulty with delivery.

During the week we were there, the weather was brutally cold. There was just a light covering of snow on the ground. Still, the temperatures hovered between zero and ten to fifteen below zero the whole time.

After dinner, Jim Logan and I began our first shift of watching the herd and taking care of any problems.

The canvas roof and sides on the old military truck didn't hold in the heat very well. We noted a heifer with a new calf down by the creek, separate from the main herd on the first trip around the herd. The calf had been tagged, so there was nothing we needed to do.

On this first trip through the herd, there was a heifer that needed to be brought into the barn. I got out and herded her slowly while Jim followed in the truck for most of the distance before he went ahead to make sure the gates were set up for her entrance.

She knew she was headed to the barn and that it would be warmer there, and she led me more than I herded her. Once inside, with the propane heater turned on full blast, it was slightly warmer but still cold.

Jim had things set up, and I pushed the heifer right into the chute.

Jim cleaned up the cow and checked her quickly.

"It looks like we lucked out with this one," Jim said. "I think we can pull this calf easily. We might even get an hour of sleep before our next herd check."

Jim hooked up the calf puller and jacked the calf out of the heifer as I completed the paperwork. We tagged the calf and moved the pair into the holding pen in the back of the barn. This calf was lucky. Mom would have him cleaned up and dry before he would be turned out to the cold in the morning. We headed to the house for a cup of coffee and a short nap in the recliner before our next trip.

As the evening wore on, the cold became overwhelming, and we became busier with the calving.

On our second trip through the herd, we brought two heifers into the barn. With the propane heater blowing full blast, the water still froze as it hit the ground.

"This one is going to be a tough one," Jim said. "You better check it, too."

I washed and pulled a plastic sleeve on my arm. The warmth on the inside of the cow felt good. It reminded me of morning milkings when I would lean against the cow's belly to keep warm.

"I agree, this is going to be a tough fit, but I can slide a hand between the pelvis and the calf's shoulders," I said. "I think we should try to pull it."

"What are we going to do if we get into a hip lock?" Jim asked.

"With both of us here, we should be able to turn those hips to an oblique position and get him out," I said. "I say again, I think we should pull it."

We hooked the calf jack onto the front feet and started the calf out. He slid through the birth canal with ease, and we were just about thinking we were home free, and then he came to a dead stop.

"Damn, his hips must be massive," I said.

"Okay, let's push him back a bit and get those hips on a diagonal," Jim said.

When we started pushing on this calf, we realized how big he was.

"He must be over a hundred pounds," Jim said.

After a bit of push back to disengage the hips from the pelvis, we put a twist on the calf. As we turned the hips to a diagonal position, taking advantage of the broadest measurement of the pelvic canal, the calf almost fell out the rest of the way. As his hips cleared the pelvis and the calf's weight pulled his hips and hind legs the rest of the way out, Jim had to catch his head, so it didn't bounce on the floor.

"That was close," Jim said. "I don't think his father will score very well."

We cleaned up after this heifer and ran the second one into the chute. I checked this one first, this time.

After washing her rear end and tying the tail out of the way, I ran my hand into the birth canal. I talked my way through the exam to give Jim my impressions first hand.

"These feet are massive, larger than the calf we just delivered," I said as I advanced my hand deeper into the birth canal. "There is a nose, but I can't fit my hand over the top of the head. This calf is so large, his head won't even come into the birth canal. I think this is going to be a C-section."

Jim checked the cow and agreed. We both glanced at the clock.

"We are going to have to hurry to make the last check," Jim said.

It was surprising how fast we could be with two professionals working on the same problem. We had the left flank clipped and prepped in no time. I had the lidocaine drawn into two sixty cc syringes by the time Jim finished the prep. Jim opened the surgery pack and scrubbed while I completed an inverted 'L' block. When I stepped away, he was ready to make the incision.

When we had the abdomen open, it was a little chore to roll the hind feet up to the incision. Once the feet were there, we incised the uterus and attached a set of chains to the feet.

I started to pull the calf out of the incision, and Jim carefully enlarged the uterine incision as needed. When the butt of the calf cleared the incision, I cried, "uncle."

"I am going to need a hand with this monster," I said.

Jim put the scalpel aside and grabbed one of the calf's hind legs. We both pulled hard, and the calf finally flopped out of the uterus.

"He looks two weeks old," Jim said.

I took care of the calf while Jim started with closing up the heifer.

"He is going to be on his feet before we get momma closed up," I said as I gave Jim a break and finished closing the flank incision.

We were only a few minutes late to do our two-hour herd check after getting momma and calf back in a holding pen.

The cold struck us both as we stepped out of the barn. The old three-quarter-ton turned over slowly, but it started with a cough as the battery waned. Jim started the truck down the hill, and I turned the heater up full blast, but it was still blowing cold air.

We started around our route. As I huddled over the heater vent, hoping for some warmth, Jim turned toward the edge of the herd.

"We better go check this heifer. It looks like she has a new calf," Jim said.

I glanced up and realized that this was the heifer with a tagged calf that we had noted earlier.

"Jim, she has been there for several days," I said.

"Several days!" Jim said. "This is our first night. This might be a long week."

As the week wore on, the cold was unrelenting. The only warm spot was inside a cow. Thankfully, the little house that we stayed in was kept warm as toast.

As we talked about our plans following graduation, all the guys from Colorado and Wyoming badgered me about the Pacific Northwest.

"Larsen, I don't understand why you want to work out there where it rains all the time," John said.

"It might rain a little, but it is a warm rain most of the time," I said. "And the water doesn't freeze when it hits the floor. And you don't have to find a cow's belly to get warm."

The Last Visit

The weather had been pretty good for the last couple of weeks in northern Colorado, and all the snow was gone. We had a trip home planned, and I had to visit the practice in Enumclaw, where I hoped to go to work next year. Gas was the only question mark now.

"Make sure you fill the gas tank today," I said to Sandy as I headed out the door on my way to school. "This is our day to get gas. If we fill up today, we will be able to leave in the morning."

Today was my last day before spring break, and we were in the middle of the 1974 Arab oil embargo. We had nearly twenty-four hours of driving ahead of us, and gas was a concern.

I was just finishing a two-week clinic rotation at the bull farm, and we had most of the work done for the week. I had made arrangements to skip my Friday clinics so we could get on the road in the morning and do most of the travel before the weekend.

Sandy had the car ready to go by the time I got home. She had the back seat leveled out so the girls could have level ground to play or sleep as needed. We would only need to throw the suitcases in the trunk in the morning and head out.

***

Morning came, and although we were not as prompt as I had hoped, we were on the road.

"It feels good to be on the road," I said. "I am a little excited to be going home."

"I will feel better when I know where we will get our next tank of gas," Sandy said. "I have nightmares about being stranded in the middle of Wyoming for all of the spring break."

"I think that gas is supposed to be available in Wyoming and Idaho," I said. "If we fill up in Green River, we won't have to worry about getting gas in Utah."

"I don't want to be driving across a desert with a gas tank tittering on empty," Sandy said. "I don't think we should pass up an open gas station."

"I agree, but Utah is like Colorado, they sell gas on even and odd days according to your license plate," I said. "And our plate says we can buy gas in Utah on Saturday. But I checked, and we can make it from Green River to Burley, Idaho, with no problem. Then if we top off the tank before we get into Oregon, we should be fine. Our only problem will be at Burns. We will arrive there in the early morning hours, and we might have to hang around until something opens. I don't think we would want to try to make it all the way from Ontario to Bend on one tank of gas."

Things went along great. We pulled off the freeway at Green River and right into an open gas station with no line. We filled the tank and took a break for lunch. We had planned to eat lunches out of our ice chest, but the cold wind of eastern Wyoming suggested that we find a little cafe for the girls.

The trip from Green River through Utah was uneventful. It was getting dark when we pulled off the freeway at Burley. Gas was no problem, and we filled the tank and found a restaurant for dinner.

"What do you hear about the gas situation in Oregon?" I asked the waitress.

"We don't hear much, I know they are on even and odd days," she said. "And I hear that they are really strict on that. Saturday is an even day, so if your license plate is even, you should be okay."

"That is why we filled up on Thursday in Colorado and planned to be in Oregon on Saturday," I said. "I guess I am worried about there being anything open in Burns at two or three in the morning."

The drive from Burley to Boise mainly was desert, and in the dark, it was a pretty dull drive.

"I think I need to take a short nap," I said as we approached Boise.

"Do you think we can just pull over and sleep?" Sandy asked. "I think we need to find a place with some people around."

We found a spot, I slept, and Sandy entertained Dee. At seven months, she slept too much today and was ready to play. A fifteen-minute power nap turned into almost an hour, but it was all I needed.

It was three in the morning when we were approaching Burns. Sandy had been sleeping since we left Ontario. I could see lights on the edge of town, and as we got closer, I could see that it was a gas station. I pulled in.

A guy was pumping gas, and several cars lined up at the pump. I stepped out of the car to speak with him. The wind was blowing hard, and it was cold. This young guy pumping gas was bundled up and wearing a thick stocking cap.

"Do you have gas to sell?" I asked the young man.

"I just got a delivery," he said. "I am selling to anybody for a couple of hours. Cash only sales, that way, there is no record."

"I have the cash," I said.

"Pull up to a pump, and I will fill you up," the young man said.

When I paid him, he had a big roll of bills in his pocket. He was doing a booming business for now.

We had to wait for a restaurant to open in Bend, so we could get breakfast. We were able to fill the gas tank again and sleep a bit in the restaurant's parking lot.

"We should have enough gas to get to Myrtle Point," I said.

"If we can get gas in Roseburg, I think we should," Sandy said. "Otherwise, we will run on empty when we get to Myrtle Point, and we won't be able to get any gas until Monday."

***

The trip was an obvious success. Both sets of grandparents were thrilled with getting to see the girls. They pretended they were happy to see Sandy and me, but the girls stole the show.

"I have to run up to Enumclaw and look that place over a bit," I said to Mom. "But I want to visit with Grandpa Davenport if he is up to it."

"He is doing pretty well right now," Mom said. "I will give Bernice a call and see when would be a good time for you to visit."

Mom's sister, Bernice, and her husband, Hub Haughton, had moved up from California to care for grandpa during the final years of his life. He was getting pretty frail at ninety-four and couldn't really live alone.

It was two in the afternoon when we arrived at his house on Catching Creek. Bernice had him up and dressed, and he was waiting on the couch when we arrived.

When I was fifteen and thinking I was pretty tough, this old man was eighty-one. I worked for him that summer, and he had worked my butt into the ground. He had trouble keeping the pace for a full eight hours, but the time he worked beside me showed me what endurance was all about.

On this day, I was amazed at how pleased he was to see us.

"David, how have you been?" he said as I sat beside him and shook his hand. His lower lip quivered a bit as he looked at the girls.

I introduced Sandy and Brenda, who he had seen before. But Amy was his first great-granddaughter born following my grandmother's death, who was also named Amy.

"And this is Amy," I said as I pushed a reluctant two-year-old over to a strange old man.

"Amy," he said as tears welled up in his eyes. He took her hand, and his lower lip quivered some more.

"And now we have Dee," I said as Sandy sat Dee on his knee. His sister, Auntie Dee, had been a favorite aunt for a couple of generations of his family.

"Dee," he said as he balanced her on his knee, and a tear fell down his face.

Our visit was brief but profoundly rewarding. I clearly understood that this was probably my final goodbye when I shook his hand for the last time. It made that long drive worth it.

Bernice went out to the car with us when we were leaving.

"I am so glad you could come to visit, David," Bernice said. "You know, of course, he probably doesn't have much time left. But I think he will hold this visit near his heart. We can't thank you enough."

The rest of the trip has become sort of blur in my memory. I did make an overnight trip to Enumclaw to look over the job offer. And we did manage to navigate the gas crisis on our return trip to Fort Collins.

My grandfather passed away on June 14 of that year, just as I started my senior year of vet school. There was no possibility of attending his funeral. But this trip had served as my goodbye to this significant role model in my life.

Is He Dead Yet?

W e were right in the middle of a story when the phone rang. Rod was closest, so he picked up the call. Everyone else on night duty tried to look busy. Our last couple of years in vet school was a little more strenuous than regular college. Clinic rotations made it like an eight to five job—actually, an eight to five job that started about six-thirty and lasted until seven. Then every couple of months, you had a week of night duty with ten seniors. Most of the time, we were busy, but there were many slow hours. We were at the hospital until at least ten, then on call for the rest of the night.

Rod hung the phone up and called Dr. Snow on the intercom. We had two interns on nights with us; one large animal intern, and one small animal intern.

"Dr. Snow, you have a turtle on the way in for an emergency exam," Rod said on the intercom. "The lady wants to know if it is alive or not."

Several of us headed to the small animal section to help with the call. This sounded interesting.

Hazel and Matt came through the door carrying a small desert tortoise. Hazel was supporting it chin as the tortoise appeared limp.

241

We ushered them into an exam room and placed the tortoise on the exam table. I put a towel under the tortoise and positioned its legs and head in what appeared to be a comfortable position.

Dr. Snow came in and introduced himself. Dr. Snow was known to the students to be sort of a flake. A flake, but also pretty knowledgable about species that we would never see in a practice situation.

"Tell me about Henry's problem," Dr. Snow said to Hazel.

"Well, last night, when I was feeding him his vegetables, I noticed that he had a little bit of a runny nose," Hazel said. "He has never been sick since we have had him, which is about three years."

"So last night he had a runny nose, and tonight he looks dead," Dr. Snow said. "What happened between then and now?"

"I knew I had to give him some medicine last night," Hazel said. "I searched through our stockpile of old medication. The only thing I could find was some phenobarbital. It was given to help me sleep when I was sick a couple of years ago. Or I think that is what it was given to me for. Anyway, that is what I gave him. But I thought he was smaller than me, so I cut the pill in half."

"You gave him 125 mg of phenobarbital for his runny nose?" Dr. Snow asked.

"Yes, that is about right," Hazel said. "Do you think that was all right?"

"Looking at Henry, I would guess, no, that was not all right," Dr. Snow said.

"I just want to know for sure if he is dead before we bury him," Matt said.

"The problem is that phenobarbital is known to put some reptiles into hibernation," Dr. Snow said. "We might have some difficulty deciding between death and hibernation."

We turned Henry over and listened, but could not hear any heart sounds. We clipped a toenail and did get a drop of blood.

"Maybe we could try to get an electrocardiogram on him," Dr. Snow said.

"Oh, how much is that going to cost?" Hazel asked. "We are on a pretty limited budget. That is why we tried to treat his runny nose ourselves."

"A phone call would have been a good idea," Dr. Snow said. "We are pretty free with information around here. Whoever may not have known what to give a tortoise for a respiratory infection, but they would have known that phenobarbital was not a good idea."

"What are we to do now?" Hazel asked.

"Okay, I will let these students take Henry in the back, see if they can detect a heartbeat," Dr. Snow said. "If we do that, you have to promise you will not tell anyone here in the hospital that I did that, or I will get into trouble. Do you agree with that?"

"That sounds fair," Hazel said. "How are they going to find a heartbeat?"

"We will try to get an electrocardiogram on him," Rod said. "If we use some needles as electrodes, that should be pretty sensitive."

"Okay, but will you hurt him?" Hazel asked.

"He is going to have a few needle pokes," I said. "But in his condition, he won't feel a thing. We will have him back here in a couple of minutes."

We picked up Henry carefully and moved him back to the treatment room. We used aluminum needles, poked through the skin, and hooked the leads of the ECG to the needle hubs.

"We just need to do a lead two," Rod said. "Any wiggle will mean he might be alive."

There was not much on the tracing. But every once in awhile, there was a small blimp.

"What does an ECG on a tortoise in hibernation look like?" I asked.

We settled the question by handing the strip to Dr. Snow when we returned Henry to the exam room.

"There is not much here to suggest he is alive," Dr. Snow said. "But I have to admit, I do see a regular deflection that occurs about two or three times a minute. I think Henry is in very deep hibernation. I doubt if he will wake up from it."

"Just what are you saying, young man?" Matt asked.

"I think Henry is near death," Dr. Snow said. "I don't think he is going to wake up. I think he will be dead by this time tomorrow."

"So, I guess I should plan to bury him tomorrow," Matt said.

"But what if you are wrong, Doctor?" Hazel asked.

"The other thing to do is to take Henry home, make him comfortable on the kitchen counter, and if he starts to smell, you can feel better about burying him," Dr. Snow said.

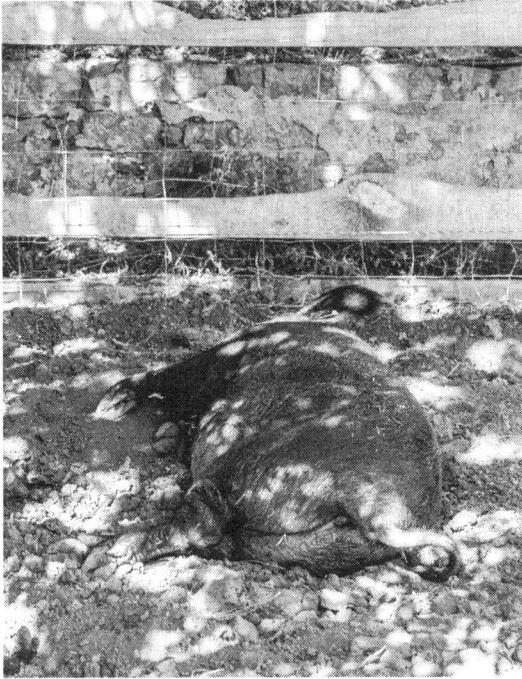

'Twas the Night Before Christmas

My first experience with a sick pig occurred during my senior year in vet school. At Colorado State University, we would only see an occasional pig. If you were not in a midwestern school, your swine medicine instruction came mostly from the book. During one of my weeks on night duty, I accompanied the intern on a farm call to look at this sick sow.

It was the night before Christmas in central Colorado, eleven o'clock and very cold, meaning about minus twenty degrees. The wind was blowing hard, and the blowing snow was obscuring the highway's surface as we headed east out of Fort Collins.

"I hope she's in a warm barn," I said as I snuggled down into my parka.

"Don't bet on it. We wouldn't even be on this call if it wasn't for Dr. Voss. He is apparently friends with this family. We have never seen them before," young Dr. Sanders explained. Dr. Voss was one of the horse doctors at the teaching hospital and carried a lot of weight, especially with the young interns.

We pulled onto the small farm and were met by two young boys. Their parents were not at home. The boys had found the sow in trouble and called Dr. Voss. The cold was almost unbearable, with the wind blowing like it was.

"Where is she?" We asked, hoping to be led to the barn.

"She is in the back of the pigpen," the older boy replied, pointing to the low sprawling shed on the north side of the barn.

This pig pen was a fenced area with about a four-foot roof covering it. The entryway was in the middle of the shed, on the roof.

Hanging his head through the hatch, the young boy pointed to the far corner.

"She's lying over there," he said, pointing with a weak flashlight.

We went back to the truck and loaded our pockets with everything we thought we might need, hoping we would not have to spend any more time exposed to this weather than necessary.

Dr. Sanders handed me the flashlight after I jumped into the pigpen. Then he scrambled in after me. The wind still stung our faces as it blew through the wide slats in the fence. We duck walked back toward the corner the boys had pointed out to us. At least all the manure was frozen solid. "This would be just as interesting in the summer," I thought.

We found the sow right where the boys said she would be. We could see the older boy hanging his head through the hatch, watching our progress. The sow was flat out. She had some mastitis and, obviously, an advanced pregnancy. The chance of helping her in this situation was nil. The possibility of getting her out of here tonight did not exist.

"What do you think?" Dr. Snyder asked me as we examined the sow on our knees. He was trying to maintain a teaching situation, but we were both freezing.

"I think we should give her a big dose of penicillin. Tell them to bring her into the hospital in the morning," I replied in a typical cold student fashion.

"I agree," Dr. Sanders said. "Let's do it and get the hell out of here before we freeze."

We both knew this sow needed more care than a couple of shots, but there was no way we could do anything for her in this situation. This treatment would at least give her a chance of living through the night.

"I wonder how they found her?" I asked as we headed back to the hatch. This would prove to be a question often on my mind in the years to come as I would treat animals in the middle of the night in all sorts of situations and environments.

"You guys did a good job to find her and call Dr. Voss," Dr. Sanders praised the boys. "If she's alive in the morning, you have your dad bring her into the hospital," he instructed.

We jumped into the truck, it was cold, but we were instantly out of the wind.

"Get that heater going," I said as Dr. Sanders started the truck.

It would take the whole night to warm up. We probably were close to hypothermia that night. I never heard if the sow lived through the night. I doubt very much that she did.

Where is the Volar Pouch?

D r. Adams was a massive man, both in his physique and in his professional reputation. He was not tall, less than six feet, but very muscular. His rugged facial features made him appear to have a scowl on his face in the best of times. In those moments, when he was mad at a horse or a student, some would say he was fearsome.

There was a story while we were in school about Dr. Adams attending a meeting of equine veterinarians. The first presenter was doing a ground-up portrait of the perfect equine veterinarian to liven up the audience.

He started with the feet, then the legs, on up to the chest and arms. The picture was that cartoon gorilla. In actuality, it portrayed Dr. Adams pretty close. Dr. Adams was in the front row and was becoming red in the face because it seemed everyone except the presenter recognized the similarity to

Adams. I have no idea if the story was true, but it was told a lot in those years.

However, he was a great teacher. When I was assigned to him for my senior rotation in large animal surgery, I was thrilled. That thrill did not last long.

On the first Monday morning of my two-week rotation, the junior student and I waited in front of the large animal surgery room. Finally, Dr. Adams arrived at eight o'clock sharp.

"Good morning, guys," Dr. Adams said. "You two are lucky. We have a busy couple of weeks coming up. I want to get off to a running start here."

He throws up an x-ray of the lower leg of a horse on the viewer.

"Where is the volar pouch, Larsen?" Dr. Adams asked.

"Um," I stammer.

"Jon, same question?" Dr. Adams said to the junior student.

"I guess I don't know," Jon replies.

"Okay, let's get started on the day," Adams said. "But you two have an anatomy test in my office at one o'clock, right after lunch on Wednesday. If you fail that test, you fail the rotation."

And if the rumors of Adams' power were correct, we will play hell graduating if we fail the rotation. This was not only intimidating, but it was also damn scary.

When the casework was done for the day, Jon and I were in a rush to get home. I had managed to get through the first three years of vet school with little studying outside of the classroom and clinic. Now, I had a couple of nights to review the anatomy of the horse in exquisite detail.

Dr. Adams was the author of Lameness in Horses and enjoyed the reputation as the leading authority on the horse's legs. That gave us a clue. Make sure you know every detail of the anatomy of the horse's legs.

For the next two nights, I reviewed my anatomy notes from my freshman year. I committed the equine section of Sisson's book, *The Anatomy of Domestic Animals*, to memory. My memory is pretty much photographic. I can save pictures in my mind, but not text. On occasion, I can save captions to the photos for a brief time.

Finally, Wednesday came. We had surgery scheduled for the morning. Dr. Adams was a skilled surgeon. In this jumper, there was a chip fracture of a carpal bone. A significant amount of the time involved was getting the horse under anesthesia and positioned on the surgery table. The surgery was brief in Dr. Adams' hands. The chip was removed, and Dr. Adams left the closure to his intern and senior student, me.

"Don't forget the test in my office at one," Adams said as he pulled off his surgery gloves.

"We're looking forward to it," I replied with an unseen smile, but I am sure it reflected in my eyes.

Adams smiled and departed the surgery room.

When the horse was recovered and back in the stall, Jon and I had a full hour and a half for a final review.

"I am going to take Sisson and go grab a coffee and a sandwich over at the MU," I said.

"That might be good," Jon said. "I will join you, but I think I have had my quota of coffee for the week."

There was no real conversation at the table. We ate a quick sandwich, and both did a final review of Sisson. My pages turned much quicker than Jon's. When the time came, we got up and walked back to the hospital.

Dr. Adams' office was on the second floor of the hospital. When we turned the corner to his office, we ran into a crowd of classmates. Word of our test had spread through the classes, and everyone wanted to watch. It must be like a crowd viewing a hanging. We worked our way through the crowd and took our seats in the office.

These professors all tried to present themselves as intimidating as possible. I found it almost laughable. In my last year in the Army, it was common for me to make presentations at general staff meetings, for generals with two or three stars on their collars. They were much more formidable than any professor. So in this situation, I was pretty relaxed. Jon was not so much.

Dr. Adams wasted no time. He started firing questions, some oral, some with x-rays on the viewer, and some with pictures from slides projected onto the wall. Like all tests, they are easy, if you are prepared. I think the fact that both of us didn't miss a question was getting to Dr. Adams.

"You haven't asked about the volar pouch," Jon said.

"I figured that would be the question you studied first," Dr. Adams said. "But since you mention it, why don't you tell me where it is located and what it is, and why it is important on that x-ray I had Monday morning."

"The volar pouch is an extension of the joint capsule and is located between the canon bone and the suspensory ligament, just above the sesamoids of the fetlock. If it is distended, it indicates inflammation in the joint."

"That's a good answer, Jon," Dr. Adams said. "You should not overlook that on an x-ray."

"If you did an adequate clinical exam, you should know it is distended before the x-ray is ever taken," I said.

"That's a good point, but in this business here, I am often looking at x-rays of horses that I didn't examine," Dr. Adams said.

Finally, he puts a picture on the wall. This was a picture of the two plantar nerves on the lower front legs of a horse. There is a nerve that communicates between these two nerves. It crosses the leg at an angle. You could tell which leg you were looking at by the direction that this nerve was running between the two primary nerves. This was a picture right out of Sisson.

"Larsen, what leg is this?" Dr. Adams asked.

"The left leg," I said. "The left front leg," I added.

"How do you know that?" Dr. Adams asked.

"That is the picture out of Sisson," I said. And then, looking at a blank wall, I used my finger to trace the words in the caption of that picture as I read the caption.

The hallway audience erupted in laughter.

Adams shook his head and smiled. "That's all I have, I can't top that."

That could have been the only time I ever saw the man smile. There was never a mention of the test in the remaining days of the rotation. We learned a lot, and even though I was not fond of horses, I learned everything I could from the man.

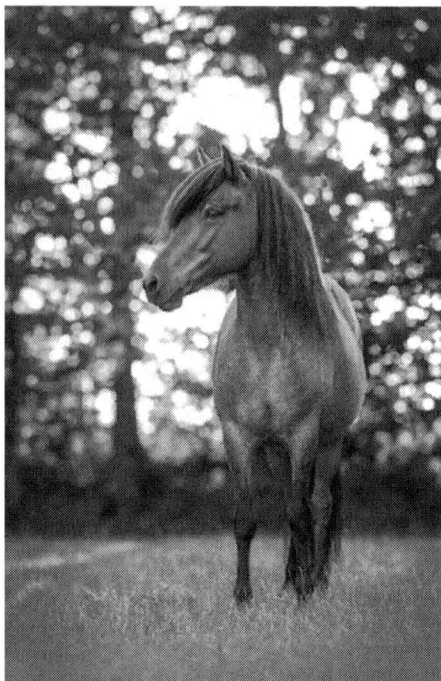

Hold the Horse Down

Mike was sitting behind the desk in the large animal hospital, his standard position during every one of our weeks of night duty at Colorado State University.

"Mike, you seem to like the desk job," I said.

"Naw, not so much, I just need the experience of talking to people on the phone," Mike said.

This was Thursday evening, nearing the end of our week of night duty. Seniors were assigned night duty every couple of months. Ten of us ran the hospital from closing at five until ten o'clock. We were managed by two interns, one on the small animal side and one on the large animal side of the hospital. We got to go home at night. The interns slept over at the hospital. But they had our telephone numbers if the need arose.

"Larsen, you need to get the whole group together for a quick conference here," Dr. Reese, the intern on duty, said. "We are going to have an issue tonight."

I headed out to the small animal side of the hospital and started gathering everyone for this conference.

"Conference?" Rod asked. "What is going on?"

"I have no idea what's up," I said. "Dr. Reese needs us all together to discuss the night."

"Is he going to keep us here all night?" Rod asked.

"I say again, Rod," I said. "I have no idea what's going on. I'm just the go-for out getting everyone over to the large animal office."

"It looks like we are missing a couple of guys," Dr. Reese said.

"Chuck and Rod are finishing up doing the evening treatments over on the small animal side. They should be here shortly," I said.

"I'll wait till they get here. I don't want to have to repeat everything twice," Dr. Reese said.

The two latecomers came through the door just as Dr. Reese made that statement.

Chuck sat on the corner of the desk "What's up, Doc?" Chuck asked.

"Okay, for those of you who don't know it," Dr. Reese started, "Dr. Adams had an emergency surgery today. He had the American champion endurance horse come in with a fractured humerus."

"That is almost an automatic euthanasia, isn't it?" Jim asked.

"In most cases, yes. But this horse has an exceptional value. So it was decided to give the repair a try," Dr. Reese said. "It was a complicated surgery, even for Dr. Adams. Repairing a fractured humerus in the horse is almost an unheard of surgery."

"So, how does that affect us?" Chuck asked.

"It was a seven-hour surgery," Dr. Reese said. "Seven hours lying on its left leg, and on recovery, there is radial nerve paralysis in the left leg."

The radial nerve controls all the muscles that extend the front leg. Without radial nerve function, the animal cannot stand on that leg. I had never heard of it in a horse. In the dog, the leg drags along, wearing the skin off the top of the paw in short order.

"That's another automatic euthanasia in the horse," Jim said.

"So the surgery team has been holding the horse down in the recovery stall all evening," Dr. Reese said. "The plan is to let them go home at ten tonight. We will be responsible for holding the horse down tonight. We will pull two-hour shifts with two of you on each shift."

"I'm not sure I understand the plan," I said. "I mean, if we had radial nerve paralysis with the horse on its side during surgery for seven hours, can we expect anything different if we hold the horse down on the other side for ten or twelve hours?"

"It is the only option we have," Dr. Reese said. "They gave the horse a big dose of dexamethasone. The hope is to see some return to function by morning so they can get the horse in a sling. I will agree, the odds are not good for the horse. But, Larsen, if you want to discuss the plan with Dr. Adams, you can just march right down there and talk with him."

Dr. Adams was almost a god in the world of lameness and orthopedics in the horse, and he had a massive influence in the veterinary school. He could kick a person out of school in a heartbeat, and there were rumors of him doing just that in the past. True or not, the potential threat made students conduct themselves with an extra measure of decorum.

"I think Jim and I will volunteer for the first shift," I said.

"Okay," Dr. Reese said. "We need to get everyone signed up for a shift. You guys take a phone into the recovery stall with you. There is a phone plug-in there. You give the next shift a phone call a half hour before they are due to be here. Everybody needs to take the responsibility to make it here for your shift. That way, all of us can get some sleep tonight."

"I need to call Sandy and let her know I am going to be late tonight," I said.

"You other guys go ahead and head home now," Dr. Reese said. "Jim and Dave, gather the clipboard with the list and bring a phone. We can go down to the recovery stall and get instructions for the night."

The recovery stall was a large room, maybe twenty feet square. It was padded with thick rubber mats, like a wrestling mat, on the floor and all sides. Once you were in the room and the door was closed, it was just you and the horse, and no place to duck for cover if the horse was flopping around.

"You guys have had a long day," Dr. Reese said as we squeezed through the large door that was opened only a crack for our entry. "We are set up with two-man shifts at two-hour intervals. We just need some instructions."

"All you need to do is have somebody sitting on his neck all the time," Dr. Adams said. "He is fully recovered and will try to jump up if he gets a chance. His left leg has no radial nerve function, and bone plates on his right humerus will not hold his weight. His only hope is to get enough return to function so we can get him in a sling tomorrow."

Jim placed his knee on the horse's neck as Steve stood up, and then Jim swirled around and sat down on his neck. It looked like an easy maneuver, but the horse did try to raise his head during the change of position.

"I'm about beat," Steve said as he pushed past me. "I don't think I will be going into equine orthopedics after today. We have been working on this horse since ten o'clock this morning. You should have been in on that surgery. I will never complain about the surgical approach of the humerus on a dog again."

"Retracting the muscles must have been a chore," I said.

"I don't think most people could have done the surgery," Steve said. "Dr. Adams is so strong, and he made some of it look easy. But, a seven-hour surgery is almost too much for this kid."

The surgical team filed out of the recovery stall.

"Call me if you need anything. I will try to get some shut-eye," Dr. Reese said as he left the stall and shut the door.

I plugged in the phone and laid the clipboard down in the corner, and set the phone on the clipboard.

"I guess if we hold the horse down, the phone will be safe in the corner," I said.

"I hate being closed in this room with a horse," Jim said. "There is no way to be safe if the horse is really flopping around."

"Well, it's one thing if you are recovering a normal horse," I said. "This horse has almost zero chance of recovery, and here we are, stuck in this recovery stall with it."

"The thing that I don't understand is how are they going to get this horse in a sling anyway?" Jim asked.

"I don't know. I would guess they will have to sedate him to lift him into it," I said. "I don't know why they didn't do that this evening. By morning, the nerve on the repaired leg will be shot too."

"I think Adams just wants to be able to write up this repair," Jim said. "I doubt if it has been done before."

"I don't think so," I said. "If it has, it hasn't been done very often."

"Have you heard of a radial nerve paralysis ever returning to function?" Jim asked.

"I haven't heard of it occurring in the horse before, but in the dog, the leg gets ruined before there is any return to function," I said. "At least that is the impression that I get from Dr. Creed."

"It's probably about time we switch positions," Jim said. "My butt is getting tired."

I moved around the horse and knelt with my knee on his neck. Jim stood up and stretched, and I tried to turn on my knee and sit down on the horse's neck. The horse swung his head up at the same time, knocking me off his neck, and suddenly I am lying on my back beside his front legs. I scrambled away from his legs, and he was immediately up on his sternum. In an instant, he tried to stand.

His left leg hung uselessly, and he placed his repaired right leg out to stand. It held together for a brief moment, and then the leg collapsed as the repair broke apart.

I looked at Jim and shrugged my shoulders.

"I wonder what Adams is going to say about this?" I said.

"We better call Dr. Reese," Jim said as he picked up the phone and dialed the intern quarters.

Dr. Reese was there in a flash.

"Oh, boy," he said. "Not much to do now. I will go call Dr. Adams."

It didn't take Dr. Adams long to get to the hospital. I have no idea where he lived, but I would guess he drove fast.

He entered the recovery stall with a frown and knelt down to examine the horse's leg.

Jim and I stood aside, not saying a word but waiting for Adams to explode.

"I have to go call the owner," Dr. Adams said. "Then we will put him to sleep."

That was all that he said. I could hear Jim take a deep breath when Dr. Adams left the room. Dr. Reese looked relieved also.

It was maybe five minutes later when Dr. Adams returned with a bottle of euthanasia solution.

"It was a long shot anyway," Dr. Adams said as he drew up the solution into a couple of large syringes. "I have never seen radial nerve paralysis in a horse before. Too bad, I really wanted this repair to work."

With that, he gave the injections and patted the horse on his head.

"We can move him back to necropsy in the morning," Dr. Adams said as he left the room.

We stood there a couple of minutes, nobody said a word.

"I will call the others," Dr. Reese finally said. "You guys can go home."

"I think this was the best outcome for the horse," Jim said. "But somehow, I feel like we dodged a bullet tonight."

"Dr. Adams likes to look mean," Dr. Reese said. "But he is really a nice man, down deep."

Notes on My Brother, Larry Larsen

I started writing bits and pieces in the 1990s. Those writings were brief, maybe all my papers are brief, but those were two hundred to four hundred words. They helped preserve some of those moments, and I still refer to those notes when pondering a topic.

About this same time, my oldest brother started writing a weekly column in The Myrtle Point Herald, the local weekly newspaper. His column was short stories of his early years in the woods (or the logging industry for those unfamiliar with the vernacular). His column chronicled his life in the woods, and as a small gyppo logging company owner, and then later as a log scaler.

He enjoyed a high level of local notoriety. To think, he didn't even know how to type, let alone run a computer.

He would write those stories in longhand, and the paper would type them out and publish them. With some encouragement, he compiled them into a small paperback book. He printed several hundred copies, at considerable expense for him. He managed to sell them all for twenty-two dollars a copy.

When they were sold, he was reluctant to go through the printing expense again. I encouraged him to put it on Amazon as an e-book.

If anyone wants a different perspective of life in a small West Coast logging town and the work that goes on in the woods. That book is still available on Amazon.

My brother passed away in 2017 from lung cancer. The events leading up to his death were a story fit for a novel.

Larry had one set of numbers that he played in the Oregon Lottery. He played those numbers every drawing, and he won a lot, winning four numbers several hundred times and five numbers a half dozen times. He absolutely knew he was going to win the big pot sooner or later.

After he was sick and waiting for some diagnostics the following week, he had trouble finding the shower Thursday night. His wife would not let him go to town to buy his lottery ticket on Friday morning. He managed to sneak out of the house and drove the eight miles to town. He made it into the store and purchased his ticket. Then he collapsed. The store called his daughter and daughter-in-law, the ambulance, and the police. Of course, there was a lot of commotion.

Larry managed to recover enough to get back on his feet and get back into his pickup. He was going home. The police were reluctant to allow him to drive. The daughters tried to talk him into the ambulance.

With much hesitation on his part, he finally consented to an ambulance ride. He died in the early morning hours of the following day.

What about that final lottery ticket? Would that not be the final irony of a man's life, if that ticket was the winner?

As it turned out, it was not the big winner, but what an ending to a novel or a life, if it had been.

Link to Larry's book, *Back in the Day*, by Larry Larsen

https://www.amazon.com/Back-Day-Larry-Larsen-ebook/dp/B0050VK9ZK

George and Martha Washington

The girls raced ahead of Sandy and me as we walked down the aisle at the Fort Collins K-Mart. They were headed to the pocket pets. We had just moved into an off-campus apartment, and we could have pets.

That was a big decision for a student family. We were only going to be here for another couple of years. What our living situation would be after school was anybody's guess. But we had decided on a couple of guinea pigs. We were lucky. Had Dee been older, we would be picking out three.

"Brenda, you pick one, and then we'll let Amy pick one," Sandy said.

Brenda made her selection in a snap. "I want the fluffy yellow and white one," she said, pointing to a young male in the bottom cage.

Amy was standing, jumping up and down and pointing at a little tricolored female in the upper cage.

"Be patient. We need to find a clerk. We have to buy a cage and all that kind of stuff," Sandy said as she entertained Dee in the shopping cart seat with her left hand.

***

260

I entered the apartment the next afternoon through the utility room door and discarded my clinic clothes.

The cage was set up on the dryer, and the two guinea pigs seemed well adjusted to each other and their surroundings. I could see that Amy and Brenda had been pushing carrot sticks into the kennel through the wires.

"What are we going to name these two?" I asked.

"I have been talking with the girls, and we have decided on George and Martha Washington," Sandy said.

So George and Martha Washington became a part of the Larsen family. The girls enjoyed playing with them, especially when we would allow them out of the cage. A few times, I would have to retrieve one of them from under a bed, but that was the biggest issue with them.

***

Some months later, when the girls were having some floor time with George and Martha, I noticed that Martha was getting a little heavy.

"We might have to deal with a litter of guinea pigs before too long," I said to Sandy when the girls were out of earshot.

"I guess that shouldn't be a surprise. After all, we knew they were male and female when we got them."

"Yes, but what are we going to do with six guinea pigs?" I asked.

"Do you think she will have four babies?" Sandy asked.

"I know nothing about guinea pig babies, but the cages at the store are pretty full all the time. That would suggest that they are pretty prolific."

"Maybe you better do some reading in some of those expensive textbooks stacked in there on your study table," Sandy said.

***

It was probably two weeks later when I parked my bicycle and stepped into the utility room. Both Amy and Brenda were there to greet me.

"Look what we have now," Brenda said.

"We have Betsy Ross," Amy squealed.

"Betsy Ross, who is Betsy Ross?" I asked.

The girls pointed at the third guinea pig, running around the cage. Only a half a dozen hours old, she was fully functional and nearly half Martha's size.

"Who came up with that name?" I asked.

"Mom thought it would fit nicely with George and Martha Washington," Brenda said. "She made our flag."

"Yes, I know Betsy Ross," I said. "But I didn't expect her to be half-grown at birth. I guess I have some reading to do."

So, it turns out that guinea pigs have an average litter of four babies, but that number can vary between one and thirteen. A standard litter weight is typical. A litter might weigh four ounces. If there are four babies, each one will weigh one ounce.

If there is one baby, as was the case with Betsy Ross, the baby will weigh four ounces, also, as was the case with Betsy Ross. She was, indeed, half-grown when she arrived.

It turns out that we managed our guinea pigs correctly, even if it was by accident. Young females reach sexual maturity at two months of age, and they must be bred before they are six months of age.

After six months, their pelvic bones will fuse, and giving birth to a large baby, like Betsy Ross, will be impossible without a C-section.

The young Martha's pelvic bones were able to disarticulate and allow a large single baby's birthing. The babies nurse for several weeks but can survive without nursing after about five days. I never witnessed Betsy Ross nursing on Martha Washington. It could have happened at night. But I suspect that Betsy Ross was large enough to survive on her own from day one.

Three guinea pigs became a burden on the tight quarters of the utility room. With my school completion on the near horizon, we were forced to find new homes for our patriotic group. That was a difficult day for the girls but little did we know that Ralph would be waiting for us in our new home in Washington.

A Full Belly Comes to Those Who Seek It

Preface:

This short story comes from my family's lore, and I write it now because it has implications for the current times. Today young mothers are having extreme difficulty in obtaining commercial baby formula to feed their infants. The medical profession and the social media "fact-checker" caution them not to resort to homemade recipes. So what are they supposed to feed a kid if there is no breast milk and no baby formula?

***

Annie Coats was born in January 1880. She was the oldest of a family of eight children. This story takes place on a small farm outside of Juliaetta, Idaho, a small town in the southern panhandle of western Idaho. It is the spring of 1891.

"Annie, we will be in town all day today as your father takes care of some banking business, and then we have to buy supplies for the spring planting," Sarah Coats explained to her daughter. "You will be fine with the kids, and Mollie is old enough to help you out if there are any problems. After you kids help your father with the morning chores, you just keep everyone in the house. I will nurse Tommy before we leave, so he should be okay until we get home in the evening. You can mash some carrots for him at lunchtime."

"Okay," Annie said. "But what do I do if you don't get home?"

"Nothing is going to happen," her mother said. "We just can't take all you kids with us on this trip."

Annie, Mollie, who was almost nine, and Lewis, who was six, went with their father to the barn to do the morning chores while Sarah nursed Tommy and tended to the two younger girls. The final two family members would not arrive for another few years.

Thomas, Annie's father, and Sarah crawled into the buckboard, and Thomas snapped the rains against Old Joe's rump.

"Giddy up," he commanded the team.

"We will see you kids this evening," Sarah yelled back to the kids. "You mind your sister. She is the boss today."

The kids stood at the cabin door and watched the wagon disappear as the trail to town turned into the trees.

"Okay, mom wanted us to stay inside today," Annie said as she ushered the kids into the cabin. "Mom has a full basket of darning to get done, and it's time you guys learned how to do some of the stuff around the house."

The day wore on, and the little kids tried to be helpful, but Annie learned that sometimes it is easier to do things yourself than to have little hands helping.

At lunchtime, Annie boiled a carrot and a couple of potatoes. That was served to the kids along with some ham that she had trimmed off the new ham hanging in the smokehouse.

Dave Larsen

She smashed the carrot into a mush with some added butter. Tommy started to reject Annie's attempts to spoon some of the carrot mush into his mouth, but he must have realized that it was all he would get.

As the afternoon turned into evening, Annie spent more and more time outside, watching for the wagon.

"Mom said they would be home this evening," Mollie said. "Tommy is getting hungry, and I don't think you can nurse him."

***

In town, Thomas and Sarah were putting the last of the supplies into the wagon when Sarah heard a 'snap.'

"What was that?" Sarah asked.

Thomas walked around the wagon, and there it was, a broken spoke in the right rear wheel.

"We can't haul this load home without fixing that wheel," Thomas said. "I guess I better go talk with Josh at the livery stable."

"Tom, I can fix that wheel, but not until morning," Josh said as he pumped the bellows to his forge. "I promised Mel I would get this job done tonight."

"We have the kids home alone, and the baby will be starving if he doesn't get to nurse his mother tonight," Thomas said.

"Sorry, Tom," Josh said. "It can't be helped. You can pull the wagon over here and put your horses in a stall. I have a small room in the back that you and the missus can use. It ain't much, but it is better than paying the hotel."

"Okay, I guess the kids will survive," Thomas said. "Annie is pretty smart, and she will figure something out for the baby."

***

"We need to get the animals fed before dark," Annie said. "Lewis, you and Sarah, come give me a hand. Mollie can stay and take care of Tommy and Lillie."

Annie was rushing through the chores to get back in the house and figure out what she was going to feed Tommy. She thought she could try to mix up some flour and water. Their milk

266

cow was getting ready to calve, and they wouldn't have milk again for another couple of weeks.

When Annie got to the pigpen, she noticed the sow laid out on her side with eight little piglets nursing. She watched her for a moment, thinking.

"Sarah, you run to the house and have Mollie bring Tommy out here," Annie said. "And have her bring an old blanket. And hurry!"

Little Sarah was off like a shot.

"Lewis, we need to spread some new straw down in this pigpen," Annie said. "And we need to be careful not to disturb the old sow."

When Mollie arrived with Tommy and the other kids, Annie and Lewis had just finished bedding down the pigpen. Annie was standing in the pen.

"Hand me Tommy and the blanket," she instructed Mollie.

"What are you going to do?" Mollie asked.

"Tommy needs some milk, and this sow is the only girl on the place giving milk," Annie said. "I will be careful, but Tommy is going to nurse this sow."

Annie took Tommy to the middle of the line-up of piglets. She moved two piglets from the middle of the pack to the sides. She spread out the blanket and laid Tommy down beside the piglets in the middle of the group.

The old sow didn't seem to mind as Annie stripped some milk from a teat into Tommy's mouth. She pushed Tommy's mouth against the teat, and he hooked on and started sucking.

Annie sat back and relaxed, watching the sow and Tommy. The piglets that had been moved to the side were starting to fight for a better position. The hind teats were not the most favorable. When one of the piglets pushed against Tommy, Annie began to intervene, but she didn't have to do anything. Tommy pushed the piglet away. He wasn't going to miss this meal.

When Annie felt Tommy was getting full, she picked him up and brushed him off before handing him back across the fence to Mollie.

"Now, what are we going to have for supper?" Little Sarah asked.

"We are going to have eggs and maybe a potato," Annie said.

"Lewis doesn't like eggs," Mollie said.

"I will scramble them, and I have a little of the ham left from lunch that I can cut up and put in the eggs," Annie said.

"But Lewis doesn't like eggs," Mollie said.

"Scrambled eggs and ham with some fried potatoes are what we are having for dinner," Annie said. "If Lewis doesn't want any, I guess he is just not hungry enough."

The kids returned to the house and cleaned up Tommy. Annie fixed a supper of scrambled eggs and ham with some fried potatoes. Lewis had figured out that this was all there was, and he ate his dinner with the other kids.

***

Morning came, and Tommy was hungry. Annie made another trip to the pigpen with him, and he was an old pro this morning. snuggling into the line-up of piglets and fighting for his teat,

With the wagon wheel fixed, Thomas and Sarah pointed Old Joe toward home.

"I am worried to death," Sarah said. "Tommy will be starved by the time we get there. And I will feel better, getting some of this milk drained from my breasts."

The kids were dancing outside the cabin door as the wagon came into view.

Sarah took Tommy from Annie and headed for her rocking chair with a towel.

"He will hardly nurse," Sarah said. "What did you feed him when I was gone?"

"We just made do with what was available," Annie answered.

Epilogue:

Tommy survived his meals with pig milk and grew into adulthood with no significant problems. Annie showed her pioneer spirit and ingenuity by using the only milk available to her at the time.

Acknowledgments

How does one acknowledge the multitude of people who have had a positive influence on my life?

There were many teachers, but only a couple who really stand out in my memory; Ed Heath and Eli Jimenez in elementary school, Doctors Livingston, Hilliman and Storm in my undergraduate studies, and many professors and clinicians at Colorado State University College of Veterinary Medicine who spent years ensuring I was prepared for practice. There were times in my years of practice when I had shortcomings, but there was never a time that I could fault my education for those shortcomings.

Possibly by accident, the US Army provided me the maturity to continue and complete my education. And Don Miller, the friend who never had the opportunity to return home, provided me the inspiration to do the same.

The friends and family who offered encouragement for me to write. And to continue to write, even when my stories were the mere scribbles of an amateur.

Scott Swanson, owner and editor of The New Era, Sweet Home's weekly newspaper, who has provided column space in his paper.

Joan Scofield, a long-time Sweet Home resident, for her excellent proofreading.

Laura Davis, my niece, who gives me another perspective on proofreading; thus making my job more enjoyable.

And lastly, Eva Long, of Long on Books, for the cover design, and who continues to be most helpful in teaching me the ins and outs of this book business.

Photo Credits

My First Sick Cow: Carboxaldehyde/Pexels
The Broadbent House: Kathy Larsen
Gary's Accident: Dolores Larsen/1949
Jerd: Sergio Souza/Pexels
The Plank Road: Antranias/Pexels
Chicken Wars: Quang Nguyễn Vinh/Pexels
Tripping Up The Bully: Aaron Larsen
The Dreaded Pox: Michael Gane/Pexels
The Young Boy and the Creek: David Mark/Pexels
Fast Ball Pitch in the Bullpen: Damir Spanic/Unsplash
The Camping Trip that Wasn't: Dolores Larsen
A Leap of Faith: David Larsen, DVM
The Big Horse Race: Zachariah Smith/Unsplash
Notes on My Mother: Family picture
Columbus Day Storm, Oct 12, 1962: Benamin Elliott/Unsplash
I Are One: David Larsen, DVM
One Day at the Cheese Factory: Polina Tankilevitch/Pexels
I Presume?: Kennell-Ellis
Howard Daniel Vandenacre: Holly Mindrup/Unsplash
US Army, Basic Training, 1965: US Army
KP, Basic Training, Fall 1965: Rap T/Pixabay
The Game: Mark Williams/Unsplash
Just Don't Eat the Apple Pie: Anastasia/Unsplash
A Day at the Track: Midia/Pexels
South Korea, Winter 1966 to 1967: Clarence Nishihara
Dumb and Dumber: Victor Hugo
My Christmases in the Army: Clarence Nishihara
That Last Glass of Milk: Alexas Fotos/Pexels
Fort Dix Transfer Company: David Larsen, DVM
Rothwesten, West Germany, December 1967: Uriel Castellanos/
Pexels
Rothwesten Operations: Bruce Richard/http://brucerichards.com/
army/kasselpics3.htm
Trip to Münster: KarinKarin/Pixabay
Power Line Splice in Yellow Snow: Alexander Ermakov/Pexels

A Wrong Turn: Bruce Richard/http://brucerichards.com/army/kasselpics3.htm
Events of August 20 to 23, 1968: Irina Balashova/Pexels
Die Schwarze Katze: James Milstid
A German Ice Storm: Corbin Richardson/Unsplash
A Change of Pace: Kathy Larsen
The Value of a Valid Complaint: Family picture
They Look Like Their Owners: David Cain/Unsplash
Notes on My Father: Dolores Larsen;
1934 OSU Rooks: OSU Archives
Robert W. Davis, DVM: Barbara Olsen/Pexels
The Budget Book: Northfolk/Unsplash
All on Number One: Jannk Selz/Unsplash
Don't Be Too Smug: Zahoba/Pexels
Always have Rabies at the Top of Your List: Barbara Webb/Pexels
Cowboy Education: Brett Sayles/Pexels
Financial Aid: Family picture
Once in the Wilds of Afganistan: Hansbenn/Pixabay
The Last Visit: Hub Haughton
Is He Dead Yet?: Ludvig Hedenborg/Pexels
'Twas the Night Before Christmas: Ibiza Ibiza Ibiza on Unsplash
Where is the Volar Pouch?: Laila Klinsmann/Pexels
Hold the Horse Down: Missi Köpf/Pexels
Notes on My Brother: Kathy Larsen
George and Martha Washington: Scott Webb/Usplash
A Full Belly Comes to those Who Seek It: Family picture
Cover: Jonathan Petersson/Pexels

About the Author

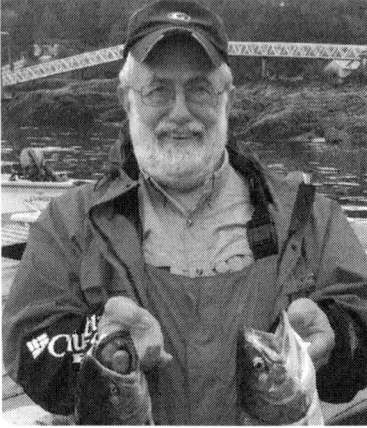

D r. David Larsen grew up on a farm in the Coquille River Valley of Southwestern Oregon. Animals and their care have been a part of life from the very beginning. Veterinary Medicine was always on his radar but it took four years in the Army to provide the maturity for him to complete his education.

First graduating from Oregon State University with a degree in Zoology, he then attended Colorado State University, receiving a degree of Doctor of Veterinary Medicine in 1975 at the age of thirty.

With a growing family, he moved first to Enumclaw, Washington where he practiced for a year and a half. Then he moved to Sweet Home, Oregon where he started Sweet Home Veterinary Clinic. He was in practice for over forty years at Sweet Home Veterinary Clinic.

Today he spends his time with his family, writing and doing a little fishing. He and Sandy travel when they can. There is much yet to see in Oregon and the rest of this country.

*The Making of a Country Veterinaria*n is the fifth book in Dr. Larsen's *Memoirs of a Country Vet* series.

Other books in the
Memoirs of a County Vet series

1 • Last Cow in the Chute

2 • Widow Woman's Ranch

3 • Lambs & Crab Legs

4 • The Daughter's Horse

Made in the USA
Monee, IL
05 September 2022

12289347R00153